Chaucer

Brian Stone entered the teaching profession after the war, and taught English in boys' schools for eleven years. He then trained teachers for ten years at Loughborough and Brighton, before becoming a founder member of the Open University as Reader in Literature. Besides writing and broadcasting there on medieval drama, he has to his credit five verse translations in the Penguin Classics: *Sir Gawain and the Green Knight*, *Medieval English Verse*, *The Owl and the Nightingale/Cleanness/St Erkenwald*, Chaucer's *Love Visions* and *King Arthur's Death* (*Morte Arthure* and *Le Morte Arthur*).

Penguin Critical Studies
Editor: Bryan Loughrey

Chaucer

Brian Stone

Penguin Books

PENGUIN BOOKS

Published by the Penguin Group
27 Wrights Lane, London W8 5TZ, England
Viking Penguin Inc., 40 West 23rd Street, New York, New York 10010, USA
Penguin Books Australia Ltd, Ringwood, Victoria, Australia
Penguin Books Canada Ltd, 2801 John Street, Markham, Ontario, Canada L3R 1B4
Penguin Books (NZ) Ltd, 182–190 Wairau Road, Auckland 10, New Zealand

Penguin Books Ltd, Registered Offices: Harmondsworth, Middlesex, England

First published in Penguin Masterstudies 1987
Reprinted in Penguin Critical Studies 1989
10 9 8 7 6 5 4 3 2

Made and printed in Great Britain by
Richard Clay Ltd, Bungay, Suffolk
Filmset in Monophoto Times

Contents

Critical Studies: Chaucer

Part V: Chaucer's Cultural Resources

Foreword: The Use of this Book

This contribution to the Masterstudies series has been planned with several considerations in mind, two of which may distinguish it from other introductory books on Chaucer. The first is that the main bulk of the book, Parts II, III and IV, is written to be read continuously, and the second is that some idea of all Chaucer's work, together with the beginnings of a critical approach, is given, with these reservations: only a representative handful of the few short poems is discussed, and the prose works receive brief notice only. The *Roman de la Rose* is discussed in Part V not with reference to the translation of parts of it ascribed to Chaucer and included in the Oxford edition of *The Complete Works of Geoffrey Chaucer* as *The Romaunt of the Rose*, but with reference to the full French work in modern English translation.

The aim of this plan is to offer the reader a developing narrative sense of Chaucer's verse stories, both separately and in succession, and, with regard to *The Canterbury Tales*, to follow that aim closely by presenting discussion of them in the context of the characters who tell their stories and of their interaction as the pilgrimage to Canterbury proceeds. Thus students may see the particular poems with which they are concerned in relation both to other poems of the same genre, and to Chaucer's whole work.

After some hesitation, I decided to present *The Canterbury Tales* first, not because most readers may be drawn to them first, but because F. N. Robinson, the editor of the Oxford Chaucer from which all my quotations are taken, presents them first. It then seemed logical to follow this with Chaucer's masterpiece, *Troilus and Criseyde*, in a separate Part. All the rest of the poetry then follows in Part IV, and readers who prefer with this book in hand to move chronologically, or nearly so, through Chaucer's work should read Parts II, III and IV in reverse order.

The short Part I is introductory, as the subheading titles of Chapter I indicate. Part V, 'Chaucer's Cultural Resources', deals as economically as possible with the formidable range of learning upon which Chaucer drew in writing poetry. Most of this learning is lost on the average modern reader, and where it is not entirely lost, the forms and details of the different branches of medieval knowledge are often different from those current today. Probably, the reader's understanding and enjoyment of every poem Chaucer wrote will be increased if he or she has read, or can easily consult, the four chapters of Part V.

The Bibliography is deliberately limited, and lightly annotated: all the works mentioned both there and in the text of this book contain their own full bibliographies, and I am sure I do not need to urge serious readers in their direction.

The index is highly selective and I hope that it nevertheless works well enough to compensate for the sparsity in the text of cross-references, a full array of which would probably have produced a more cumbersome apparatus for finding one's way about this book and the poetry of Chaucer.

All quotations from Chaucer are glossed, and occasionally annotated, for the convenience of readers who are not familiar with his language.

In the writing of this book I declare my own critical preferences and choices for detailed treatment; but proceeding, as I recognize, with limited originality, I own that I rest heavily on perceptions and knowledge drawn from the great stock of scholarship in English medieval literature. Besides works quoted and acknowledgements made in the text, I wish especially to acknowledge the Chaucerian scholarship of F. N. Robinson's *The Works of Geoffrey Chaucer.* And I am particularly grateful to the editor of this series, Stephen Coote, a true Chaucerian whose generosity with his ideas and spirit of shaping encouragement have made this a better book than it would have been otherwise.

Brian Stone
Kensington, 1987

Part I: Introductory

Chapter 1. The Poet, His World and His Language

General Introduction

Chaucer is the chief adornment of English medieval literature, and one of the three greatest English poets. Like Shakespeare and Milton after him, he took English poetry into a new phase, and profoundly influenced the thinking and writing of poets of several succeeding generations. Though he wrote no plays, and his surviving output of short poems is scanty, as a narrative poet he excelled both Shakespeare and Milton owing to the originality, volume and variety of achievement in the *genre*: as a storyteller in verse he has no equal in English.

However, he treats a more limited subject-matter than either Shakespeare or Milton: for example, on the pre-eminent subject of government. By this I mean the spiritual as well as temporal regulation of human affairs. While they expound with dramatic or visionary insight its contemporary workings, and go far to specify ways in which it should work – though Shakespeare suggests rather than prescribes – Chaucer seems content to record the consequences to particular characters of the exercise by others of various sorts of power.

Chaucer's main interest is love, and he channels his compassion into celebrating the diversely manifested nobility of those who undergo hard fates, especially in love. The compassion, the interest in love and the awareness of the workings of Fortune and Fate, characteristically produce a lofty pathos which is arguably Chaucer's highest expression and best gift: the conclusions of *The Book of the Duchess* and *Troilus and Criseyde*, and Part V of *The Clerk's Tale* are cases in point.

Chaucer is as scholarly a poet as Milton, in that all the learning of his age – classical, contemporary, religious, scientific – seems to sit easily in his poetry, and to be fully absorbed into the drift of argument and the currents of character conflict. But unlike Milton, and arguably unlike Shakespeare, Chaucer appears not to advance, except by implication, any moral or philosophical system of his own, though he uses other people's systems, or busily translates into English the Latin, French or Italian texts in which they appear, as such works as *Boece* (Boethius), his own *Tale of Melibee* and *The Parson's Tale* attest. In much of his poetry, the influence of Boethius is marked.

Chaucer was not saluted by his French contemporary, the poet

Eustache Deschamps, as 'grant translateur' for translating works of philosophy or religion, however, but for his transformations and referential use of poetic narratives by such classical Latin poets as Ovid and Virgil, and of earlier medieval and contemporary European writers, among whom Jean de Meun, the author of most of the *Roman de la Rose* (*The Romance of the Rose*), Dante and Boccaccio are the most important. Chaucer was a 'translator' who delightedly engaged with the cultural past and present of the Europe of his day, using them to compose poetry in new ways.

Not less interesting than his selections from the cultural heritage are his exclusions. Chaucer treats as major subject none of the old military epics and sagas of feuding – that fury of mutual destruction which seems to have been the preferred vocation of early European aristocracy – and dallies with the 'derring-do' of old Romance only to ridicule it, as in *The Tale of Sir Thopas*. Accordingly, in its occurrence in his poetry violence, both personal and institutional, tends to be viewed from the point of view of the victim, not the inflictor. So the sufferers from violence and oppression in his poetry are mostly women, with just the occasional child or man, and the reasons for their suffering tend not to be military but sexual, as in rapes or male domineering in marriage, or religious, as when Christians maintain their faith against pagans, Jews and Moslems. Overwhelmingly, Chaucer's sufferers are women whose options in life are limited. But it was not this factor that led Chaucer's contemporaries, John Gower and Thomas Usk, to celebrate him as the true servant of Venus, goddess of love, but his delineation of women as the prime upholders of passionate natural life.

Another area of exclusion in Chaucer's handling of his classical source stories appears in the poems which comprise *The Legend of Good Women*, and in the tale-within-a-tale of Ceyx and Alcyone in *The Book of the Duchess*: to retain the purity of the pathos, Chaucer omits the consoling endings of the originals.

Still more instructive of his use of sources than the inclusions and exclusions are his major changes of structure and emphasis, as in his 'translations' from Boccaccio. *The Knight's Tale* is a romance only a quarter as long as the *Teseida*, and favours the love interest by omitting much of the combat and ceremonial material of the source; and *Troilus and Criseyde*, for which Chaucer admittedly drew on other material besides that in *Il Filostrato* (meaning he who is struck by love), presents a loftier theme and far more interesting characterization than the Italian poem.

Chaucer's compassion for people who suffer, and his detached absorption in the great story-telling past of Europe, are leavened by a sense of humour which equals Shakespeare's: at its lowest levels, it is more uproarious and bawdy, and when it appears as gentle irony, it is as subtle and delicate, and possibly even more humane in its understanding of the predicaments of life. Its achievements range from the joyous bawdry of *The Miller's Tale* to the sustained mixture of knockabout farce and intellectual humour, grounded in moral sense, of *The Nun's Priest's Tale* of the Cock and the Fox. Chaucer is our greatest comic poet, his practised resort in writing on almost any subject, even a potentially tragic one, being to reveal and exploit the humour in it. The pathos of his finest single achievement, *Troilus and Criseyde*, is often laced with it. The resulting alternations of tone and mood can surprise and even shock. Often, and even in the *Troilus*, a poem proceeds with, say, underlying deep feeling overlaid by gentle irony, and all of a sudden, like a subliminal flash of pornographic advertising, the reader is aware of a rubious, tufted nakedness; he blinks, and there again is the familiar understanding compassionate gaze and the continuous graceful smile.

It may be understood from the foregoing why Chaucer never wrote an epic, which is historically the loftiest form of poetry: most classical and medieval epics are strong on battle scenes and the fates of societies or nations, and their heroes fulfil roles more public than private.

Chaucer's humour and apparently uncommitted intellectual and ideological eclecticism combine to produce a unique effect. I suggest above that whatever moral or philosophical position is taken by Chaucer it is advanced only by implication. But though formally undefined, his purpose generally appears to be as Derek Pearsall defines it in regard to *The Canterbury Tales*, 'always to give the advantage to a humane and generous understanding . . .' (*The Canterbury Tales*, 1985, p. xiv). Of course 'humane' and 'generous' may be defined in different ways, but Pearsall's choice of those epithets underlines what are evident concerns of Chaucer: to assess experience in a spirit of sympathetic realism, balancing it always against the desire of human beings to express themselves in their own ways; and to imply always a kindly and flexible morality, especially when faced by the rigidities of authority, whether they be religious, social or personal. Chaucer's articulate and rebellious creation, the Wife of Bath, succinctly comments on this matter of experience and authority in relation to her own concern, which happens to be how to achieve a good marriage relationship:

> Experience, thou noon auctoritee
> Were in this world, is right ynogh for me
> To speke of wo that is in mariage;
>
> (*The Canterbury Tales*, III, 1–3)

Her experience is a touchstone of such valid force to her that she ignores prescriptions of authority concerning the state and nature of holy matrimony; her preference in being guided not by authority but by experience accords with that of other Chaucerian characters, though her expression of it is excessive.

Chaucer's life and times have traditionally occupied the opening chapters of books on his work. But since there is no mention of his having been a poet in the Life Records, and there are few references in his poetry to the great events of his times, only a skeleton chronology of the main known events of his life is tabulated below, while political, social and religious matters are discussed in connection with the poems in which reference to them appears. Nevertheless, a brief characterization of the fourteenth-century world in which Chaucer lived and worked may be found useful.

Chaucer worked as courtier, civil servant and occasional diplomat under three kings: Edward III (1327–77), Richard II (1377–99) and Henry IV (1399–1413). The transition of his service from king to king was smooth, even during and after the upheaval of Richard's deposition, usurpation and murder by Henry, which is familiar through Shakespeare's tragic history play, *Richard II*. But during Richard's minority, when the Duke of Gloucester presided over the regency, it seems probable that Chaucer was out of favour at court during the three years' absence in Spain of his chief patron, John of Gaunt (1386–9).

In foreign affairs, the century was dominated by the Hundred Years War against France, which began in 1337. In its early years there were English battle triumphs such as Crécy (1346) and Poitiers (1356) and much of the disputed French countryside was laid waste. But as Edward III grew feebler, English battlefield superiority diminished, and during the period of Richard's enthusiasm for the war, England lost most of her possessions in France and the French made several punitive landings on the south coast. These wars helped to establish the modern nationalistic rivalry between England and France.

At home, four related matters are important enough to be mentioned here: the growth of London, the rise and increasing power of the middle classes, the plague and the Peasants' Revolt. The development of the wool industry, and later of the cloth trade, together with a general increase in wealth in the first half of the century, made London into a European entrepôt and a national capital ranking in size and influence with major continental cities. The comparatively new class whose accelerated rise was part of this process of urbanization was composed of the mercantile, technical and legal personnel required for large-scale commercial undertakings in a Europe still largely free of the political restraints associated with modern nationalisms. Its members are well represented in *The Canterbury Tales*: the Sergeant of Law, the Merchant, the Franklin, the Shipman, the Wife of Bath, the Physician and the five Guildsmen, as well as such characters within the *Tales* as those two cuckolds, the merchant of *The Shipman's Tale* and the 'riche gnof' (lout) of a carpenter in *The Miller's Tale.*

The Black Death (1348–9) was an epidemic of the plague which in two years killed more than a third of the population of Western Europe, and recurred in less severe outbreaks in subsequent years. In 1369 it killed John of Gaunt's Duchess, whose death is lamented in *The Book of the Duchess*. It is hard to imagine the terror, suffering and grief, as well as the social dislocation, wherever the plague attacked, but the economic consequences are known. Agricultural and industrial production fell, and the scarcity of labour caused wages to rise sharply.

These factors, together with the exactions levied in order to pay for the increasingly expensive war against France, helped to bring about the Peasants' Revolt of 1381. Matters came to a head slowly but inevitably, as the ruling classes, that is to say the leaders of State, Church and Manor, resisted demands for a living wage, and the government laid increasingly unbearable burdens on all taxable members of the community, not just labouring people. The peasant leaders of Kent and Essex were the spearheads of a mass revolt.

Chaucer does not treat any of these matters as main subjects in his poetry, but occasionally makes incidental reference to them: the Squire fought, as the young Chaucer had done, 'In Flaundres, in Artoys, and Pycardie'; and in *The Nun's Priest's Tale* the mass pursuit of the fox at the end is compared with a crowd led by Jack Straw looking for Flemings to kill. The reference is to the Peasants' Revolt: Edward III had encouraged Flemish weavers to settle in England, and in time of stress and social unrest, they were liable to be attacked as foreigners who threatened English livelihoods.

Those English concerns do not seem to have touched Chaucer with such galvanic effect as his cultural and travelling contacts in other countries which, in spite of the protracted wars which kept rulers aggressively posturing at one another, were evidently the norm for the upper and mercantile classes in fourteenth-century Europe. Scholars, writers and artists all knew Latin, and easily learned each other's vernacular languages. Chaucer's English, French and Latin appear to have been secure from the time of his first writings; he was already deeply read in the literary heritage of Rome and the French literature of his own times and the two or three preceding centuries. The works of the Frenchmen, Froissart (known as 'Sir John' owing to his service to English royalty), Deschamps and Machaut were well known to him, and as they exchanged compliments, he probably met them personally. As his contacts with, and visits to, Italy brought the works of Dante, Petrarch and Boccaccio to his notice, his borrowings from them took his poetry into a wider world of ideas and greater refinement of poetic expression. We do not know whether he met Boccaccio and Petrarch, and it remains a mystery why he never mentioned Boccaccio by name, although two of his major poems, *Troilus and Criseyde* and *The Knight's Tale*, draw on Boccaccio's poetry. Petrarch and Dante he often mentions, and always with intense respect. Chaucer, at his most serious, sometimes creates his most sublime poetry by paying the ultimate compliment to Dante of imitating him. Like Byron, another poet who was deeply affected by Dante's *Divina Commedia*, Chaucer dared

> ... to build the imitative rhyme,
> Harsh Runic copy of the South's sublime.
> (Byron: Dedication to *The Prophecy of Dante*)

But the self-deprecating 'harsh Runic' is true of neither Byron's nor Chaucer's imitative compliments. As Piero Boitani says, whenever Chaucer invokes the great Italian, 'Chaucer works a continuous counterpoint to Dante's text, first drawing close to him and using some of his words or images and then distancing himself so that Dantean echoes are only half-heard' (*Chaucer and the Italian Trecento*, 1983, p. 117). Chaucer took into his own work the inspiration of Dante's *dolce stil nuovo* (sweet new style), and it is partly his stylistic freedom from the Gothic elaboration of typically medieval English literature that makes us think of him as our first modern poet.

It used to be common to refer to Chaucer's 'French period' and 'Italian period', but those terms are of limited value since, to take a single example, Chaucer continued to draw heavily on the French *Roman de la Rose* until the end. But the two great influences on his poetry of France and Italy were followed by a third: although knowledge of the religion of his day figures in Chaucer's work from the very first, his recognition of its workings and significances, as well as his power to evoke its innermost meanings and even make fun of its rigidities and pretensions, increase as his career progresses.

It may be appropriate to allow the question of religion to usher into the last paragraph of this introduction three mild warnings to readers of

Chaucer who may find themselves occupied with background material for much of the time which ought to be spent on reading the poetry. It seems to me not worth expending energy, as some critics do, on trying to save Chaucer's soul, six hundred years late, by trying to prove him to have been devout. Then, while study of his sources is necessary to complete the work on his poetry, it has in my view been overemphasized at the expense of literary appreciation. Lastly, one of the effects of giving isolated prominence to the *General Prologue* to *The Canterbury Tales*, with its description of characters and their occupations, has been to divert literary study and enjoyment into delving, through the examination of historical material, into Chaucer's life and times. But we require to experience his own creation of characters, and his own evocation of the times in which he lived, in his poetry, through which he lives for us today.

A Short Chronology of Chaucer's Life

c. 1343	Born.
1357	Is page to the Countess of Ulster, wife of Prince Lionel.
1359	Campaigns in France as a squire, is captured near Rheims.
1360	Is freed on payment of ransom, to which King Edward III contributed £16.
1361–6	Possibly accompanies Prince Lionel in Ireland.
c. 1366	Marries Philippa Roet, sister of Edward's mistress, Katherine Swynford.
1366	Visits Spain.
1368	Is enrolled as Squire of the Royal Household.
1369	Campaigns in Picardy.
1372–3	Visits Italy for the first time.
1374	Becomes Controller of Customs. Rents house above Aldgate, on the city wall of London.
1376–81	Often travels abroad on royal business.
1377	Is in France, possibly for peace negotiations.
1378	Second Italian visit.
1385	Is appointed Justice of the Peace in Kent.
1386	Elected Knight of the Shire in Kent. Controllership of Customs is terminated. Gives up house over Aldgate.

1387	His wife dies (conjecture).
1389	Richard II comes of age. Chaucer is appointed Clerk of the King's Works, and oversees building and repairs of royal buildings for two years.
1391	Is appointed Deputy Forester of North Petherton in Somerset.
1392–1400	Receives various gifts, emoluments and pensions from Richard II and Henry IV.
1400	Dies and is buried in Westminster Abbey.

A Selective Literary Chronology of the Century of Chaucer

1300–50

∩ c. 1302–4	Dante's *De Vulgari Eloquentia* (*Concerning Literature in the Common Tongue*). Use of vernacular in writing high poetry is justified.
c. 1304–7	Dante's *Convivio* (*Banquet*), a philosophic commentary on lyric poetry.
✓ c. 1307–20	Dante's *Divina Commedia* (*Inferno, Purgatorio, Paradiso*). Christian perfection is attained through the guidance of the idealized poet, Virgil, and love for the ideal woman, Beatrice. An allegory of Christian redemption which is Europe's greatest, and probably most influential, post-classical poem.
1321	Death of Dante.
c. 1320	The *Harley Lyrics*, both secular and religious, written in the form of French stanzas, heavily rhymed, but also alliterative.
1340	The *Auchinleck Manuscript*: Romances, including *Kyng Alisaunder* and *Sir Orfeo*, a 'Breton lay' in octosyllabic couplets on the Ovidian theme of Orpheus and Eurydice.
c. 1343	Chaucer born.
1349	William of Ockham (see p. 203) and Bishop Bradwardine (see pp. 203–4) both die of the plague. Bradwardine's *De Causa Contra Pelagium* (see The Nun's Priest's Tale, and pp. 203–4). Throughout the century: Mystery plays, especially at York, Chester, Coventry, Wakefield.

1350–80

c. 1350   *Wynnere and Wastour* (*He who acquires and he who wastes*),
           a 500-line alliterative dream vision on contemporary events.
/ 1349–51 Boccaccio's *Decameron* (see p. 28).
  c. 1350 Bromyard's *Summa Predicantium* (see p. 205), a long ABC
           of material for use in sermons.
  1358–70. Boccaccio's *Filostrato* (see **Troilus and Criseyde**, pp. 123–4)
           and *Teseida* (see **The Knight's Tale**, p. 36).
  1362   English supersedes French as language of law courts.
  1363   Parliament opened in English for the first time.
✓ 1363   *Piers Plowman* (A-Text) by William Langland. An extended
           spiritual allegory and social satire in alliterative verse, in the
           form of linked dream visions. West Midland English.
  1365   Alliterative *Morte Arthur*, a long tragic epic on Arthur's
           death following his successful wars against Rome.
  1369   **An ABC, The Book of the Duchess.**
  c. 1372–80 **St Cecilia (The Second Nun's Tale). The House of Fame.**
           Most of **The Monk's Tale**, excluding the 'modern instances'
           (see pp. 67–70). **Anelida and Arcite.**
  1374   Death of Petrarch, early Italian humanist and most popular
           Italian poet in medieval and Renaissance England.
  1375   Death of Boccaccio.
  1376   Barbour's *The Bruce*, an epic of 13,000 lines on Robert the
           Bruce, with its account of the Scots' victory over the English
           at Bannockburn (1314).
  1377   B-Text of *Piers Plowman* (three times as long as the A-Text).
  1376   Gower's *Mirour de l'Omme* (in French). An allegory of
           fallen man in 32,000 lines of octosyllabic couplets.
  1379–81 Gower's *Vox Clamantis* (a Latin poem on contemporary
           political events).

1380–90

c. 1380   **The Parliament of Fowls.**
1380   First Lollard Bible, instigated by Wycliffe.
c. 1382   *Palamon* (later to become **The Knight's Tale**).
c. 1383   **Boece.**
1384   Death of Wycliffe.
c. 1383–6 **Troilus and Criseyde, Boethian Ballades, The Legend of
           Good Women.**

1385–6	C-Text of *Piers Plowman*.
c. 1386–90	Gower's *Confessio Amantis* (*A Lover's Confession*), in English. A collection of 141 moralized love stories, many on subjects Chaucer treated, many drawn from Ovid.
1387	John of Trevisa's translation into English of Ranulf Higden's *Polychronicon*, a universal history in Latin, with a comment in the introduction that grammar schoolboys no longer know French. Higden is popularly supposed to have written the Chester cycle of Mystery plays.
1388	Lollard Bible is revised in more accessible English. Execution of Thomas Usk, author of the prose allegory *The Testament of Love*, which borrows from *Boece*, *Troilus and Criseyde* and *Piers Plowman*.
/ 1370–90?	Works of the Gawain-poet: *Pearl*, a dream-vision religious allegory on the death of a child, in 101 heavily rhymed and alliterating twelve-line stanzas; *Patience*, an alliterative Bible epic on the Book of Jonah; *Cleanness* (or *Purity*), an alliterative Bible epic in which homily material based on New Testament teaching about spiritual and sexual purity binds the Old Testament accounts of the Flood, Sodom and Gomorrah, and Belshazzar's Feast; *Sir Gawain and the Green Knight*, the masterpiece of alliterative literature. A sophisticated Arthurian romance, rich in event, atmosphere and moral seriousness. All four poems were written in north-western English.

1390–1415

√ 1387–92	**General Prologue** and earlier **Canterbury Tales.**
1391–2	**A Treatise on the Astrolabe.**
1392	**The Equatorie of the Planets.**
√ 1393–1400	Later **Canterbury Tales.**
1394	(Probably) revised **Prologue** to **The Legend of Good Women.**
1396	Death of Walter Hilton, writer of the mystical *Scale of Perfection*.
1400	Death of Chaucer.
1402–4	Hengwrt manuscript of *The Canterbury Tales*.
1408	Death of Gower.
c. 1410	Death of Froissart, French poet and chronicler of English and French chivalric exploits.
1410–12	Ellesmere manuscript of *The Canterbury Tales*.

An Approach to Chaucer's English

. . . the words preserved in a text are the immobilised testimony to a vital language system which has now disappeared.

(David Burnley: *A Guide to Chaucer's Language*, 1983 p. xiii)

Notwithstanding Burnley's daunting truth, which applies to all literature of the past, but may seem to bear especially heavily on the reading of works written six hundred years ago in the language of south-eastern England, Chaucer's poetry can be read quite easily by modern readers who lack linguistic expertise, provided a few simple ground rules are followed. These firstly concern matters of spelling and vocabulary.

Spelling was not standardized in the fourteenth century, and was not to be fully so for another quarter of a millennium. So take the varied spellings lightly; even a demand of rhyme or metre may produce a new spelling. In vocabulary, the number of obsolete words is not great, but you must ascertain their meanings, either from the glossary of an annotated text or the accepted full Chaucer Glossary (see Bibliography). Then there is the admitted difficulty of what George Steiner (in *Babel*, 1975) calls 'false friends'; that is, words which are still in use today, but at that time had different, further, or more restricted meanings. 'Free', for example, usually connoted the qualities associated with aristocracy and is hence translated 'noble', but is occasionally found with its modern meaning. Lastly, there are the occasional trap-words such as the adverb 'uprighte', to which have been given downright opposite meanings because lexicographers seem, in some cases, to work pragmatically from the context: 'His slepy yerde in hond he bar uprighte' is translated as 'his sleep-inducing wand he (the god Mercury) carried in the vertical position' (*The Knight's Tale*, I, 1387); whereas in 'This wenche lay uprighte, and fast slepte' (*The Reeve's Tale*, I, 4194) it means facing upwards, that is, flat on her back. There is only one way to deal with 'false friends'; keep looking them up, and be especially suspicious of words which define concepts, like 'gentilesse', for example. Eventually, your developing sense of the culture the language reflects may be trusted to some extent, but even then, keep on checking.

Grammar presents much less of a problem, unless the reader, and especially the student, wishes to study the language besides reading and enjoying Chaucer. Such a reader will at once run into the problem posed by the varieties of medieval English which are occasionally found in Chaucer, but proliferate in the work of his contemporaries. Next, and more important, there are a few idioms and syntactical constructions

21

to be learnt and thereafter recognized when they occur. Also, the reader is constantly aware of inflexions in the final syllables of words both familiar and strange; inflexions of which few now remain in our language: in the conjugation of verbs, and in the case and gender indications of nouns and the adjectives which qualify them. These are survivals from Old English which in Chaucer's time were fast withering away.

The Pronunciation

More important to the reader of poetry than any of the above matters, apart from knowing the vocabulary, is the skill of reading Chaucer aloud in a reasonably correct way. There is a fair consensus concerning the pronunciation, which means that we know approximately how the poetry sounded. It is only by reading it – or any poetry for that matter – aloud that the lexical and metrical qualities can be brought fully into the experience. To take a single important detail first: in modern times, until the nineteenth century, it was not appreciated that final -e and -es of words were usually syllabized. I take my examples at random from *The Knight's Tale*:

1 2 3 4   5 6 7 8 910 11
I mene nat the goddesse Diane,

(I, 2063)

(in which the final unaccented 'e' is, as invariably, syllabized so that the line reads as a hendecasyllable, with a feminine ending)

1   2   3   4 5   6   7   8 9 10

With hym ther wenten knyghtes many on;

(I, 2118)

In Chaucer's day, vowels had the general sound values which we hear today in Western European languages like French. That was before the great vowel shift, the process during the fifteenth century by which modern English vowel sounds began to emerge, and to be represented in writing – especially by Caxton and others when printing came into use – by standardized letter symbols which did not have regular phonetic equivalents. The table below is offered as a guide to reading Chaucer aloud.

Approximate pronunciation of vowel sounds

Spelling in Chaucerian word	Pronunciation in modern English example	Chaucerian word
1 a, aa	*father* (N)	f*a*der, n*a*me
2 a	c*a*t (N)	th*a*t, f*a*t
3 e, ee (closed)	d*a*ze	sw*e*te, n*ee*de
4 e, ee (open)	th*e*re	b*e*re, h*ee*th
5 e	b*e*d	b*e*d, w*e*pte
6 e (neutral)	*a*bout	yong*e*, tabl*e*
7 i, y	mach*i*ne	bl*i*the, f*y*nde
8 i, y	k*i*t	l*i*st, kn*y*ght
9 o, oo (closed)	b*oa*t (N)	d*o*m, g*oo*d
10 o, oo (open)	b*oa*rd	s*o*rwe, d*oo*n
11 o	c*o*t	s*o*fte, j*o*ly
12 ou, ow, ogh	f*oo*l	h*ou*s, h*ow*, sw*o(u)*gh (noise of wind)
13 u, o	b*oo*k	f*u*ll, n*o*nne
14 u, eu, ew	t*u* (Fr)	vert*u*, Pr*u*ce
15 ai, ay, ei, ey	s*ay* or *ai*sle (diphthong)	f*ai*r, d*ay*, f*ei*th, w*ey*e
16 au, aw	m*ou*se (diphthong)	c*au*se, dr*aw*e
17 eu (closed)	kn*ew* (diphthong)	r*eu*le, kn*ew*
18 ew (open)	f*ai*r plus b*oo*k (diphthong)	f*ew*e
19 oi, oy	b*oy* (diphthong)	p*oi*nt, c*oy*
20 ou, ow	l*ow* (diphthong)	th*o(u)*ght, s*ow*le

Notes

(a) In the middle column, (N) means that the modern example should be pronounced as in northern forms, not standard southern English, and (Fr) that it should be pronounced as in French.

(b) Doubling the vowel in Chaucerian English usually lengthens the sound.

(c) The distinction between 3 and 4, between 9 and 10, and between 17 and 18 is neither certain nor absolute.

Consonants

Consonants were all pronounced, including letters which in certain positions have now become silent, and with the exceptions given here, were pronounced as they are today:

in words of French origin (such as 'honour') the initial 'h' was silent, as was also the 'g' before 'n' in words such as 'digne' and 'deigne';

'ch' was always pronounced as in modern 'church', not as in 'machine';

initial letters of words such as 'knyght' and 'gnof' were pronounced;
medial 'l' in words such as 'calf' and 'folk' was pronounced;
'gh' in words such as 'knyght' was pronounced as in Scots 'loch';
'r' was always trilled; such word endings as '-ion' or '-ioun', and in
'-ious', were disyllabic;
'gg' was pronounced as a hard 'g' except when in modern spelling it has
become 'dg'; then it has the sound of 'j' for instance in 'jugge' which has
become the modern 'judge' (verb).

Part II: The Canterbury Tales

Chapter 2. Introduction and the General Prologue

The Canterbury Tales is a collection of twenty-four stories of different kinds – romance, fabliau, saint's legend, homily – ranging from extended bawdy joke to elevated religious treatise, told by members of a company of pilgrims on their springtide journey from the Tabard Inn in Southwark to Canterbury. The *Tales* are preceded by the *General Prologue*, in which Chaucer briefly describes the appearance, character and occupation of twenty-two of the twenty-nine pilgrims, the remaining seven being merely listed; and they are linked by connecting passages, including Prologues to all but two of the tales. The grand design, as stated in the Tabard the evening before departure, by Harry Bailey, the Host, is that each pilgrim shall tell four stories, two on the way to Canterbury and two on the way back, with a free supper at the Tabard as a prize for the best story-teller. This plan is far from completed; it appears that Chaucer adjusted it as he proceeded, so that towards the end of *The Canterbury Tales* as we have them, the reader can easily accept that only one more tale remains to be told.

The best surviving manuscripts, the Hengwrt (1402–4) and Ellesmere (1410–12), contain ten fragments of sequences of tales, all of them with some internal linking passages. *The Canterbury Tales* occupied Chaucer for the last dozen or so years of his life, probably from 1387 onwards, and it seems clear that he died before putting even what he had written in final order and revising it accordingly; so that both the above manuscripts are the result of conscientious compiling and editing by a single knowledgeable scribe. Although most editions of Chaucer's work are based on Ellesmere, which is beautifully written and more complete, it is now thought by many that Hengwrt, though possibly put together more hurriedly, is often freer from scribal emendation. Quotations from the *Tales* here are referenced as in the standard work, *The Works of Geoffrey Chaucer* (ed. F. N. Robinson, second edition, 1957) that is, by letter indication of Fragment, followed by line number.

Even as we have it, incomplete as a whole and unfinished in some of its parts, *The Canterbury Tales*, taken as a single narrative work, stands possibly without equal among the greatest long English poems: works such as Spenser's *Faerie Queene*, Milton's *Paradise Lost*, Wordsworth's *Prelude* and Byron's *Don Juan*, and of course Chaucer's own *Troilus and Criseyde*.

Collections of stories had been popular in classical antiquity, and there were several medieval examples, both in Europe and the Near East. Of the classical collections, perhaps the best known is Ovid's *Metamorphoses*, in which the unifying factor was the requirement that the subject of each story should include a change of being, such as from human to animal or plant or stellar body; Chaucer drew heavily on the *Metamorphoses*, especially in the early and middle parts of his career. The best known of the medieval collections are the Arabic *Thousand and One Nights* and Boccaccio's *Decameron.* The formal unifying factor in the first is the person of the teller, the bride of an oriental ruler who habitually murdered his wives after consummating marriage on the first night, but spared Scheherezade because he could not resist the lure of her nightly story-telling; and in the second, the *Decameron*, the story-tellers are young nobles of both sexes whiling away the time as country refugees from an outbreak of plague in their home city. The originality of Chaucer's collection lies in formal requirements more varied and especially more dramatically dynamic than any of those just mentioned.

The story-tellers are a diverse company of English people – members of the minor nobility, professions, religious orders, trades and lower classes, excluding serfs – on pilgrimage to Canterbury, where the shrine of Thomas à Becket was one of the busiest in Europe. Thus, to a degree which varies from character to character, each *Tale* may be seen as the expression of a particular pilgrim's personality, and is accepted as such by the company, though readers well understand that all is mediated through the overruling poetic art of Chaucer. The relation between tale and poet-teller, which is so richly productive elsewhere in Chaucer's narrative poetry, is thus further, and often enigmatically, enriched in *The Canterbury Tales* by the existence of this third factor, the added fictitious narrator together with his or her fictional audience.

Twenty-two of the twenty-nine pilgrims tell stories, Chaucer himself being the only one to tell two. In addition, the Canon's Yeoman, who joins the pilgrimage late, tells a tale, so that twenty-four in all are told. When the last tale, that of the Parson, begins, the impression is given that the pilgrims are not far from Canterbury on the outward journey. Those who do not tell stories are the Yeoman accompanying the Knight, the Plowman and the five Guildsmen – the Haberdasher, Carpenter, Weaver (Webbe), Dyer and Tapestry Weaver (Tapycer).

Two of the binding elements in *The Canterbury Tales* are the progress towards the cathedral city – stages of the route, places stopped at, times of day – and the interaction of members of the company, both within and outside the tales they tell. The first element is chiefly formal; it gives a satisfactory impression of a continuing journey by, for example, providing the names of towns on the way to Canterbury – Deptford, Greenwich, Rochester, Sittingbourne – and does not provide deep meanings, except, notably, when the Parson, in the *Prologue* to his tale, gives significance to the idea of pilgrimage as the progress of the soul, by praying Jesus to allow him to show the pilgrims, as they near Canterbury,

> ... the wey, in this viage,
> Of thilke parfit glorious pilgrymage
> That highte Jerusalem celestial.

(X, 49–51)

The interaction among the pilgrims provides a continuous drama so potent that the reader looks for its special excitements before and after every tale. First of all in the *General Prologue*, and then in the introductions, prologues and other linking material, the developing harmonies and antipathies within a company on the move are vividly expressed, together with their responses to what they hear. Probably this linking material was written at a late stage of composition, when Chaucer started to put together, and to allot to particular narrators, stories which he himself had written at various times, and also to create stories for particular tellers, and tellers for particular stories. But the Links are even less complete than the overall scheme of *The Canterbury Tales*; the connections and sense of continuity that they establish are intermittent, though they are especially strong at the beginning, in the sequence of tales told by the Knight, Miller, Reeve and Cook and in Fragment VII, which contains the tales of the Shipman and the Prioress, Chaucer's tales of Sir Thopas and Melibee, and the tales of the Monk and the Nun's Priest. The Links, which are dominated, as might be expected, by the Host in his role of master of ceremonies, are both entertaining and illuminating, and it is a pity that, since students are usually asked to concentrate on the *General Prologue* and on individual tales, they are not given the wide admiration they deserve. They give particular life to the whole.

As they appear in the *General Prologue*, Chaucer's characters make such a vivid gallery that artists, most prominently among them William Blake, have been stimulated to show the group of thirty on the move, each habited and characterized as Chaucer's text and the artist's ideas about medieval manners and modes suggest. But for the reader, no such partial and limited conspectus should prevail because, to state it in dramatic terms, the *General Prologue* is like the formal parade of the characters in a theatre at the beginning of a play, such as appears in, say, *The*

Revenger's Tragedy; the appetite of the audience is whetted, but will only be satisfied by the action which follows. The *General Prologue*, read as an isolated literary phenomenon, demonstrates chiefly a particular aspect of Chaucer's art: his ability to make a thumbnail character sketch live powerfully and subtly. That is a minor though essential part of his equipment as a great narrative poet. For this reason, I treat the characters in the direct context of the tales they tell and the linking passages connected with them while, in this introduction to *The Canterbury Tales*, I discuss broader matters concerned with the *General Prologue* and the *Tales* as a whole.

Chaucer exercises some freedom in describing his characters, being by no means bound by the schemes of character portrayal favoured by classical authors such as Theophrastus, or by medieval rhetoricians and moralists. Variously, he draws on literary, religious, scientific and pseudo-scientific sources which depict and moralize upon types of people; on the literature of social satire in both lay writing and sermon; on his knowledge of public and private life in his own times; and on his own direct observations of individuals. He keeps no set order in selecting from these elements, but treats each character according to his special purpose for him or her: a process which allows him to achieve instant vital detail as well as significantly revealing juxtapositions. For example, the Pardoner has only just been introduced when, in the third and fourth line of his description, this key observation is made:

> . . . That [he] streight was comen fro the court of Rome.
> Ful loude he soong, "Com hider, love, to me!"

(I, 671–2)

There his formal religious function and his shameless libertine exhibitionism are placed in a single couplet with an outrageous rhyme (though 'Rome' was pronounced as a disyllable ending in the neutral vowel sound).

The order in which the characters appear does not seem to have been rigorously planned, but five broad groups may be noted. First comes the Knight with his Squire and Yeoman. There follow three members of religious orders, the Prioress, the Monk and the Friar, the Prioress with her entourage of two who are not described: the Nun who tells *The Second Nun's Tale* of St Cecilia, and the Priest who tells *The Nun's Priest's Tale* of the Cock and the Fox. Next comes a diverse group of people from the professions and trades whose main concern is with money: Merchant, Clerk, Sergeant of Law, Franklin, Shipman, Doctor of Physic, five Guildsmen with their Cook, and the Wife of Bath; among these the Clerk, an idealized scholar figure, is the odd man out. The penultimate group is composed of only two, the poor Parson and his brother the Plowman, both of whom are entirely idealized types. Of the final six, five are rogues: Miller, Manciple, Reeve, Summoner and Pardoner; and Chaucer, with silent laughter, introduces himself as a member of the group. So there is some progression from the upper reaches of society to the lower, encompassing first those who fight, then those who pray, and lastly those who work, while the concluding ragbag contains the least worthy among those who pray and work.

The Knight, who seems slightly severe and old-fashioned in spite of being presented as typical and apparently ideal, and his son the Squire who, besides being accoladed with loverly youth and its accomplishments, appears more modern and sophisticated than his father, are accompanied by a Yeoman, who does not tell a tale and is not depicted in the illustrations to the Ellesmere manuscript. The Yeoman is presented as a huntsman and forester, his green clothing, weapons, horn and even his St Christopher badge being typical of the occupation of one who works for his Knight, both on the estate and in the field. His efficiency, close-cropped head and sunburnt face are mentioned, but nothing more personal of appearance or character.

The pervasiveness of religion in *The Canterbury Tales* appears not only in the subject matter of many of the stories, but also in the preponderance of characters whose main concern is, or ought to be, the Christian religion. Thus we have a Prioress, a Monk, a Friar, a Nun, a Priest, a Parson, a Summoner and a Pardoner besides the two idealized laymen who respectively represent holy studies and holy labour – the Clerk and the Plowman. The Prioress is endearingly satirized, while the soft-living, hunting Monk and the lecherous, acquisitive Friar are penetratingly exposed. The next three are idealized either by description in the *General Prologue* or by the nature of the tales they tell and their behaviour in the Links, and the Summoner and the Pardoner are savagely satirized. That makes ten characters out of the twenty-nine (the Host makes the thirtieth). While the tales told by these ten are not necessarily religious in the strict sense, though those told by the Prioress, Nun, Pardoner and Parson are, it should be noted that two laymen, the Man of Law and Chaucer himself, do tell religious stories: the Man of Law's tale of Constance exemplifying unwavering faith and Chaucer's *Tale of Melibee* exemplifying charitable forbearance and forgiveness.

Chaucer is more forgiving of those who err in their worldly occupations, such as the Merchant, Sergeant of the Law, Doctor of Physic and Shipman, than of those whose formal care is for souls, though in his description of their modes of operation he still points to abuses of the age and their effect on individual character, while giving a clear account of practical worldly life in the late fourteenth century. But two of this group seem largely uncondemned: the generous Franklin, who eventually tells the tale which seals the so-called marriage debate with its recommendations of mutual trust and equality, and the Wife of Bath, a character so unusual in conception, and so particularized in the detail of her feeling, thinking and doing, that to apply a simple moral yardstick to her is too limiting to be useful. To judge by references to her in other parts of *The Canterbury Tales*, and in other poems by his contemporaries as well as by Chaucer himself, she instantly caught the fame that she has never lost.

In Chaucer's gallery of characters, and the people in the stories they subsequently tell, three main categories may be discerned: the good, the worldly-striving and the depraved. The good, like the idealized types mentioned so far, are fortified by their faith, and on the whole, are not such interesting human beings as those in the other two categories, though the insight of the patient Griselda, in *The Clerk's Tale,* into the mentality of sexual tyranny displayed by her husband Walter, and the combination of fantastic humour, wit and intellect in *The Nun's Priest's Tale*, are exceptions. Those I call worldly strivers fascinate the reader because, though not necessarily fundamentally evil, they show common fallibility in being unable to resist the lures of wealth, power, formal status, sex, or a brew of two or more of these. The Wife of Bath with her drive for social status, love and sexual equality, the hag-ridden Merchant concealing his debts while playing rich, and the Prioress insisting on the luxuries and graces of worldly aristocratic life while ruling her cloister, are cases in point.

The depraved, such as the Miller, Pardoner, Reeve and Summoner, astonish and delight the reader, the first two for the brilliant energy with which they prosecute their immoral lives, the last two for their comprehensive unattractiveness. It is interesting that Chaucer has no pilgrim of the lowest social rank, that of serf: no serf could go on an expensive pilgrimage except as a servant. When a serf does appear in one of his tales – such as Griselda's father in *The Clerk's Tale* – he is allowed the dignity of those to whom unremitting work and casual oppression are the main rewards of life. All the depraved are independent people of substance.

Every character, whether good, or worldly-striving, or depraved, throbs with a life which is real and rooted in an actual society, not fantastically conceived or determined by abstract moral considerations alone. Against his faithful sense of that ever-present religion which dominates so much medieval literature, Chaucer poses a broad and compassionate humanity over which Nature, goddess of creation and the good potentiality in all living things, may be said to preside.

Chaucer's prime theme in *The Canterbury Tales* is love. In ten of the twenty-four stories, men and women on the way to, or in, marriage or bed provide the ostensible subject, and in six more tales they figure largely. In the comic tales, sexual activity is consentingly relished; in the romances and religious tales, the high ideal of a love relationship between man and woman, confirmed by vow and faithful practice, is time and again presented as one of relaxed and trusting harmony, as in *The Franklin's Tale*: 'Thus been they bothe in quiete and in rest' (V, 760). In that line Chaucer is expressing what is, for him, a dominant idea, for Troilus and Criseyde, having first consummated their love, also relate to each other 'in quyete and in reste' (III, 1680). Even the Wife of Bath affirms, though admittedly after establishing mastery over the male, this Chaucerian recommendation. She is the one who has most to say on the subject of love, and insists against religious precept that her sexual organ is for use rather than moral control.

Although formal philosophical and religious themes are perennial components of the *Tales*, and are of concern to particular pilgrims and characters in the stories, they appear to me less important than Chaucer's observation of human beings within the society and the literary culture that he knows, and still less important than his story-telling art, in which he extended the bounds and the variety of known genres. To give point to this assertion: *The Nun's Priest's Tale*, though formally a beast fable about a cock, a hen and a fox, uses a discussion about the prophetic value of dreams and a Boethian debate about free will and predestination to further a highly comic vision of a loving couple. The man in the case (the cock) becomes overbearingly confident as a result of successfully exercising his passionate love in the sexual act, and that is a profound observation of humanity at large, to which philosophical theories, however amusingly applied, are incidental. The same sort of thing could be said of the two young men in *The Knight's Tale*, which is often advanced, unjustifiably in my view, as a 'philosophical romance'. Through Chaucer's admittedly learned persiflage, whether in the widow's smallholding in *The Nun's Priest's Tale* or Theseus's tournament arena in *The Knight's Tale*, the passions and preoccupations of real people in real medieval English life stand in their superb particularity. Every detail is carefully selected. In the *General Prologue*, it is important what sort of horse a character rides (Knight, Monk, Clerk, Shipman, Wife of Bath,

Reeve) and what musical instrument he plays (a lover's flute for the Squire, a learned man's 'rote' – possibly a fiddle upon which he 'harped' – for the Friar, rural bagpipes for the Miller who plays the pilgrims on their way).

The *General Prologue* significantly opens with an eighteen-line sentence which is a paean to spring, reminiscent of the beginning of a dream vision on the subject of love; and that is a sophisticated joke by a poet who proceeds to present a gallery of original characters, and to spill a cornucopia of diverse narratives before his audience. At the end, after a formal apology from the poet for having to be true to each of his story-tellers' styles, 'Al speke he never so rudeliche and large' (However crudely and with licence he speaks), the *Prologue* closes with the start of the pilgrimage and its management by the Host, a big and bright-eyed man who is used to responsibility and at once makes forceful play for leadership of the group. The evening before departure he suggests the story-telling, and the next morning, when the company has gone only a little way, to 'the watering of Seint Thomas' (I, 826) on what is now the Old Kent Road, he halts them to draw lots to decide who shall begin. In sermon literature, pilgrimages are often described as inviting loose life, and the telling of tales on pilgrimages is specifically condemned.

Chapter 3. Tales of the Knight, the Miller, the Reeve, the Cook and the Man of Law

The Knight

The Knight is presented as the true pattern of chivalry in his dual capacity of noble warrior and devout Christian. Since his tunic is still stained with rust from his coat of mail, he has evidently just come from the wars to go on this pilgrimage. His distant campaigns include some waged 'for oure feith'. But he has also engaged in prestigious single combat, and apparently in wars on behalf of one lot of pagans against another:

> Somtyme with the lord of Palatye
> Agayne another hethen in Turkye.
>
> (I, 65–6)

He is humble, and not showily dressed and equipped. Naturally, as the only male aristocrat in the pilgrimage party, he is the first character to be described, and also the first to tell his tale. The text implies that the Host discreetly helped on the 'foreward' (agreement) and 'composicioun' (arrangement) by which the Knight's priority was fixed, perhaps by determining the length of the cut the Knight drew in the lottery to decide who should be first to tell a tale. The Knight does not obtrude himself into the story, although near the beginning Chaucer puts into his mouth an *occupatio*[1] in which he modestly excuses himself from describing the wars and marriage feast of Theseus and Hyppolita on the grounds that

> ... wayke[2] been the oxen in my plough,
> The remenant of the tale is long ynough.
>
> (I, 887–8)

It has been justly remarked how little interested in the subject of warfare Chaucer seems to be. Appropriately enough, it is only in this tale told by the professional soldier that accurate accounts of sustained mortal combat and of tournament practice are given.

The Knight's Tale seems to have received its final form in about 1382, that is, several years before Chaucer started work on *The Canterbury*

---

1. the rhetorical device of expressing an intention not to deal with a subject while in fact referring to it briefly. Chaucer often uses it, and sometimes lengthens the brief references with humorous intention   2. weak

Tales and decided to incorporate it there, and not long before the time that he was working on *Troilus and Criseyde*. The *Knight's Tale* has affinities with the *Troilus*, being essentially a romantic tale of love set in classical times and conceived on an epic scale, and also owing much of its philosophical thought to Boethius. The main source of the story of Palamon and Arcite is Boccaccio's romantic epic, the *Teseida* (1340), a work of almost ten thousand lines, only seven hundred of which are clearly recognizable in Chaucer's poem of 2250 lines. Chaucer also drew on the episodic Latin epic about ancient Thebes by the first-century poet Statius, the *Thebaid*, and, in addition, probably on French versions of both Statius and Boccaccio. For the philosophical content, Chaucer drew not only upon Boethius, but also on Macrobius. However, his lovers are driven by the motives and values of courtly love, and lack individuality of character to such a degree that the beauties and excitements of the poem must be sought elsewhere than in the depiction of their states of mind. The narrative frame of the poem remains concerned with a vital 'question of love' in the courtly code: 'which lover will, or should, win the lady?' The verse throughout is iambic pentameter rhymed in couplets, the form favoured by Chaucer for *The Legend of Good Women* (which was probably begun in 1386), and subsequently for many of the Canterbury narratives.

The *Knight's Tale* opens with the high pathos of a group of black-clad noble widows, victims of a downward turn of Fortune's wheel, pleading on their knees to Duke Theseus. They want his help to ensure that the bodies of their husbands, slaughtered in battle by Creon, King of Thebes, are given honourable obsequies. Theseus responds at once: he sends back to Athens his wife Hyppolita and her younger sister Emelye, and kills Creon in battle. When the enemy corpses are being stripped of their equipment and looted of their valuables, two royal knights, both badly wounded, are found still alive among them: the joint heroes of this *Tale*, the cousins Palamon and Arcite. As enemies of Athens, they are denied ransom and are imprisoned in a tower from the window of which, one May morning, first Palamon and then Arcite sees Emelye in the garden below doing observance to the spirit of the season, and falls violently and irrevocably in love with her. Prison and garden are pervasive in Chaucer's love poetry, and are rarely juxtaposed as here: in the prison the lover languishes, and in the garden he seeks, and sometimes finds, fulfilment. Oddly enough, in *The Legend of Good Women*, it is an imprisoned Theseus, a very different character from the reasonable and humorous one in this tale, who languishes in the Cretan dungeon above which Ariadne and Phaedra plot his salvation.

Palamon and Arcite quarrel: Palamon says that he saw Emelye first, and claims the help of his kinsman in his love pursuit, which Arcite counters with 'Who shal yeve a lovere any lawe?' (I, 1164). After a while a visiting duke, Perotheus, persuades Theseus to release Arcite, whom he has long known and loved. Arcite is freed, with the proviso that, if he is ever found in a country ruled by Theseus, his head will be cut off. Each lover in turn laments: Arcite in Boethian style against Fortune because, being banished from Athens, he may no longer see Emelye daily as Palamon may; Palamon because he correctly judges that Arcite will somehow be able to use his freedom to woo Emelye. Palamon blames Saturn, the malignant god, for his imprisonment, Juno for the destruction of his native city, and Venus for his jealous misery. Part I ends with the narrator asking a key question in the love debate: 'Who hath the worse, Arcite or Palamoun?' (I, 1348).

Part II opens with Arcite wasting away for love. When the god Mercury tells him in a dream to go to Athens, where his woes will end (a nice ambiguity in view of his unexpected and violent death there), Arcite judges from the mirror that he will not now be recognized. In disguise, under the name of Philostrate, he first works as page to Emelye, then rises to be a squire under Theseus, a post he keeps for three years. Meanwhile Palamon has languished in prison for seven years, and then, typically on a night in May – the conventional month for love exploits – he escapes and hides in a grove outside Athens. There, again typically, comes Arcite 'to doon his observaunce to May', lamenting his fate at the hands of Juno and Mars, and conveniently narrating aloud his life story. As he begins, an authorial comment, which ought to be in the style of the Knight as the ostensible narrator, but sounds more like Chaucer from behind his own mask, ludicrously compares Arcite's loverly up-and-down mood to the motions of a bucket in a well. Palamon, over-hearing all Arcite's words, emerges from the bushes to challenge Arcite either to fulfil the proper role of a kinsman in supporting him in his love-quest and giving up his love for Emelye, or to prepare to die. Un-fortunately Palamon has no weapon. Arcite repeats his old argument that 'love is free', insists on continuing his love-quest and promises to bring weapons and armour the next day so that, Palamon choosing the best if he wishes, they may decide the matter in mortal combat.

In a passage redolent of battle descriptions in Arthurian romance, Chaucer describes their duel as they fight first with spears and then with swords. The moment when Theseus, who has come to the same grove hunting accompanied by Hyppolita and Emelye, finds them at it is particularly vivid:

> Under the sonne he looketh, and anon
> He was war of Arcite and Palamon,
> That foughten breme,[3] as it were bores[4] two.
> The brighte swerdes wenten to and fro
> So hidously[5] that with the leeste strook
> It semed as it wolde felle an ook.[6]
>
> (I, 1697–702)

Theseus intercedes, threatening death to either if he deals another blow. Palamon, who is throughout the more tragic and death-centred of the two lovers, reveals all, and Theseus swears by Mars that both shall die. For the second time the course of events is deflected by kneeling and pleading women, and Chaucer, in allowing the plea for clemency of Hyppolita and Emelye to succeed, puts perhaps his most famous pathetic line in the mouth of Hyppolita, who thus expresses her 'verray [true] wommanhede': 'For pitee renneth[7] soone in gentil[8] herte' (I, 1761). In yielding the ladies grace, Theseus reveals a profound but unavoidably comic sagacity, which puts the love theme, and hence the whole poem, in another light: one foreshadowed by the thought of that bucket going up and down in the well. He exclaims: 'Who may been a fool, but if he love?' (I, 1799; Who can be a fool, unless he is in love?) and finds further amusement in the fact that Emelye, the motive for their murderous conflict

> ... woot namoore of al this hoote fare,[9]
> By God, than woot a cokkow or an hare!
>
> (I, 1809–10)

The third point Theseus makes is that his niece by marriage, for whom he is responsible, cannot wed two men, however worthy they may be. One of them 'moot go pipen in an yvy leef' (must pipe in an ivy leaf, that is, go whistle). He decrees that in a year's time the matter must be decided by mortal combat in the lists, each contender being supported by a hundred knights. With both lovers rejoicing in that judgement, Part II ends.

So far, despite the courtly stances and plaints of Palamon and Arcite, the narrative impulse has carried the story forward in a pagan tone – that is, with the mythology, names and settings of Graeco-Roman antiquity, though there are such quaint medievalisms as calling the two kings, Theseus and Perotheus, 'dukes'. But Part II imposes a rich and yet more pagan stasis upon the developing tale of love rivalry. This arrest of the narrative concerns the setting up by Theseus of the arena in

---

3. furiously   4. boars   5. terribly   6. oak   7. runs   8. noble   9. knows no more of all this furious going-on

which the love conflict is to be decided, and the use of the arena before battle. The style rises to the epic mode as Chaucer describes how Theseus orders his mile-wide circular theatre for the great event, with altars and oratories at three of the four compass points: to Venus at the eastern gate, to Mars at the western gate, and to Diana in the northern wall. Palamon will enter the lists from the east and Arcite from the west. Readers or listeners who wish to know which lover would win the lady are now held up, and no doubt diverted, by a fireworks display of epic writing lasting six hundred lines.

The first of the three sections of Part III is given to descriptions of the three sets of altars and oratories, and of their characteristics which fit their presiding deities. The temple of Venus is first described: depicted there ('wroght on the wal') is all the physical and allegorical apparatus of disordered love, from abstract characters drawn from the *Romance of the Rose* (Desire, Bawdry, Jealousy and so forth), through such sensuous love-pursuits as dancing, singing and personal adornment, to such absurd likelihoods as cuckoldry, symbolized by the cuckoo. Lastly, the goddess herself and her attendant son Cupid are described in language of ravishing sensuousness:

> The statue of Venus, glorious for to se,
> Was naked, fletynge in the large [10] see,
> And fro the navele doun al covered was
> With wawes [11] grene, and brighte as any glas.
>
> (I, 1955–8)

Chaucer, as the poet of love, enjoys dallying with its presiding deity.

The bleak and terrible temple of the god of war, Mars, is next described. A continuous roaring din, bare northern light, and ghastly hard iron, steel and adamant characterize this appalling place; Felony, Ire and Dread, Madness, Mischance and Outrage, are among its allegorical inhabitants, who accompany

> The smylere with the knyf under the cloke;
> The shepne [12] brennynge [13] with the blake smoke;
> The tresoun of the mordrynge in the bedde;
> The open werre, with woundes al bibledde; [14]
>
> The sleere [15] of hymself yet saugh I ther, –
> His herte-blood hath bathed al his heer; [16]
> The nayl ydryven in the shode [17] a-nyght;
> The colde deeth, with mouth gapyng upright. [18]
>
> (I, 1999–2002, 2005–8)

10. wide 11. waves 12. stable 13. burning 14. covered with blood 15. slayer 16. hair 17. temple 18. face upwards

To conclude the horror, Mars himself is painted, on a cart, with a man-devouring wolf at his feet.

The temple of Diana, goddess of chastity and hunting, is the last to be described. The myth of Actaeon, who spied on Diana naked, and for his lust was turned into a stag and torn to pieces by her hounds, is depicted, and the goddess herself, with her attributes of hounds, moon, and bow and arrows, is described. Chaucer does not forget that as Lucina, Diana is also the goddess of childbirth, for the last picture in her temple is of a woman in labour crying out for help.

The second section of Part III contains an account of the allies recruited by Palamon and Arcite for the battle, and their equipment, and the entertainment of the contestants by Theseus in his palace. Palamon's chief ally is the black-haired King of Thrace, who is accompanied by wolf-hounds as big as bullocks, and Arcite's is the fair-haired King of India, around whom run tame lions and leopards. The setting and social rituals preceding the trial of strength are medieval, the tone still power-fully pagan. Part III ends with a bravura description in epic style of a triple ceremony conducted before the battle, which reveals clearly a main structural element of the whole *Tale* that has, up to this point, been only lightly implicit: the three main characters pray to the deities with whom they feel affinity, and receive prophetic signs from them. After-wards the gods in heaven discuss how the apparently conflicting pro-phecies can be fulfilled. Divine partisanship resolves human predica-ments.

Before dawn, at lark-rise, Palamon prays to Venus that, whatever the outcome of the battle, he may have Emelye's love; and the statue of Venus shakes, whereby Palamon knows that his prayer is granted. Next Emelye, at sunrise and attended by her maidens, offers sacrifice to Diana and prays firstly that she may keep her virginity and that her suitors' passion for her may be turned in another direction. Failing that, she prays that if she must marry either Palamon or Arcite, it shall be the one who most desires her. Blood issues from the sacrificial fire, and Diana appears, to tell her that she is bound to marry one of her suitors, but she does not know which. Lastly, Arcite prays to Mars for victory, which Mars grants. In the ensuing debate among the gods, Saturn, the president over human disasters, describes to Venus his typical achievements, and promises to fulfil the prophecies which have been made in such a way as to reconcile differences among the gods and goddesses:

> I do vengeance and pleyn correccioun,[19]
> Whil I dwelle in the signe of the leoun.[20]
> Myn is the ruyne of the hye halles,
> The fallynge of the toures and of the walles
> Upon the mynour or the carpenter ...
> Now weep namoore, I shal doon diligence
> That Palamon, that is thyn owene knyght,
> Shal have his ladye, as thou has him hight.[21]
> Though Mars shal helpe his knyght, yet nathelees
> Bitwixe yow ther moot be som tyme pees ...
>
> (I, 2461–5, 2470–74)

So the humans have become protagonists of the wishes of the gods which, with due regard to the necessary astrological timing, will be realized in the imminent final action.

Part IV opens with a graphic account of the people gathering early in the morning for the tournament. When Theseus appears,

> ... at a wyndow set,
> Arrayed right as he were a god in trone[22]
>
> (I, 2528–9)

he causes a herald to announce that, since he doesn't wish any of the contestants to be killed, weapons for close fighting shall not be used, and only one charge shall be made by any knight using a sharp spear. In addition, a knight who is worsted in combat may not be killed, but must be taken to a stake, where he must remain for the rest of the fight. The contest shall end when one of the two principals is so staked.

All this is very much according to fourteenth century usage. Tournaments, besides being dangerous and extraordinarily expensive aristocratic games, provided training for war, and even if they were fought with limited or bated weapons, like this one, casualties were often heavy. So it is not surprising that the Church outlawed them, though by the fourteenth century, in face of their growing popularity, it gave up trying to enforce its rule that men killed in tournaments should not be buried in holy ground.

Chaucer's description of the tournament is probably the best in all medieval English literature and, for part of it, he takes into his iambic pentameter the alliterative force and stern language of earlier romance:

> In goon the speres ful sadly[23] in arrest;[24]
> In gooth the sharpe spore[25] into the syde.[26]
> Ther seen men who kan juste and who kan ryde;

19. exact vengeance and ... penalty 20. lion 21. promised 22. throne 23. firmly 24. into their socket(s) 25. spur 26. horse's flank

> Ther shyveren shaftes upon sheeldes thikke;
> He feeleth thurgh the herte-spoon[27] the prikke.
> Up spryngen speres twenty foot on highte;
> Out goon the swerdes as the silver brighte;
> The helmes they tohewen and toshrede;[28]
> Out brest the blood with stierne[29] stremes rede;
> With myghty maces the bones they tobreste.[30]

(I, 2602-11)

The blond King of India and twenty of his men drag Palamon to the stake, in which action Palamon unhorses his royal opponent. But he has lost the battle, and up in heaven Venus weeps at her defeat and disgrace. Saturn promises her redress, and as Arcite takes off his helmet to gaze up at the approving Emelye, Pluto, at Saturn's request, causes an infernal fury to terrify Arcite's horse. The tournament victor is thrown, and fatally lands on his head. Before he dies in the arms of Emelye – and Chaucer accurately describes the medical measures taken to try to save his life, and to treat the wounds of all others hurt in the combat – he commends Palamon to her.

The entire community, 'old folk, and folk of tender yeeres', is grief-stricken, and Theseus and his father, Egeus, give the grief Boethian expression: 'this worldes transmutacioun', says the old man, brings 'joye after wo, and wo after gladnesse'. But the stately formal grief of the ensuing funeral is presented in a double focus: on the one hand the erection of a huge pyre, into the towering flames of which mourners throw jewels, and round which a mighty company of Greeks ride with clattering spears; on the other, an immoderately extended *occupatio* as Chaucer repeatedly says, while describing the details of the funeral, that he will not describe it. Even among the noble elements of the description, one detail of comic exaggeration suggests the detachment of the author, who is clearly Chaucer and not the Knight. The latter would not see anything funny in the idea of so much wood having to be cut down to make the funeral pyre that the 'Nymphes, fawnes and amadrides' (hamadryads) who had lived in the trees fled the scene, terrified and homeless.

In a long philosophical speech at the end of which he instructs his niece to take Palamon as husband out of her 'wommanly pitee', Theseus counsels everyone 'to maken vertu necessitee' – a phrase commonly still used today by people who have no idea of its origin. Theseus attributes the events to 'The Firste Movere of the cause above' who made 'the faire

---

27. hollow at base of breast-bone   28. hack in pieces   29. cruel   30. shatter

cheyne of love'. Unlike the ending of *Troilus and Criseyde*, there is no philosophical transition from pagan to Christian. Theseus advises:

> What may I conclude of this longe serye,[31]
> But after wo I rede[32] us to be merye,
> And thanken Juppiter of al his grace?
> And er that we departen from this place
> I rede that we make of sorwes two
> O[33] parfit joye, lastynge everemo.

(I, 3067–72)

The order in human affairs which Theseus thinks of as bound by the 'faire cheyne of love', and has been striving and legislating for throughout the poem, has now been achieved, but only at heavy cost, and that is due to the chief of the gods, whose will must be accepted.

The loverly lover has triumphed over the martial lover – a romantic upshot whose political corollary, seized on by Theseus and specified by Chaucer (I, 2967–74), is that Thebes conveniently becomes amicably dependent on Theseus's Athens.

The Miller

The Miller, who insists on following the Knight by telling 'a noble tale' of his own, although the Host wishes the Monk, a person of substance, to be next, apologizes in case he should 'mysspeke' on the grounds that he is drunk. His story, a fabliau,[34] fits the grotesque fellow described in the *Prologue*: he is big-boned and red-headed, has black flaring nostrils and a skull so thick that he can butt a door through. He leads the pilgrims, playing his bagpipes. As he declares the subject of his *Tale*, which is the cuckolding of a carpenter, he makes an enemy of the Reeve, whose trade in his youth happens to have been that of carpenter.

The Miller's Tale, a masterpiece of comic sex and intrigue, presents a figure conventional in classical and medieval literature and drama: the

---

31. process 32. advise 33. one 34. A fabliau is a comic short story in verse which in France, where it flourished in the twelfth and thirteenth centuries after developing from remote and probably oriental origins, was usually written in octosyllabic couplets, the metre of the *Roman de la Rose*. Chaucer not only extended the scope of the genre in English, through such tales as those of the Miller, Reeve, Shipman and Merchant, but joined its essence with that of other kinds of comic writing derived either from Ovid or medieval scabrous and bawdy anecdote: the tales of the Manciple, Friar and Summoner are cases in point. The fabliau is a comic and usually bawdy relation of an incident from middle-class life; an extended satirical anecdote, the targets of which are often cuckolds or clerics, and which is most often cynical.

old man who marries a young wife and fears to be cuckolded. In his orbit swing three unprincipled and sexually potent youngsters. First, there is his eighteen-year-old wife Alison, 'wylde [lecherous] and yong', who is described in terms of faunal and floral imagery, which give her a sweet and compliant sensuality and beauty. Then there is their student lodger Nicholas, an intelligent and crafty psaltery-player who violently desires her, and grabs at her sex ('caughte hire by the queynte') as soon as he gets her alone. Thirdly, there is the parish clerk Absalon, with his pretentiously biblical name, and hair as lovely as Absalom's (see 2 Samuel XIV, 25–6), who visits taverns where he is squeamish about farting. He uses his position in the Church to size up the wives of parishioners, and he too longs to have Alison.

Nicholas, being in occupation, quickly gets Alison's agreement to be his lover as soon as John the carpenter can be got out of the way. The story is a masterpiece because of the brilliant absurdity of the plan by which Nicholas and Alison are enabled to enjoy each other, and the way in which Nicholas nevertheless receives at least some come-uppance when exuberant in his satiety.

First of all, Absalon fails in his loverly pleas, singing and playing the guitar under Alison's window on a night when John is at home, acting the part of Herod in a Mystery play in order to impress her, and sending her presents. Meanwhile Nicholas develops his plan. Since he could have had his Alison on any one of the absences of John mentioned in the *Tale*, and his plan depends for fulfilment on John's very close presence, Nicholas and Alison must be seen as creatively esoteric adulterers in spicing their pleasure as they do. Taking supplies of food and drink upstairs, Nicholas pretends to be in an astrological trance, and when the solicitous carpenter eventually gets into his room, he finds him gaping skywards, apparently possessed. When Nicholas can speak, he says his prognostication shows that on the next Monday night there will be a downpour of rain that will dwarf Noah's Flood. As God thought of the Ark to save Noah and his family, so he, Nicholas, has thought of three vessels in which John, Alison and himself, can float to safety. Each is to climb into a big tub which is to be suspended from the roof and stocked with food – the tubs being separate so that John and Alison shall not endanger their salvation by having sex, and so that all shall keep the appropriate silence. They are to take axes to cut the ropes when the flood level rises, which will allow them to float away through the roof.

As soon as John is asleep, Nicholas and Alison creep down their ladders, which, ironically, have been specially made by the carpenter, and go to bed to frolic. Absalon, who has checked that nobody has seen

John for some hours and therefore assumes that he is away from home, dresses up, sweetens his breath, and comes wooing at Alison's low window. She tells him to go away, and when he pleads at least for a kiss, she has a brilliant idea. Out of the window she sticks her well-used tail, which he kisses. Absalon, furiously wiping his mouth as he overhears the chortling of the inventive couple, goes away vowing vengeance. He rouses Gervays the smith, who rightly supposes that Absalon is prosecuting a late night amour, and borrows a red-hot coulter which he promises to bring back soon. He takes it to Alison's window and promises her a ring if she will kiss him again. Nicholas, having 'risen for to piss', thinks he will improve the joke, and putting his back-side out of the window, lets fly a thunderous fart; but Absalon unerringly places the red-hot iron, and Nicholas shouts for water to ease the scorching pain. It may be noted at this point that bum-baring, often with fart, was a common gesture of contempt in folk literature and art; bum-branding and unwary kissing of the lower beard also figure, though less commonly.

The carpenter, hearing the cry, 'Water!' cuts the ropes, and in the fall breaks his arm. The neighbours, awoken by the din, are told by Alison and Nicholas that John is out of his mind for fear of the Flood and, believing them, collapse in laughter. The biblical account of the Flood has been obscenely parodied: the tub has facilitated activities for which God busily drowned licentious humankind below the keel of the Ark in which the righteous Noah and his family were preserved; water, which in the religious context both drowns sinners and washes away sin, cools the burnt bum of a sexual sinner; lastly, social retribution for adultery, which should parallel God's punishment of the licentious, is frustrated by wit and scepticism. With his 'noble tale', the Miller has capped the lofty tale of the Knight. The love rivalry of Nicholas and Absalon parodied that of Palamon and Arcite, and was helped to final expression by conventions less tedious than those of courtly love; conventions which not only allowed the Lady to be actively pleasure-bound with the lover, but also gave listeners vicarious delight in happy sex and in the comic procedures which sometimes further it.

The Reeve

Oswald, the Reeve, is twice characterized, once in the *General Prologue* and again out of his own mouth in the *Prologue* which precedes his *Tale*. As we see him in the *Prologue*, he travels last of the pilgrims, at the opposite end from his enemy the Miller, who leads, playing his bagpipes. The Reeve is 'a sclendre colerik man', with physiognomical characteristics which indicate, notes Robinson (p. 665), 'wit, irascibility and wantonness'. He has done well out of corruptly managing his lord's lands and terrorizing those in his power, and has a pleasant tree-shaded house; he is close-cropped, and wears a monk-like gown which, however, is tucked up, revealing his long matchstick legs.

But when the laughter of the company at *The Miller's Tale* subsides, and Oswald, who does not laugh, has reproved the Miller for mocking the craft of carpentry, and has disclaimed any intention of taking revenge by telling an answering ribald tale, he gives a portrait of himself in what V. A. Kolve in *Chaucer and the Imagery of Narrative* (p. 223) calls 'a series of swift, ugly and humiliating similitudes'. He bitterly lists his own white hair, his decaying heart and his impotent lechery in terms of rotten fruit, incontinent bowels and a leek which, having a white head and a green tail, is like an old man who cannot perform sex. He concludes this savage catalogue with another list of the vices a man near death exercises – boasting, lying, raging and avarice. The abundant life of the young in *The Miller's Tale* is thus at once challenged by the Reeve's sour view of 'the streem of lyf' dripping away into death; and when the Host, solicitous for the morale of his company, reproves him for offering a gloomy sermon as if he were a priest, Oswald at once says that he will answer the Miller in his own 'cherles termes', and launches into his *Tale*.

The Reeve's Tale is a brilliant fabliau which seems less brilliant than it is only when it is compared with *The Miller's Tale*. That was a town fabliau, with two sophisticated young fellows going to work on a beautiful, high-spirited and lecherous girl; this is a country fabliau, with two down-to-earth students who speak a northern dialect avenging themselves on a swindling miller by bedding the two ugly, stuck-up and thickwitted women of his household. Those interested may care to note that *The Miller's Tale* is set in Oxford, and the Reeve's near Cambridge.

Symkyn, the miller, and his set-up are first described. He has married the illegitimate daughter of the local parson, who wants to make his granddaughter, the offspring of Symkyn and his wife, heiress to his property and to negotiate her a blue-blooded husband.

> For hooly chirches good [35] moot been despended
> On hooly chirches blood, that is descended.
> Therfore he wolde his hooly blood honoure,
> Though that he hooly chirche sholde devoure. [36]

                                                        (I, 3983–6)

35. wealth   36. i.e. destroy by devouring its values

It is savage anti-clerical satire. Because of that plan, the miller's daughter Malyne is still unmarried at the age of twenty. There is also a six-month-old baby.

One of Symkyn's regular jobs is grinding the wheat and malt of a Cambridge college ('Soler Halle': that is, King's Hall, which was later merged with Trinity) and one day, when the college manciple is too ill to bring the produce to the mill at Trumpington, two northern scholars, John and Aleyn, undertake to bring it and to take special care, by watching as the stuff is ground, that the miller does not swindle the college as he usually does.

They watch the hopper so closely that they do not see Symkyn sidle out, untether their horse and shoo it off into the fens where, being one of the animals in medieval iconography which represent unbridled lust, it proceeds to frolic with wild mares. When the students have gone to retrieve their horse, the miller laughingly gives half their flour to his wife to make a cake. Not until nightfall is the horse caught, and then it is too dark for the students, who know at once that they have been robbed, to travel back to Cambridge. Symkyn smugly feasts his victims and has a bed made up for them in the communal bedroom.

Satisfied with their day's pillage, miller and wife go to bed, he pale-drunk, she with her whistle well wet, and start snoring. Aleyn, smarting under defeat, determines to take at least some revenge and, brushing off the objections of the cautious John, quickly gets into the compliant Malyne's bed and proceeds intently to spend the night copulating with her. John, left alone, ponders being thought a wet later, when Aleyn's triumph is told. So he quietly moves the baby's cot from the foot of the miller's bed to the foot of the students' bed, and a few minutes later, when the miller's wife 'wente hire out to pisse,/And cam agayn, and gan hir cradel mysse' she uses the new position of the cradle to find her way into the wrong bed where John, after letting her settle:

> ... up leep,
> And on this goode wyf he leith on soore.
> So myrie a fit ne hadde she nat ful yoore;[37]
> He priketh harde and depe as he were mad.

(I, 4228–31)

Towards dawn, the sated Aleyn says goodbye to Malyne, who fondly tells him where her father has hidden the cake. Going to find his bed, he is deceived, as the miller's wife was, by the new position of the cot, and gets in beside Symkyn, to whom, thinking he is John, he tells what he's

37. for a very long time

been up to with Malyne. In his waking rage, the miller is appalled at the affront to his daughter's rank:

> Who dorste be so boold to disparage
> My doghter, that is come of swich lynage?

$$(I, 4271-2)$$

The ensuing fight wakes the wife and John, and grabbing a staff, the wife aims a blow at what she thinks is Aleyn's white nightcap; but it is Symkyn's bald head, and he goes down and is beaten by the students before they ride away with both ground meal and cake. The miller 'hath ylost the gryndynge of the whete', a metaphor for what happened to his wife and daughter during the night, and the Reeve has had his revenge on the Miller.

The Cook

The company has no general reaction to *The Reeve's Tale*. Perhaps they remain stunned by the ease with which the lofty atmosphere engendered by the Knight has been perverted by the churls' take-over of the pilgrimage. At any rate, Roger the Cook fastens on one common aspect of the Miller's and Reeve's tales, that of the lodger fornicating with the wife. He moralizes on the Biblical injunction 'Ne bryng nat every man into thyn hous', and offers his tale which, though it ends before it has properly begun, starts as if it is to be on that subject. In giving the Cook permission to speak, the Host urges him to tell a story that is good, and not like the twice-heated pasties he sells in his fly-plagued shop. This perception of the Host accords with the description in the *General Prologue* of the Cook who, though he serves the needs of five reputable guildsmen – the haberdasher, carpenter, weaver, dyer and tapestry-weaver – has a gangrenous sore on his shin, a 'mormal' which evidently betokens unclean living.

The Cook's Tale stops after fifty-eight lines, at which point the scribe of the Hengwrt manuscript wrote, 'Of this Cokes tale maked Chaucer na moore'. The hero is Perkyn Revelour, a riotous apprentice whose master, a victualler, sacks him for repeated misbehaviour which has more than once landed him in prison. Perkyn goes off to shack up with an associate whose wife is a prostitute – so the *Tale* offers to be the lowest yet. Sudden end of story.

The Man of Law

The Man of Law is an august personage, the Sergeant of the Law of the *General Prologue*. The description indicates one of the sixteen senior barristers who were special servants of the Crown. He is recognizable in the illustration to the Ellesmere manuscript by the white coif such sergeants wore. He is picked by the Host, in the *Introduction to the Man of Law's Tale*, to correct the licentious buffoonery of the Miller, Reeve and Cook. Noting that the party is well on in its journey, the Host calls a stop to such idleness as dwelling on the loss of 'Malkynes maydenhede' (Malkyn and Malyne both mean 'Molly', a name which can still indicate a loose woman, as in the phrase 'gangster's moll').

Among the characters in the *Prologue* to whom critics have appended actual identities, the Sergeant of Law is perhaps the most prominent: Thomas Pynchbek became Sergeant in 1377 and in 1388 signed a writ arresting Chaucer for debt. Line 326 of the *Prologue* can be read as a pun on his name: 'Ther koude no wight pynche [38] at his writyng'. This sergeant remembers all the significant judgements since the Norman Conquest, and his prodigious memory enables him also to recall all the tales of Chaucer that he now proposes not to re-tell. He has garnered enough wealth in his practice for his methods to engage Chaucer's irony concerning his fees and many robes. In his own *Prologue*, the Man of Law, in words drawn from Pope Innocent III's *De Contemptu Mundi*, praises wealth and condemns poverty as a state which deprives one of social honour. About voluntary religious poverty, which is meritorious, he says nothing. The absolute purity and dependence on God of Constance, the heroine of his *Tale*, also stands as an ironic comment on the Man of Law's kind of Christian morality.

The Man of Law's Tale may have been composed before the idea of revising it and putting it into *The Canterbury Tales* came to Chaucer. It is in rhyme royal, the metre of *Troilus and Criseyde*, and is based on the *Anglo-Norman Chronicle* of Nicholas Trivet (1335), about one-fifth of whose story Chaucer uses. It is a Christian romance, akin to a saint's legend set in late Roman and early British times. It begins and ends in Rome, and has as historical background Christian attempts to convert the pagan Near East (here, anachronistically, Moslem), and the arrival of Christianity in a Northumberland under pressure from still more northerly pagans. The heroine, Constance, the daughter of the Emperor of Rome, through her unwavering trust in God survives marriage to a

38. find fault with

49

Moslem, as well as massacre, attempted rape, repeated betrayal and, above all, the murderous hostility of two successive mothers-in-law.

The dominant image is of Constance at sea in a rudderless ship ('a ship al steereless'), the unseen but trusted pilot of which is God. Twice she is so cast away during a period of eight years – a time span not mentioned in the sources but probably specified by Chaucer because eight is the special number of eternity and the Resurrection (see p. 219) – at the end of which she is brought to Rome, which is allegorically the place of the saved soul, that is, heaven. This is one of many instances of doctrinal precision imposed by Chaucer on his source story, which, by the way, was supposed to be a true one, its truth enhancing its religious veracity. The holy marine aspect of a heroine sailing in her soul-ship corrects the abuse of the water theme in the spurious Flood of *The Miller's Tale.*

The story of Constance, which exemplifies not only absolute faith, but the fortitude needed to sustain it in adversity, is terse and graphic in the description of repeated evil and catastrophe, and shot through with flashes of intensely humane insight which illuminate the heroine. The Moslem Sultan of Syria hears of Constance's beauty, and determines to marry her even if it means that he and all his people must become Christians, upon which conversion the Pope insists as a condition of the union. In Constance's grief on leaving for Syria to be married the reader catches the plangent note of Chaucerian pathos:

> 'Fader,' she seyde, 'thy wrecched child Custance,
> Thy yonge doghter fostred up so softe,
> And ye, my mooder, my sovereyn plesance
> Over alle thyng, out-taken Crist on-lofte,[39]
> Custance youre child hire recommendeth ofte
> Unto youre grace, for I shal to Surrye,[40]
> Ne shal I nevere seen yow moore with ye.[41]

> (II, 274–80)

The Sultan pays for being converted to Christianity for the wrong reason of carnal love: his mother and her confederates, after taking baptism in blasphemous scorn of that holy water ('Coold water shal nat greve us but a lite!'), massacre Sultan and followers and turn Constance adrift in a rudderless boat. God, who cares for her as he did for Daniel in the lions' den and for Jonah in the belly of the whale, takes her through the Straits of Gibraltar and miraculously feeds her until she lands in Northumberland. There she begs the local constable to end her life, speaking

39. except Christ above   40. Syria   41. eye

– a nice historical touch this – 'a maner Latyn corrupt' that he can understand. She conceals her identity, and by her example converts her pagan rescuer and his wife Hermengyld.

A knight lusts for Constance and, being repulsed, kills Hermengyld and lays the bloody knife by the sleeping Constance. At the ensuing inquiry before King Alla, Constance is described as one on the way to execution:

> Have ye not seyn somtyme a pale face,
> Among a prees,[42] of hym that hath be lad[43]
> Toward his deeth, wher as hym gat no grace,
> And swich a colour in his face hath had,
> Men myghte knowe his face that was bistad,[44]
> Amonges alle the faces in that route?
> So stant Custance, and looketh hire aboute.

> (II, 645–51)

Her prayer for help gets her grace, for when the false knight is swearing to her guilt, a hand from heaven smites his neck-bone. Together with many present, King Alla is converted, and soon marries Constance. But his mother detests the union, and when her son is away campaigning against the Scots, she substitutes two messages carried by a negligent and drunken courier with counterfeit letters. The first tells Alla that Constance has given birth to a monster, and the second commands the constable to set her adrift with her baby in the very boat in which she first arrived in Northumberland.

Her little boat eventually touches on a heathen shore, where the steward of the local castle tries to rape her, but is pushed overboard and drowned, thanks to the strength God gives her. She sails away. Meanwhile – a very long while! – the army of the Roman Emperor has been campaigning in Syria to avenge the slaughter of the Christians at Constance's first marriage feast. Sailing back to Rome victorious, the senator leading the army happens upon Constance in her boat, and once again she will not say who she is. In Rome neither her aunt, who is the wife of the victorious senator, nor her father recognize her, but the saintly behaviour of mother and child again wins hearts. When King Alla, who killed his mother for her crimes against Constance and himself, visits Rome as a pilgrim in order to receive his penance, he sees his child at a feast and is reminded of Constance.

Conjecturing that God has sent Constance to Rome by sea, just as he formerly sent her to Northumberland, Alla seeks her out and, in a

42. crowd 43. led 44. who was in peril

moving reconciliation scene, explains everything. Constance is reunited with her father before returning with King Alla to Northumberland where, after a year, her husband dies. 'Finally to seye', Constance, now defined as a 'hooly creature', goes on the last of her journeys, back to Rome; not to 'live happily ever after' like the heroes and heroines of Romance, but to await death, the dawn of everlasting bliss.

The key to the religious sense of *The Man of Law's Tale* is the heroine's absolute refusal, even by such a small act as declaring who she is, to take any step to save herself: God must do everything: produce miraculous food, deliver condemnatory blows, stir the minds of others to virtue and compassion and, archetypical of all, steer her soul's boat.

What is named in the Oxford Chaucer as *The Epilogue of the Man of Law's Tale* is thought to be a rejected draft; it contains no reference to the *Tale* just concluded, but does seem to function as a Shipman's *Prologue*, and that is how I treat it. This arrangement is fully discussed by Derek Pearsall (*The Canterbury Tales*, pp. 20–21).

Chapter 4. Tales of the Shipman, the Prioress, Chaucer's Tales of Thopas and Melibee, the Monk and the Nun's Priest

This group of tales is probably the one in which Chaucer most nearly realized the aim of making each story arise from a continuous dialogue among the pilgrims, each teller being nicely impelled by the group's social dynamic to contribute in such a way that the new story either contrasts with the previous one, or fulfils its underlying theme in a different way, or simply provides new diversion. Except for the headlink to the first of these tales, and a few other minor discrepancies, the links, prologues and epilogues provide a rich foil within which the *Tales* sit, setting off both the sequential plan and the characters in the company.

The problem with the first headlink, which ends with the Shipman introducing his story, is that in only one manuscript does it appear immediately before *The Shipman's Tale*. In others, it either does not appear, having been cancelled, or comes after *The Man of Law's Tale*, to which, however, it contains no clear reference. It is therefore called either *The Epilogue of the Man of Law's Tale* or *The Shipman's Prologue*, and I follow common practice in treating it as the latter. Its twenty-eight lively lines open with the Host praising the useful morality and the learning of whatever tale has just concluded, and asking the Parson to speak next. The Parson rebukes him for swearing, whereupon the Host accuses him of being a Lollard (see p. 206), swears again yet more blasphemously, and prepares the company to hear a Lollard sermon. The Shipman cannot stomach this, and interrupts forcibly with a promise to tell such a story

> That I schal clynken you so mery a belle,
> That I schal waken al this compaignie.
>
> (II, 1186–7)

The Shipman

The Shipman, a sea captain, is one of the most forcefully drawn characters in the *Prologue*. Almost every detail of his appearance, character and mode of operation can be confirmed by reference to historical

53

records of sea-faring in the fourteenth century. His home port was Dartmouth, whose sailors, 'besides holding from the king a blanket privateering commission, took the lead as freebooters, and were known as such throughout England' (Muriel Bowden, *A Commentary on the General Prologue to the Canterbury Tales*, 1967, p. 193). And there actually were ships in the last twenty years of the century called 'Maudelayne' and 'Magdalen', a fact which has led to speculation that Chaucer depicts a particular ship's captain.

The Shipman's double occupation as trader and fighter by sea was normal for the time, and both of the practices which Chaucer mentions were common. The first is that of stealing wine from his cargo while the wine merchant was asleep, and the second is that of drowning prisoners taken at sea; both establish him as ruthlessly unprincipled. But the objective and knowledgeable Chaucer also records the Shipman's familiarity with Northern European coasts and tides, his skill as a pilot, and his dependability and courage in storm or other adversity at sea.

As for the Shipman as a land-faring pilgrim, Chaucer lightly indicates the fish-out-of-water impression by mounting him on a 'rouncy' which, if the illustration on the Ellesmere manuscript is a good guide, is a thickset carthorse. His exotic quality shows in his heavy sun-tan, his dagger slung at the ready, and Chaucer's summary character evaluation: the Shipman is a 'good felawe' (smart rascal) who disregards matters of 'nyce conscience'.

The Shipman's Tale is remarkable for several reasons. To start with, as we have it, at least the first few lines are told not by a man – certainly not the Shipman, who would probably know little of the world of the story, though the immorality of the characters lies parallel to his own and the sardonic brevity of narration also seems appropriate – but by a woman. It opens with a shrewdly cynical analysis, in the style of the Old Woman ('Vekke' in Chaucer) of *The Romance of the Rose*, of middle-class marriage from the wife's point of view:

> The sely[1] housbonde, algate[2] he moot paye,
> He moot us clothe, and he moot us arraye,
> Al for his owene worshipe richely,[3]
> In which array we daunce jolily.

(VII, 11–14)

Consider the triple effect of that 'moot' (must), followed by the lurid triumph of 'we daunce jolily'. The *Tale*, which has undetected cuckoldry

1. hapless 2. in any case 3. honourable repute

at its centre, is often supposed to have been allotted first to the Wife of Bath.

The three characters in *The Shipman's Tale* are people of substance who aspire to wealth and honour: a monk outrider (that is, a monk licensed to conduct the business of a monastery with the society outside – and 'business' is the right word because a monastery, besides being a religious house, was a commercial undertaking with functions and rights in the surrounding secular world) and a merchant of international operation, together with his wife.

An unusual feature is the absence of the conventional ending of a fabliau, that dénouement or summary authorial judgement resoundingly celebrating with the audience the concluding poetic justice of the upshot, which is usually a wild kind of retribution such as the branding of Nicholas's arse in *The Miller's Tale*.

The moral critique, a subtly implicit one, appears indirectly in the imagery which, featuring terms associated with the salvation of the soul and moral behaviour generally, encompasses the two related worlds of lust and avarice. Lustful and avaricious as all three characters are, Chaucer constantly attaches to them, ironically, epithets associated with aristocratic virtue: 'noble', 'good', 'fair', 'gentle'. The motif of *The Shipman's Tale* is a common one in folk stories: the Lover's Gift Regained.

A merchant of Saint Denis, preparing to travel on business, invites to his house a monk, 'daun John', who has so ingratiated himself there that he is accepted as 'cousin'. One morning before leaving, the merchant orders that he is not to be disturbed, and goes into his counting-house to determine how his affairs stand; both the privacy and the making up of accounts parody the religious process of meditation and prayer. At the same time, John is saying his prayers in the garden. To him comes the wife, whom the monk chides for rising so early, since she must need rest seeing that

> ... oure goode man
> Hath yow laboured sith the nyght bigan,
>
> (VII, 107–8)

and at the thought of that copulating, 'he wax al reed' (red). But she replies that she gets so little sex that she is thinking of committing suicide, whereupon he invites her to tell all in secrecy, a parody of the confessional. In her 'confession' she complains that her husband is mean, and begs the monk to lend her a hundred francs that she owes for clothes. He promises to do so when her husband has left, and physically seals his promise, as their mutual endearments have threatened for some time:

> And with that word he caughte hire by the flankes,
> And hire embraceth harde, and kiste her ofte.

(VII, 202–3)

The monk then demands to be fed, and the wife, after instructing the kitchen to prepare a meal, interrupts her husband, cursing his absorption in money affairs ('The devel have part on alle swiche rekenynges!', VII, 218) and his failure to be a good host to daun John. The merchant defends himself by lamenting the difficulties of the business life and mentioning various ways by which a merchant can deal with crises, including absenting himself on pilgrimage:

> For everemoore we moote stonde in drede
> Of hap and fortune in oure chapmanhede.[4]

(VII, 237–8)

He then advises her how to support his business interest by behaving well in his absence, and comes down to dine having, as it were, fasted over his accounts. The monk wishes him well – in something like a parody of a blessing – and in confidence asks him for a loan of a hundred francs to buy livestock for his monastery. The merchant happily parts with his money, and lectures the monk on its use; money is the businessman's plough – a sexual innuendo that Chaucer's listeners would recognize. Meditation, prayer, fasting, confession and blessing have been crowned by alms-giving, and daun John goes off to his monastery.

The merchant being gone, John turns up, freshly shaved, and the wife, in return for the hundred francs, enjoys him busily in bed 'in myrthe al nyght'. The merchant returns, calls at home to pick up money which he must repay in Paris, and on his way calls on John to ask how his business has prospered during his absence. He does not mention the loan, but John does, before abruptly terminating the meeting, casually remarking that he was able to pay over the very same gold to the wife. When the merchant finally returns home, happy that his business has prospered on all fronts, he is now able and willing to make love to his wife:

> And al that nyght in myrthe they bisette;
> For he was riche and cleerly out of dette.

(VII, 375–6)

In the morning, still amorous in bed, he reproves his wife for not telling him that daun John has repaid the loan. Boldly invoking mercantile values, she answers that she thought the money was a gift to her, by

4. bargaining

which John was honouring the husband and repaying the hospitality of the house, and that she had already spent the money on her 'array', which is 'honour' to her husband. She asks him to forgive her and says she will not repay him except by being good to him in bed; a moment earlier she had said of her debt to him, 'score it upon my taille' ('notch it on my debt tally'), a *double entendre* which crowns the union of lust and cupidity in the *Tale*. The unstated poetic justice is achieved at the expense of the unwitting merchant.

In religious terms, a man pays the debt of marriage to his wife when he makes love to her. If he fails to pay that debt, as the merchant failed at the beginning, then if the wife falls into fornication, as the merchant's wife did, it is the opinion of Aquinas that her sin can in some way be imputed to the husband (discussed by Robert Adams, to whom I am indebted here, in 'The Concept of Debt in *The Shipman's Tale*', *Studies in the Age of Chaucer*, Vol. 6, New Chaucer Society, 1984, pp. 85–102). A person's sins, by this way of thinking, are debts owing to God: 'Forgive us our debts . . .' runs one version of the Lord's Prayer. Those debts must be repaid by prayer, fasting, penance and alms-giving. The narrator binds the whole process with both the open and covert meanings of his final word-play, which is cast in the form of a conventional concluding prayer:

> Thus endeth now my tale, and God us sende
> Taillynge ynough unto oure lyves ende.
>
> (VII, 433–4)

The Prioress

The Prioress is appealed to courteously by the Host to tell the next tale, in terms which suggest that she may have been grieved by the slur on clerical folk contained in the Shipman's depiction of daun John, and she graciously responds. The Prioress, as befits her high social status – for a prioress had the same prestige as a noble – is the fourth character to be treated in the *Prologue*. The description of her there is so exquisitely poised on sympathetic observation and soft light satire that our judgement, if it is based on the number of respects in which she falls short of the religious ideal, founders on our appreciation of her richly ambiguous character.

To begin with, the Church would disapprove of a prioress going on pilgrimage at all. Then, the first two epithets relating to her are 'symple and coy', terms conventionally applied in romances to noble heroines, the elaborated meaning of which is 'innocently open and quietly well-bred'. But Chaucer uses them not of her character, but of her 'smylyng', which admits the interpretation that that is the impression of herself that she wishes to convey, and not necessarily what she is. Next we are given her name, Eglantine (sweet briar), which again is drawn from Romance. The long description of her fine table manners is taken directly from the *Roman de la Rose*, where it follows its source in Ovid in making such graces the means by which a woman may entice a lover. Her beauty is also described in Romance terms except that, unlike Romance writers and no doubt in deference to her religious status, Chaucer does not proceed to any part below the face except to note, in general terms, 'hardily [assuredly] she was nat undergrowe [short]'.

The Prioress sings divine service nasally, in the style of the period, and speaks French not like a Parisian but with the Anglo-Norman accent learned in her nunnery, which is generally thought to have been St Leonard's. This was within walking distance of Chaucer's house over Aldgate and we know from the records that some of the nuns of St Leonard's, like this prioress, wore jewellery and fine clothes, which was contrary to religious rule. But in a period when it was common for dowerless daughters of breeding to go into religious houses, a little licence in such matters is not surprising. Though 'ful plesant and amyable of port', the Prioress is careful to preserve the graces of nobility and the dignity of her rank: she

> ... peyned hire to countrefete cheere [5]
> Of court, and to been estatlich [6] of manere,
> And to ben holden digne [7] of reverence.
>
> (I, 139–41)

But (and the 'but' is Chaucer's) she would cry if she saw a mouse trapped, bleeding or dead, and keeps little pet dogs (how many is not stated) which she feeds luxuriously. Such keeping of pets in convents, let alone giving them food which might have kept poor humans alive, was repeatedly condemned by the Church. The last detail of the Prioress's person is that she wears, among other jewellery, a gold brooch inscribed *Amor vincit omnia* (love conquers all). In Virgil, whence it comes, this phrase refers to profane love or *eros*, but the Church early took it over as referring to *agape*, so that the Prioress would justify parading it as signifying spiritual loving-kindness – a nice ambiguity for the modern reader to cope with.

We are left with an intriguing conception of a good-looking and conventional aristocratic woman expressing herself within the firm but semi-

5. imitate the behaviour   6. dignified   7. worthy

transparent frame ordained for senior female religious. She travels with a 'chapeleyne' (nun assistant) and, most critics agree, one priest, not three as stated in the text (besides being highly unorthodox, three would take the numbers on the pilgrimage to thirty-one, two more than the twenty-nine indicated; *Prologue*, 24).

The Prioress's Tale recounts a miracle of the Virgin. The Prioress first offers a prayer to invoke the Virgin Mary's aid in the telling, as the Second Nun does later in her prologue to her story of the life of St Cecilia. Thus two of the three devotional stories in *The Canterbury Tales* (the other being *The Man of Law's Tale*) are characteristically allotted to female religious, while the contributions of the virtuous male religious, the Parson and the Clerk, are stronger in homiletic and moral tone. Both invocations and both tales are written in rhyme royal, the metre Chaucer used for lofty subjects. *The Prioress's Tale* seems to have been the most popular of *The Canterbury Tales* after *The Clerk's Tale*, sixty manuscripts having survived; and, like the Shipman's, it is thought to have been written after 1387 but, unlike the Shipman's, to have been written specifically for its narrator.

Both *Prologue* and *Tale* are shot through with references to the Bible and the liturgy, and especially to the Mass for 28 December, Childermas or the Feast of the Holy Innocents (the babies slaughtered by Herod in an attempt to kill the Saviour). The poetic intensity of medieval adoration of the Virgin Mary is caught by Chaucer in the Prioress's opening prayer, which is built not only upon Church texts, but also upon their poetic evocation by Dante in the *Paradiso*. Here is the third stanza, which should be declaimed with a devout passion, modulating to the urgent plea in the last line:

> O mooder Mayde! o mayde Mooder free! [8]
> O bussh unbrent, brennynge in Moyses sighte, [9]
> That ravyshedest [10] doun fro the Deitee,
> Thurgh thyn humblesse, the Goost that in th'alighte,
> Of whos vertu, whan he thyn herte lighte, [11]
> Conceyved was the Fadres sapience,
> Help me to telle it in thy reverence! [12]

> (VII, 467–73)

8. O mother Virgin! O noble virgin Mother!   9. The burning but unconsumed bush that Moses saw was a common symbol of the Virgin, who was impregnated with Christ without losing her virginity   10. drew forcibly down   11. By whose power, when it illuminated thy heart,/Was conceived (i.e. as Christ) the wisdom of God the Father   12. so that it honours thee reverently

The *Tale* is Chaucer's rendering of a story, many examples of which survive in manuscript, which was popular during the period of the later Crusades, when there were massacres of Jews in York, King's Lynn and Stamford associated with Richard Lionheart, who was crowned in 1189. In 1290 the Jews were banished, and so from then until Cromwell allowed new Jewish settlement in England in 1655, there was no Jewish community to be the target of what we now call anti-Semitism. The Jews in the tale of a miracle told by the Prioress are the villains because they do not accept Christ.

The 'litel clergeon' (schoolchild), who is seven, has been taught by his widowed mother to reverence the Virgin Mary. When, during his first term at school, he hears the anthem 'O Alma Redemptoris Mater' (Gracious Mother of the Redeemer), he likes it so much that he learns the first verse. Then he begs an older pupil, a choirboy, to tell him what it is about, as he does not understand the Latin. The schoolfellow does not either, but he knows he sings it in praise of the Virgin, and he has all the words by heart. He teaches them to the little fellow, who sings the anthem every day on his way to and from school along the street where the Jews live. These find the song offensive to their religion and hire a murderer, who cuts his throat and throws his body into their privy pit. The soul of the little martyr joins the blessed virgins in the presence of the Lamb, singing the 'new song' indicated in *Revelation*.

His mother, the poor widow, distractedly searches for her lost son, praying the while to the Virgin, who unlocks her miracle, causing the supine corpse of the child to sing 'O Alma Redemptoris Mater' 'So loude that al the place gan to rynge'. Christians hear the singing and send for the magistrate, who ties up the Jews and has all of them who knew of the murder tortured to death. The child, 'syngynge his song alway', is taken to the nearest abbey where, in response to the abbot's plea, he relates the Virgin's part in his story, and her placing upon his tongue of a grain – possibly of a spice soothing to his wounded throat – with the command that he should sing until it is taken away. Thus prompted, the abbot removes the grain, whereupon the child's corpse gives up the ghost, the congregation prostrate themselves weeping and praising the Virgin, and entombment of the child in bright marble follows.

The narrator concludes with one plea to God that the pilgrims may meet where the 'litel swete body' now is, and another to the sainted martyr Hugh of Lincoln, a nine-year-old boy supposed to have been ritually slaughtered by Jews in 1255, to pray for God's mercy on them for their sins, 'For reverence of his moder Marie' (VII, 690).

The structure of this little poem of only twenty-nine seven-line stanzas particularly reveals Chaucer's art in synthesizing the popular doctrinal

Christianity of his day. The *Tale* is like a many-layered sandwich, in that its several elements recur to make a tasty and balanced whole; it contains realistic common life with its aspirations, activities and emotions, simple declarations of faith, hate of the common enemy, and scriptural or liturgical reinforcement. First comes the description of the setting, the city in Asia where Jews are

> Sustened by a lord of that contree
> For foul usure and lucre of vileynye,
> Hateful to Crist and to his compaignye.
>
> (VII, 490–92)

The Church's prohibition of usury, which resulted in rulers relying on Jews for loans to finance their enterprises, to the annoyance of their subjects, explains these lines. Secondly come the Christian children, learning their way to God through adoration of the Virgin Mary, among them the innocent seven-year-old whose mother is at once established as a figure of sympathetic deserving on two counts: she is a widow, and has brought up her child in true Christian style. Thirdly comes the development of the child's faith, in which love of the Virgin strengthens through his singing of the anthem he has learnt. It is time for the hate layer to be tasted again: the Jews entertain in their hearts the wasps' nest of Satan, and justify their intended murder as a defence of the Jewish Law against the false doctrine ('sentence') sung by the little boy. Against the frightful circumstances of the murder and the disposal of the body is juxtaposed the soul's immediate ascent from the 'litel body swete' to heavenly bliss, and then three stanzas of sentimental pathos are given to the sorrowing and searching mother:

> With moodres pitee in hir brest enclosed,
> She gooth, as she were half out of hir mynde,
> To every place where she hath supposed
> By liklihede hir litel child to fynde ...
>
> (VII, 593–6)

Wonder at the miraculous singing follows, and praise of God, who

> ... parfournest thy laude [13]
> By mouth of innocentz, lo, heere thy myght!
>
> (VII, 607–8)

Chaucer is responding to the often-quoted 'Out of the mouth of very babes and sucklings . . .' (Psalms VIII, 2). The punishment of the religious 'adversary' (the exact translation of the Hebrew 'Satan') is briefly

13. performs thy praising

described with horrible satisfaction before the virtual apotheosis of the child in his final address to the congregation. Beginning with the appalling 'My throte is kut unto my nekke bone', he describes the Virgin's benign intervention in the case: nowhere in the *Tale* has she anything to do with the horrors, her layers of the confection being kept inviolate.

Many readers of *The Prioress's Tale* today find the typological presentation of the Jews – their standing for all hostile non-Christian believers – too near modern anti-Semitism for comfort, and resent the attendant sentimentality about the choirboy and his mother, which seems psychologically to counterbalance the violent hostility to the Jews in a now familiar way. So it is worth considering the extent to which the detail and sentiment in the Prioress's story fit the fashionable creature of the *Prologue*. There she lavishes pity and generosity on mice and little dogs; here on a saintly little boy. However harmless her pretensions of manner and appearance in the *Prologue*, they show a moral indifference which is an affront to her calling and invite the suggestion that her passionate adoration of the Virgin Mary and her violent hatred of the Jews may indicate a crude and undeveloped religious sensibility. Chaucer should be given credit for demonstrating both that 'true doctrine' and prayers of great beauty may well figure in a popular religious narration, and that such a Prioress as he portrays in the *Prologue* might well profess such excessive sentiments as we find in her *Tale*.

The Tale of Sir Thopas

The *Prologue* to *Sir Thopas* nicely bodies forth Chaucer's irreverent wit in placing his own tales of Thopas and Melibee immediately after *The Prioress's Tale*. Observing the company's solemn reception of the miraculous legend of the Virgin, the Host wants to cheer up his charges, and so his pervasive desire for mental ease makes him turn to Chaucer, who at this point, if the order of *Tales* followed here is correct, is briefly but penetratingly and humorously described for the first time in *The Canterbury Tales*.

> Thou lookest as thou woldest fynde an hare,
> For evere upon the ground I se thee stare.
>
> Approche neer, and look up murily.
> Now war yow, sires, and lat this man have place!
> He in the waast is shape as wel as I;
> This were a popet [14] in an arm t'enbrace

14. pet

For any womman, smal and fair of face.
He semeth elvyssh by his contenaunce,
For unto no wight dooth he daliaunce.

(VII, 696–704)

The preoccupied look, the impression of subtle perception and mystery in that 'elvyssh', and the absence of the impulse to fraternize noted in the last line, crowned by the physical idea that his fat belly would make him a cuddlesome prospect for a pretty little woman, work on the threefold audience in different ways. For Chaucer, this is his wry view of himself for presentation; for the Host, this is the sort of person who might relieve the solemnity engendered by *The Prioress's Tale*; for us, it is a cartoon, and probably a truthful one, of a poet whom we might like to keep in mind as we read his poetry. Chaucer, who is asked to tell 'a tale of myrthe', accepts the invitation, but asks people not to be offended if all he can offer is a rhyme he learned long ago.

The Tale of Sir Thopas (topaz being a gem signifying purity) is a satire on metrical romance, a genre in which Chaucer wrote such sophisticated examples as the tales of the Knight and the Franklin, and the huge-scale romance of *Troilus and Criseyde*, not to mention *The Wife of Bath's Tale*, which is a fine example of an old-style romance. Though *Sir Thopas* is as short as *The Prioress's Tale*, the diversity and concentration of its absurdities have led to much interpretative speculation, of which only a little may be mentioned here.

The satire is primarily literary, in that the subject matter, metre and style of popular romance are burlesqued. Chaucer's romances are written in either rhyme royal or iambic pentameter couplets; none of them feature the short lines and heavy rhyme schemes of *Sir Thopas*, which is written mainly in six-line stanzas rhyming a a b a a b, with four feet in lines 1, 2, 4 and 5 and three in lines 3 and 6. That is the basic metre, but Chaucer occasionally embroiders it, as popular poets often did, with an extra short line of one foot, the resulting whole stanza being called 'tail-rhyme', or even with further lines, as in the following stanza, which contains both features. It describes Thopas's reply to a three-headed giant called Sir Olifaunt (elephant) who challenges him:

> The child[15] seyde, 'Also moote I thee,[16]
> Tomorwe wol I meete with thee,
> Whan I have myn armoure;
> And yet I hope, *par ma fay*,[17]
> That thou shalt with this launcegay[18]

15. knight   16. as I may thrive   17. by my faith   18. small spear

>   Abyen it ful sowre.[19]
>
>   Thy mawe[20]
>   Shal I percen, if I may,
>   Er it be fully pryme of day,[21]
>   For heere thow shalt be slawe.'[22]

(VII, 817–26)

The stanza contains no fewer than three gap-filling rhyme tags, that is, stock phrases which do not advance the meaning, to which popular romance poets could turn in their search for rhyme: 'Also moote I thee', '*par ma fay*' and 'if I may'. All help to fulfil the complicated rhyme requirement. Thopas's knightly resolve to slay the giant is not helped by such a qualification as 'if I may'; a reservation such as 'thurgh Goddes gras' would be both pious and correct. The latter phrase does occur in the next stanza, to explain how, this time, Thopas managed to flee the giant in safety!

The indecorum of some of the descriptive matter may be briefly indicated. 'Mawe' in the stanza just quoted is right for the belly of Jonah's whale, or the belly of the Shipman which, its owner tells us, contains no Latin, but is hardly right for the stomach of a mighty adversary. In knightly combat, aiming at the heart or head is noble; piercing the belly, let alone a 'mawe', though it does happen in romance, is rather a disgusting aim for a knight who, we are told, is 'the flour of roial chivalry'. The two stanzas describing Sir Thopas give him a face as white as best bread ('payndemayn'), a 'semely nose' and saffron-coloured beard and hair hanging waist-low. The flowers of the romantic forest in which he seeks adventure are herbs described with their properties as for kitchen use. The oath by which he swears to kill Sir Olifaunt after he has been armed is 'on ale and bread'. He hunts with an ungainly goshawk, a bird used by yeomen, not knights, and is good at such sub-knightly sports as archery and wrestling.

The non-story runs as follows: Sir Thopas was born at Poperinghe, near Bruges (which has led to speculation that Chaucer is satirizing Flemish pretensions to knighthood); his person and skills are described; many women are in love with him, although he is chaste; he rides out in search of adventure and, on hearing birdsong, falls in love (with whom is not stated); he gallops about until his horse sweats blood, and becomes so tired with 'prikyng [spurring] on the softe gras' that he has to lie down; he decides he is in love with an elf-queen, and sets off in search of her; he meets and runs away from Sir Olifaunt; back home, his retainers

19. suffer, sorely   20. belly   21. morning   22. killed

feed and arm him; end of the first fit (an Old English word for a section
of poem or canto) with a minstrel's plea that he be allowed to continue:

> Loo, lordes myne, heere is a fit!
> If ye wol any moore of it,
> To telle it wol I fonde.[23]

> (VII, 888–90)

Without pausing for approval, Chaucer starts the second fit with the
assertion that his hero is the most chivalrous of all knights, and sleeps
not in a house, but in the open air with his helmet for a pillow; like Sir
Percival, one of King Arthur's most famous knights, he drinks water
from the well – but the Host has had enough, and stops him.

The Tale of Melibee

The link between *The Tale of Sir Thopas* and *The Tale of Melibee* confirms the absurdity of the story interrupted by precise complaints from
Harry Bailey, who thus emerges as more than a dutiful, if forceful, Host:
here he is an effective literary critic as well:

> Thy drasty[24] rymyng is nat worth a toord!
> Thou doost noght elles but despendest[25] tyme.

> (VII, 930–1)

Chaucer has wearied him with his 'drasty speche' and 'rym dogerel', and
so he asks him to tell instead a story in prose which is either funny or
contains 'doctryne'. Brusque though his interruption is, the Host's advice
is kindly meant and critically sound, but Chaucer's response launches
another literary time-bomb, warning, by its remorseless drawn-out
prolixity, that the pilgrims are in for a verbose moral disquisition full of
proverbs. Moreover Chaucer, still smarting from the interruption of his
first effort, begs the company: 'And lat me tellen al my tale, I preye'.

The Tale of Melibee is the English translation of a French paraphrase of
a longer Latin original of the thirteenth century, by Albertanus of Bres-
cia. Since it follows the French closely and therefore has few Chaucerian
characteristics, it will not detain us for long. It is important, in my view,
for two things: the first is that within the satirical purview of the pilgrim-
poet, it is judged to be long-winded and sententious, and its telling may
thus be read as a kind of slyly humorous revenge on the Host for interrupting *The Tale of Sir Thopas*; and the second is that its wide-ranging

23. strive 24. filthy 25. waste

Christian thought is part of the essential religious content of *The Canterbury Tales*, and therefore ought not to be ignored by the reader or listener.

The scheme of the *Tale* resembles that of the Book of Job, in that an opening calamity is turned in the end into peaceful harmony by a prolonged and many-faceted debate between the powerful and rich young man Melibee ('a man that drynketh hony') and his wife Prudence, throughout which the wife takes the initiatives that bring about the happy ending. In Melibee's absence, his house is raided by 'thre of his olde foes', who beat his wife and wound his daughter Sophie (wisdom) in five places; and on his return he vows vengeance. By a slow process of reasoning and persuasion, Prudence deflects his vengeful anger and, towards the end, persuades his enemies to accept his judgement. Even then, Melibee wants to disinherit them and exile them for ever, but Prudence persuades him that if he forgives them, he will be renowned for his mercy and pity, and not have the bad name of one who misuses his power.

Prudence sustains her discourse with a wealth of Biblical references, many of which are proverbial, drawn chiefly from Solomon, but also from Paul and, in one case, from Job; and she invokes classical wisdom as well, especially that of Cicero. Her husband, too, quotes such material in his attempts to refute her arguments and maintain his right to revenge, but of course not nearly as profusely. Included in the brief suggested by her name, Prudence recommends many virtuous qualities and wise practices, among them patience, forbearance, taking advice only from close friends, right and circumspect ways of accumulating and using wealth, avoiding hasty action, not exercising private revenge but leaving vengeance to the judge, and making peace with enemies. She also gives practical advice, for example, by warning him that if he takes revenge he will be in danger. Through the debate between them runs the perennial argument between clerical anti-feminism and its opponents, which is concerned here with one main aspect: those who think women are bad say that a man should not confide in his wife because she will then dominate him with bad counsel, the counterargument to which is that, *pace* Solomon who said, 'Good womman foond I nevere', good women must exist, otherwise Christ 'wolde nevere have descended to be born of a womman.' The upshot of this particular and most politely conducted debate is that Prudence proves herself both good and true.

The daughter, who is given by Chaucer a name that she does not possess in either the French or the Latin, survives her wounds, and it would have fitted the allegorical structure within which the debate takes place to have that fact stressed at the end, because it is then that Melibee's wisdom is restored by Prudence. But it is not stressed. Thus spiritually equipped, Melibee performs to his former enemies a god-like function, receiving them into his grace and underlining that act with a conventional closing prayer:

For douteless, if we be sory and repentant of the synnes and giltes which we han trespassed in the sighte of oure Lord God,/he is so free [noble] and so merciable/that he wole foryeven us oure giltes,/and bryngen us to the blisse that nevere hath ende. Amen.

(VII, 1884–8)

In the two contrasting acts of performing *Thopas* and *Melibee*, the poet-pilgrim – a character created by the actual Chaucer – has broadened the scope of *The Canterbury Tales* by satirizing popular verse romance in a wildly funny way, and by discoursing at length on Christian material which he uses in several other tales. In addition, he has further illuminated the fictitious travelling company that he took over as audience from the Prioress, an audience slightly stunned by the Gothic horror and sentimentality of her tale. And for the real audience, us, he has further defined our relationship with our narrator. This illusionist has two *personae*: a diligently accommodating one in which he fulfils his pilgrim function to the confusion of the Host, and a wryly self-deprecating one which he inhabits in order to draw us into humorous literary and moral sophistication.

The Monk

When *The Tale of Melibee* has been heard out, it is not its sound doctrine which receives the first comment, but the dominant role of the wife. The Host explodes at the thought of the tale of this Prudence reaching the ears of his own wife. The latter is a termagant who urges him to violence in every circumstance, even when a neighbour fails to bow respectfully to her in church; and ironically her name is Goodelief (probably meaning beloved of God). The Host starts to confess that anyway, when it comes to violence, he doesn't need much urging, but wisely draws back and starts to arrange the telling of the next tale.

He turns to the Monk, whom he addresses in terms which, although some critics find it hard to match *The Monk's Tale* with its teller, indubitably establish him as the fast-living Monk of the *General Prologue*. There, placed in honour after the Prioress, he appears as a well-groomed, well-fed, fashionably accoutred and vigorous lover of the chase, who wears a golden pin in the shape of a love-knot, and looks about him with glaring pop-eyes. Several of the vices that priestly writers often complained of in bad monks are mere habit to Chaucer's Monk: chiefly, he avoids monastic rules that a monk should keep to the cloister, work at holy books and labour with his hands; besides which, he is devoted to hunting, and to owning and feeding expensive animals such as horses and hounds. Yet for all that, Chaucer's opening general statement about him is that the Monk is 'A manly man, to been an abbot able'. That is also how Harry Bailey sees him, as he asks him to tell the next story. More than that, perhaps remembering the lecherous monk of *The Shipman's Tale*, the Host sees him as such a masculine fellow that if only he, or indeed any other 'mighty man' serving the Church were allowed to marry and copulate, he would inject the race with vigorous stock:

> Religioun hath take up al the corn
> Of tredyng,[26] and we borel[27] men been shrympes.
>
> (VII, 1954–5)

These comments 'This worthy Monk took al in pacience' and, tentatively offering to begin with a saint's life, that of Edward the Confessor, he proceeds to define tragedy of which, he says, he has a hundred examples in his cell. Evidently a number of these rise to the surface of his mind, because he launches into a succession of seventeen of them, begging to be excused if he gets them in the wrong order. The stanza form is ornate, and thus hard to compose in: eight lines of iambic pentameter, rhyming a b a b b c b c.

Of the seventeen instances of tragedy in *The Monk's Tale*, seven are drawn from the Bible or related literature, six from classical myth and history, and the remaining four, the so-called 'modern instances', from Chaucer's own century. The whole is preceded by a framing stanza bewailing Fortune's power, and advising listeners in admonitory sermon style not to trust in prosperity – a message the repetition of which, in slightly different words, rounds off the whole in the closing stanza of the last 'tragedie', that of Croesus:

> ... Fortune alwey wole assaille
> With unwar[28] strook the regnes that been proude;
> For whan men trusteth hire, thanne wol she faille,
> And covere hire brighte face with a clowde.
>
> (VII, 2763–6)

26. copulation 27. coarse 28. unexpected

The *Tale* consists of a standard medieval approach to a standard medieval theme: vicissitude, as exemplified by the arbitrary decisions of Fortune. Of the seventeen unlucky heroes and heroines, seven suffer misfortune because they are bad, and six fall in spite of being good, or at least admirable. God, not Fortune, is implicated in the fall of some of the Biblical characters, and it has to be said that the pattern of the whole is not clear, and that attempts to show that the conception of Fortune develops through the examples have not been widely supported. Since little masterpieces like *The Prioress's Tale* and *The Nun's Priest's Tale* figure in the same group, *The Monk's Tale* has suffered by comparison with them. But it has its own merits, as well as points to make in the overall scheme of those of the tales which are told by Church people.

It is thought that Chaucer wrote some of *The Monk's Tale*, those 'falls of princes' of the biblical and classical worlds, before he began *The Canterbury Tales*, and that he added the 'modern instances' in 1386 at the earliest, since Bernabo Visconti, who is one of them, died in prison only in December 1385. The scheme of the *Tale* is imitated from Boccaccio, whose *De Casibus Virorum Illustrium* (*Concerning the Falls of Famous Men*) is quoted in Chaucer's sub-title, and based on the Boethian thinking in that work and in part of the *Roman de la Rose*. But the scheme is incomplete; the examples illustrate the impossibility of frustrating fate, but do not deal with the religious solution to such a problem – that solution being a compound of classical stoicism and Christian doctrine which asserts that the effects of misfortune can be countered by exercising the will and so making the spirit superior to the calamity endured.

Of the separate accounts, those of Zenobia and Hugelino (Ugolino) are perhaps the most vivid. Zenobia was a third century Semitic queen who defied the Romans, but was eventually beaten in battle and paraded in Rome at the triumph of Aurelian. The story of Ugolino is taken from Canto XXXIII of Dante's *Inferno*, in which the spirit of Ugolino tells Dante and Virgil that he was kept starving in prison with his four sons, who died one after another before his eyes. In the 'tragedie' of Zenobia, who is such a warrior queen that she allows her husband to have intercourse only for specific acts of breeding, the pathos arises from contemplation of the beautiful and once powerful queen in a procession with a mock crown on her head, stared at in derision by the Roman crowd. In the tragedy of Ugolino, the pathos arises from the selflessness of the children (younger in Chaucer than in Dante) who, seeing their father gnawing his hands in an agony of grief over the death of one son, think that he does so because he is hungry, and ask him to eat them instead. As in *The Legend of Good Women*, Chaucer plays down or excludes details of his source story which are not relevant to the pathos.

The Monk's dwelling on the horror and sadness of Fortune's victims, and his failure to complete the religious meaning in each case, loosely correspond with his own behaviour, as described in the *Prologue*, in failing to attend to the essentials of his religion – although this may be an overstatement of the match between tale and teller.

The Nun's Priest

As the Host interrupted Chaucer over Sir Thopas, so the Knight interrupts the Monk, to complain of the unrelieved gloom of those seventeen personal calamities:

> ... litel hevynesse
> Is right ynough to muche folk, I gesse.
>
> (VII, 2769–70)

he observes, and opines that a tale which told of a rise in fortune rather than a fall would be 'gladsom'. The Host supports him forcefully. Exasperated by the length and 'high sentence' of the previous two tales, he cannot even demand the conventional 'som murthe or som doctryne' which he requested after *Sir Thopas*, but complains that the Monk has offered neither 'desport ne game'; and upon the Monk's dignified refusal to improve on his effort, he severely insists to the Nun's Priest, who agrees to be the next story-teller, that his 'herte be murie everemo'. The result is a tale of just over 600 lines in which the Monk's theme, the fall of princes at the hand of fortune, is adjusted, varied, and attuned to sound Christian doctrine, in a hilarious folk tale the upshot of which is deeply satisfying and would certainly leave all the pilgrims with merry hearts.

Since *The Nun's Priest's Tale* about the cockerel Chauntecleer and his henwife Pertelote is 'perhaps the best and certainly the most inimitably Chaucerian of the Tales' (Derek Pearsall, *The Canterbury Tales*, p. 230), to summarize it effectively and judiciously and to indicate its special excellences may prove beyond the scope of a short survey, but the attempt must be made.

A poor widow has a cockerel who greatly loves his wife, the chief of his seven hens. Early one morning, Chauntecleer wakes in fright from a nightmare about a dog-like creature who wants to kill him. Pertelote scoffs at the idea that dreams are prophetic and, diagnosing excessive choler (see the discussion of the Humours, p. 213) as the cause of the nightmare, proffers him herbal remedies. He declines, and gives three long and vivid examples of fatalities being anticipated in dream. We are just over halfway through the poem, and the action is about to begin. The end of the couple's philosophical discussion is signalled by the rousing of Chauntecleer's love and desire for his wife.

Unable to balance for love-making perched where they are on a roof-beam, the couple flutter down and copulate twenty times. Soon after, Chauntecleer rejoices in his power to time his crowings by the stars. Meanwhile the fox, who penetrated the boundary hedge during the night, lies in wait among the vegetables. While the hens are enjoying a dust-bath, Chauntecleer watches a butterfly among the vegetables, and suddenly becomes aware of the fox. His instinct to flee is arrested when the fox expresses a desire to hear his lovely singing voice, and he falls to the flattery, crowing his best with his eyes shut and his neck stretched out. The fox seizes him by the neck and starts to carry him off, while the farmyard, beasts and humans together, erupts in alarm behind him. Chauntecleer, though terrified, suggests to the fox that he turn to curse his pursuers and assure them that he is going to eat the cock. Off guard in the moment of his triumph, the fox complies, and the cockerel flies up a tree in safety. Each character pinpoints his offence: the cock shut his eyes when he should have kept them open, and the fox opened his mouth when he should have kept it shut.

The Nun's Priest's closing moralization which is more complex than that, is:

> Lo, swich it is for to be reccheless,
> And necligent, and truste on flaterye.

The array of ideas, and of attitudes to them, orchestrated by Chaucer provides another yet more complex layer of meaning. How that is so, and how such widened dimensions are accommodated by Chaucer's art when the base material is so limited, will now be suggested.

All the details of the animal story, from the dust-bath onwards, occur in one medieval version of the beast fable about foxes and birds which took various forms from the time of Aesop (sixth century B.C.), whose fables, among them that of the Fox and the Crow, are still current, chiefly as children's reading. By the time Chaucer wrote his *Tales*, the fox had become the popular humanized villain of beast epics and fables, many of which were pointed by religious moralization, the vice he stimulated by flattery being, as here, pride above all.

The presiding human of this story is the widow, owner of Chauntecleer's yard domain, who is presented at the outset in an idealized portrait, similar to that of one of the few good people in the *General Prologue*, such as the Clerk, the Parson and his brother the Plowman. She is virtuous, hard-working and thrifty, and concerned for the welfare of her mixed flock of humans, animals and birds. If, as seems advisable when a tale is told by a 'sweete preest, this goodly man' (for so the Host describes him), we are to look for a religious interpretation, even one short of a complete allegory, then the widow functions as the Church, and her yard is the world. And to the hero of its dusty, ditch-enclosed patch, Chaucer turns next. The vista of the central continuous joke, that a ludicrous cockerel should represent humanity's complex aspirations, pleasures and vices, opens before the listener. Even leaving aside any possible political allegory,[29] it is a scenario dense with comic and philosophic possibilities.

The Nun's Priest's first gambit is to establish, within a veiled religious context, the subject of a fundamental human preoccupation with love; he raises such matters as lovers' harmony, sensual indulgence, pride in possession, uxoriousness, and the duel fought for mastery. The lovers' harmony is expressed in the duet sung by Chauntecleer and Pertelote, which is an actual medieval love-song. The listener is seduced into the tone of the poem – if not already seduced by the occasional inclusion in the description of the birds, of terms conventional in love poetry – by the double experience: that of two chickens stretching out their necks, one to cluck and the other to crow (the latter a crucial act in the upshot of the story), and that of romantic reminiscence connected with the song 'my lief is faren in londe' (my lover has gone away).

In reproaching Chauntecleer for being frightened by his dream, Pertelote draws on popular ideas about the marriage relationship, and reminds us of Lady Macbeth ridiculing Macbeth's manhood when he is

29. Tracing contemporary allusions in Chaucer's poetry is a historical diversion rather than a specifically literary activity. Nevertheless J. Leslie Hotson's theory (*PMLA*, XXXIX, 1924), which would confirm the date of the writing of the *Tale* as late, at least goes some way to explain the odd colouring of the poem's protagonists and the use of the nonce-word 'colfox' (which still exists as a surname). The colours in the description of the cock and his hens exactly match those of Henry Bolingbroke's coat of arms, and those of the 'colfox', red and yellow but with ears and tail tipped with black, match the golden truncheon tipped with black at both ends that Mowbray, appointed Earl Marshal of England in 1397, was allowed by the King to carry. Early in 1398 Mowbray was accused by Bolingbroke (see Shakespeare's *Richard II*, I, i, 100) of sending a party (which included one John Colfox) to Calais to murder the Duke of Gloucester. Chaucer's colfox is described as a murderous traitor.

compunctious about murdering Duncan when she says, 'Han ye no mannes herte, and han a berd?' [30] Her list of essential husbandly qualities may be compared with that of the wife of the merchant in *The Shipman's Tale*. Narrator and character are virtuous in this chicken-yard, but scarcely so in that rich house 'at Seint Denys'. The things a husband should be are:

> Hardy,[31] and wise, and riche, and thereto free,[32]
> And buxom [33] unto his wyf, and fressh [34] abedde.
>
> *(The Shipman's Tale*, VII, 176–7)

> . . . hardy, wise and free,
> And secree,[35] and no nygard, ne no fool,
> Ne hym that is agast of every tool,[36]
> Ne noon avauntour.[37]
>
> *(The Nun's Priest's Tale*, VII, 2914–7)

The truth of dreams, a subject to which Chaucer often returns, is debated in the style of medieval scholastic dispute, and by apparently winning the argument, Chauntecleer successfully opposes Pertelote's bid for 'maistrie' (the upper hand) in marriage. She cites only one authority in support of her case that dreams are lies, but in his splendid speech proving dreams prophetic, which he starts by politely doubting her scholarship ('Madame . . . graunte mercy of youre loore'), he cites six authorities. Several of these are backed by *exempla*.[38] The first of these stories, in which the body of a man, whose companion dreamed of his murder but did nothing about it, is hidden in a dung-cart (2985–3062), is as grisly and graphic as anything in Chaucer. It ends with the pious moral, which is both popular and priestly, 'Mordre wol out, this is my conclusioun' (3057).

The curious thing is that Chauntecleer, having proved himself right to his own satisfaction, is not warned by his own argument. Far from trying to locate and guard against the fox, he is deflected into exercising a pleasant uxoriousness, getting to a flat surface on which he can tread his wife without overbalancing. The compliment to Pertelote with which he launches himself on marital exertion makes one of the funniest and most learned jokes in Chaucer. 'In principio', he says, introducing his Latin tag with the first words of the Gospel of St John ('In the beginning was the Word'), which were often uttered by friars as they crossed

30. beard 31. brave 32. generous 33. obedient 34. lively 35. discreet 36. weapon
37. boaster 38. An *exemplum* (example) was a story or anecdote incorporated in sermon or devotional literature which illustrated the maxim, moral or spiritual truth being recommended, often, as in *The Pardoner's Tale*, by demonstrating the bad consequences of not following the maxim.

people's thresholds, 'Mulier est hominis confusio'. This stock anti-feminist tag means, 'Woman is man's ruin', but the randy cockerel's translation is, 'Womman is mannes joye and al his blis' (3166). The love scene (uxoriousness) and the display of astrological knowledge which follows are succeeded by an expression of conventional pessimism. Perhaps Chauntecleer has begun to think about the fox, or is he just experiencing post-coital melancholy?

> But sodeynly hym fil a sorweful cas,
> For evere the latter ende of joye is wo.
>
> (VII, 3204–5)

Theologically, the whole section shows Chauntecleer allowing his intellect to be corrupted by desire, so that he falls into the sin of making love 'Moore for delit than world to multiplye' (VII, 3345).

The arrival of the fox is prefaced by a short Boethian meditation on 'necessitie', free will and God's foreknowledge which merges into a mock priestly moralization relating recent events to the question of women's 'maistrie':

> My tale is of a cok, as ye may heere,
> That tok his conseil of his wyf, with sorwe ...
> Wommennes conseils been ful ofte colde; [39]
> Wommennes conseil broghte us first to wo,
> And made Adam fro Paradys to go ...
>
> (VII, 3252–3, 3256–8)

But the Adam in this paradise, our bearded chicken, narrowly regains his abode of bliss at the end, not through virtue but through cunning bravado and wit. At the point at which we have arrived, the Nun's Priest is careful to disclaim serious belief in the priestly anti-feminist line he has just shot; he is a sermonizer and story-teller detached enough to be playful with his audience.

As the fox tempts the cock with his flattery, the dominant absurd image of the poem is seen again; the picture of Chauntecleer's father is evoked by the tempter, in order to persuade Chauntecleer to emulate his sire in beauty of song:

> Save yow, I herde nevere man so synge
> As dide youre fader in the morwenynge. [40]
> Certes, it was of herte, [41] al that he song.

39. fatal   40. morning   41. heartfelt

And for to make his voys the moore strong,
He wolde peyne hym[42] that with bothe his yen[43]
He moste wynke,[44] so loude he wolde cryen,
And stonden on his tiptoon[45] therwithal,
And strecche forth his nekke long and smal.[46]

(VII, 3301–8)

The hilarity and force of meaning are now enhanced by a bravura display of mock-heroics. As soon as the fox has grabbed by the neck the straining singer with the closed eyes – the predator's mouth, arguably representing hell-mouth, into which the sinner falls – the narrator rises to three lamenting apostrophes in the classical style; involving first destiny, who arranged that Chauntecleer should fly down from his safe position on the roof-beam; then Venus, because Chauntecleer copulated in her service of pleasure rather than for the Church-sanctioned purpose of procreation; and lastly Geoffrey of Vinsauf (early thirteenth century), in whose treatise on poetry the death of Richard I was the subject of his demonstration of the art of poetic lamentation. Furthermore, so the continuing mock-heroic vein reveals, the tragic weeping of the hens when they see their master carried off outmatches the grief of Troy when Pyrrhus killed old King Priam, the grief of Hasdrubal's wife when the Romans burned Carthage, and the grief of the Roman senators' wives when Nero killed their husbands and set fire to Rome.

The abrupt transition from cataclysm in the high classical mode to uproar on the low domestic scale is beautifully managed. Every member of the widow's establishment is mobilized to take part in that popular medieval activity, chasing the fox, the farmer's *bête noire*: the widow herself (perhaps representing the Holy Church pursuing the Evil One), her daughters, three dogs, a maidservant, the cow and calf and even the pigs, to say nothing of 'many another man'. The men carry staves, the maidservant her distaff, and all run yelling 'as feendes doon in helle'. Terrified, the ducks quack as though they are about to be killed, the geese take off over the trees, and the bees swarm out of their hive. The scene is compared with a (what we would now call racialist) massacre of Flemings in London during the Peasants' Revolt of 1381: 'It semed as that heven sholde falle.' The sudden twist of fate (or is it the cock's exercise of free will in flattering the fox as he himself was flattered?) by which Chauntecleer is freed is signalled by a joyous moralization from the narrator:

42. make such effort   43. eyes   44. had to shut his eyes   45. tiptoes   46. slender

> Lo, how Fortune turneth sodeynly
> The hope and pryde eek of hir enemy!

(VII, 3403–4)

The closing advice offered by the Nun's Priest at the end of his brilliant comic sermon may be taken by the reader of almost everything that Chaucer wrote:

> But ye that holden this tale a folye,
> As of a fox, or of a cok and hen,
> Taketh the moralite, goode men.
> For seint Paul seith that al that writen is,
> To oure doctrine it is ywrite, ywis;[47]
> Taketh the fruyt, and lat the chaf be stille.

(VII, 3438–43)

But can the 'fruyt' and the 'chaf' be so separated? In Chaucer, surely not.

The *Epilogue* to *The Nun's Priest's Tale* opens with a heartfelt compliment from the Host to the narrator, which comically but unfortunately modulates into the kind of crude appreciation the Host addressed to the Monk before that cleric slowly unfolded his catalogue of the falls of the great. This is unfortunate because nothing the Nun's Priest has said or done merits the Host's suggestion that his testicles and strong muscles must surely qualify him well as a 'trede-foul' (fornicator like a cockerel). Since one line ('Thou woldest ben a trede-foul aright') is virtually the same as one addressed to the Monk in his *Prologue*, this *Epilogue* is generally regarded as meant to be cancelled, though genuine. It does effectively round off the group of tales on the manuscript called Fragment VII in the continuous dramatic spirit of the whole, in which the Host's crude interventions, which foster the interplay among the characters on pilgrimage and help to determine the variety of the stories told, are always surprising and amusing.

---

47. is certainly written to instruct us

Chapter 5. Tales of the Physician and the Pardoner

The Physician

The Doctor of Physic of the *General Prologue* is another of Chaucer's blandly damning sketches of professional men. The account of his orthodox practice, which is 'grounded in astronomye', and his application of the theory of the Humours (see p. 213), ends with the summing up, 'He was a verray, parfit praktisour', and the information that he colludes with the apothecaries who supply medicines to ensure high profits for both them and himself. Similarly, a list of fifteen medical authorities, the study of which has made him a learned 'praktisour', is shortly followed by a list of three undesirable characteristics: 'His studie was but litel on the Bible'; he is very sumptuously clothed; and he spends little money, but keeps to himself the high profits earned during plague years. The concluding joke at his expense is that, since gold distilled in cordial is a healing agent, 'he lovede gold in special'.

The Physician's Tale begins Fragment VI, which consists only of this and the Pardoner's *Introduction*, *Prologue* and *Tale*. The story originally figured in Book III of Livy's *History of Rome*, and appears in the *Roman de la Rose*. Like *Measure for Measure*, it treats the well-known theme of the Corrupt Magistrate, the judge who uses his power to further his lustful desires. Apius sees the beautiful Virginia with her mother near a temple and decides he must have her. So he hires a 'false cherl' to swear in court that the girl was stolen from his house in infancy and, without hearing the evidence of the girl's father, orders her to be given to the churl. The father goes home grief-stricken and, telling his daughter that she must suffer death or dishonour, he says, 'My pitous hand moòt smyten of thyn heed.' After swooning at the impact of this, Virginia revives, to bless God that she will die a virgin, and her father cuts off her head and sends it to Apius, who orders that he be hanged. But the people intervene to save him, and judge and churl are punished.

The fascination of this unusually nasty story is attested by its frequent treatment by medieval writers, and by three English dramatists, all of whose resulting plays were staged – John Webster, John Dennis and Sheridan Knowles. As usual, Chaucer adds significantly to his source story and so changes its impact. He removes the political content almost entirely and, by inserting a long panegyric on maidenly virtue as exemplified by Virginia, and concluding with a brief homily on the deserved punishment of sin at the end, he brings the story nearly into line with the genre of the saint's legend. The twelve-year-old Virginia's virtues are catalogued as a creation of Nature's delight; the Physician's insistence on them is interlarded with garrulous advice to governesses, fathers and mothers on the upbringing of children. The decision of the father to enforce his daughter's death is not commented on: could he be a type of God the Father, demonstrating one of his unknowable ways?

That Chaucer took the moulding of his source story more seriously than his merely homiletic additions might indicate is suggested by the care with which he injected his characteristic pathos into the final exchange between father and daughter, before the grisly decapitation. 'For love, and nat for hate, thou most be deed' (VI, 225) are the words of the father which, if any words can, give acceptable meaning to the *Tale*. The Father would rather his beloved innocents die into everlasting bliss than live besmirched this side eternity.

The Pardoner

The *Introduction* to the *Pardoner's Tale* shows a new side of the Host; almost overcome by the pathos of Virginia, he moralizes what he has heard:

> ... yiftes of Fortune and of Nature
> Been cause of deeth to many a creature.
>
> (VI, 295–6)

His compliment to the Physician takes the form of blessing his medical paraphernalia: his 'urynals', 'jurdones' (chamberpots), boxes and medicines. In danger of losing his heart for pity of Virginia, the Host turns to the Pardoner for a 'myrie tale', but there is a chorus of objections from the 'gentils' among the pilgrims to having to listen to more ribaldry, as the effeminate fellow demands drink before performing, promising them 'som honest thyng'.

The Pardoner of the *General Prologue*, a striking original, has the last entry in the catalogue of pilgrims: Chaucer gives this perverted lecher and corrupt minor church official an unusually specialized scrutiny. With his beardless face, straggling yellow hair and voice 'as smal as hath a goot', what should the Pardoner do but sing 'Com hider, love, to me!' to the 'stif burdoun' (ground bass) of the Summoner, 'his freend and his compeer'? Is it a defensively comic brazenness which makes him suggest (*The Wife of Bath's Prologue*, III, 166) that he is thinking of getting married, and boast, in his own *Prologue* (V I, 453), of having 'a joly wench in every toun'? Such people can be found in every age and place.

His glaring eyes are a physiognomical sign of gluttony, libertinism and shamelessness, the last of which qualities he shows to excess in his *Prologue*. 'I trowe he were a geldyng or a mare' (I, 691) is Chaucer's summing up of this aspect of the Pardoner, who comes from Rouncivale, a charity hospital in Charing (on the site of the present Charing Cross station in London) for which Pardoners collected money. Tantalizingly, one meaning of 'rouncival' was 'mannish woman'. Pardoners sold Papal indulgences which released people from punishment for sin, but not from guilt, for which sacramental penance was required. But this Pardoner, like many others attacked in religious reform writings, claims that he can 'assoille' (absolve) sinners completely (*Pardoner's Prologue*, V I, 387). He also peddles sham relics, such as pigs' bones and a shred of cloth which he claims came from the sail of St Peter's boat, in order to deceive the poor and ignorant into parting with their money. Efficient in all functions in church – reading, singing, preaching – he is naturally at his best when singing the offertory.

The Pardoner's Prologue, a more conclusive act of self-exposure than that achieved by the Wife of Bath, being a detailed account of his attitude to life and the means he uses to persuade people into giving money which ostensibly goes to the Church:

> Of avarice and of swich cursednesse
> Is al my prechyng, for to make hem free
> To yeven hir pens,[1] and namely unto me.
>
> (V I, 400–402)

His constant theme is 'radix malorum est cupiditas' (avarice is the root of evils), but he both boasts of his own avarice and stimulates avarice in others by pseudo-magical persuasion which is ancillary to his Christian doctrine. For example, he offers for sale a cheap metal shoulder-bone of a sheep which, if dipped in water, will cure farm animals of diseases, give the owner wealth-creating increase of stock and cure a man of jealousy even if he knows that his wife has had two or three priests. His strongest religious persuasion lies in his clever assertion that those who are extremely sinful

> . . . have no power ne no grace
> To offren to my relikes in this place.
>
> (V I, 383–4)

1. pennies

This leaves those who do not succumb to his persuasion under suspicion of sin from those who buy his pardons.

The boldness of the Pardoner is even more breathtaking than his shamelessness. It may be that, being a social outcast by reason of his physique and temperament, he compensates by taking a daringly poetic view of his triumphs over ordinary people. Desperation at knowing what he is, and at his inability or unwillingness to change from wickedness, may be partly responsible. Here he is, dramatizing his own preaching style:

> Thanne peyne I me to strecche forth the nekke,
> And est and west upon the peple I bekke,[2]
> As dooth a dowve[3] sittynge on a berne.[4]

(VI, 395–7)

He finishes the drink the Host has provided and then reassures the audience that, as they wished, they will not have to listen to ribaldry from him:

> For though myself be a ful vicious man,
> A moral tale yet I yow telle kan . . .

(VI, 459–60)

As a man who parades and glorifies his wickedness, the Pardoner behaves like False Seeming in the *Roman de la Rose*, or as the Vice in a medieval morality play. He is a kinsman of Shakespeare's clever rogues, Falstaff, Parolles and Pompey, but is better at what he claims to be able to do than any of them.

The Pardoner's Tale is a superb sermon against avarice, the centre-piece of which is a powerful and eerie *exemplum* in which the daily sins – gluttony (to which lechery is 'annexed'), gambling and blaspheming – of three debauchees lead to pure avarice, which in turn draws all three men to become murderers, and to die murdered. Their spiritual death in the vices of life, which the 'riotoures' wish to prolong, leads them to look for Death in order to kill him when they hear that he has carried off a comrade of theirs. When directed by an old man who is himself a deathly figure, they find a pile of gold, which makes them plot against each other in order to get bigger shares; and each, planning murder, is murdered and so finds actual death. The *exemplum* follows the plan of an old oriental folk tale, which is topped with a hard-hitting homily on the three vices and tailed with a closing formula which promises heavenly bliss to

2. nod   3. dove   4. barn

those of the listeners who avoid avarice – especially those who are 'assoil-led' of it by paying the Pardoner for indulgences.

In everything except the very last detail, the Pardoner fulfils his own pretensions as an expert preacher, thus demonstrating that an effective sermon can issue from a vicious mouth. As a good story-teller, he begins by briefly introducing his three protagonists (VI, 463–82). G. R. Owst, writing on sermon technique (*Literature and Pulpit in Medieval England*, Blackwell, 1961, pp. 149–209), notes that English congregations loved the elements of narrative and marvel, both of which this *Tale* contains. The long and hard-hitting homily which follows on the three named vices (VI, 484–660) contains many instances from the Bible and the classics, and such vituperative apostrophes as this one against gluttony:

> O wombe! O bely![5] O stynkyng cod,[6]
> Fulfilled of dong[7] and of corrupcioun!
> At either ende of thee foul is the soun.[8]
> How greet labour and cost is thee to fynde![9]
>
> (VI, 534–7)

Then in only 234 lines comes the application of that homily in the *exemplum*, no summary of which can do justice to its inexorable momentum, stark horror and force of meaning.

In subtle turns throughout the spare and clear dialogue, the religious implication of events and the coming doom are insisted on. At the outset the three revellers, already drunk by mid-morning, hear a funeral bell and ask a boy who has died. His answer is that it is one of their mates, whose heart Death burst with his spear as he sat totally drunk, and that they should beware of Death:

> Beth redy for to meete hym evermoore;
> Thus taughte me my dame;[10] I sey namoore.
>
> (VI, 683–4)

Swearing blood-brotherhood, they set off to find Death, and soon meet the old man, who directs them to an oak tree with these concluding words:

> God save yow, that boghte agayn mankynde,[11]
> And yow amende![12]
>
> (VI, 766–7)

5. belly   6. bag   7. full of excrement   8. i.e. referring to belches and farts   9. how much work and expense are required to sustain you   10. mother   11. who redeemed   12. improve

The analogues do not include such an old man, who appears to be Chaucer's own idea. When the rioters challenge him, his first words bring a ghostly chill which remains until the end of the *exemplum*. He says he can neither find a man to give him youth in exchange for his age, nor escape into death:

> Thus walke I, lyk a resteless kaityf,
> And on the ground, which is my moodres gate,[13]
> I knokke with my staf, both erly and late,
> And seye, 'Leeve mooder, leet me in!'
>
> (VI, 728–31)

When the rioters find the gold, they decide to guard it until nightfall, when they may remove it safely. The youngest goes to the town for food and drink and the two left behind agree on a plan to kill him; the purchaser laces two out of three bottles of wine with poison in order to kill them. On his return, he is quickly knifed in a sham wrestling match, and the two remaining carouse to their deaths with the poisoned wine.

The Pardoner rounds off this perfect *exemplum* with a short and violent apostrophe to all the vices mentioned in his story, and a ringing command to his imagined congregation to part with their wealth and so ensure that they go to 'the blisse of hevene'. But, carried away by the art of his story, he has forgotten his actual congregation, the pilgrims, and when he remembers them he makes a bad mistake. Having exposed his nefarious practices beforehand, he barefacedly asks them to buy pardons from him, and turns first to the Host, 'For he is most envoluped in synne' (VI, 942). That poor literary critic and man of deep and often violent feeling explodes with the worst abuse in the whole of *The Canterbury Tales*:

> Thou woldest make me kisse thyn olde breech,[14]
> And swere it were a relyk of a seint,
> Though it were with thy fundement[15] depeint![16]
> But, by the croys which that Seint Eleyne[17] fond,
> I wolde I hadde thy coillons[18] in myn hond
> In stide of relikes or of seintuarie.[19]
> Lat kutte hem of, I wol thee helpe hem carie;
> They shul be shryned in an hogges toord!
>
> (VI, 948–55)

13. mother's   14. drawers   15. anus   16. stained   17. The concubine who was mother of Constantine the Great and who was credited with finding the True Cross in A.D. 326   18. testicles   19. holy object

This makes the Pardoner speechless with rage; but the Knight diplomatically pulls his rank, and makes them kiss in reconciliation. So ends Fragment VI.

Chapter 6. Tales of the Wife of Bath, the Friar, the Summoner, the Clerk, the Merchant, the Squire and the Franklin

The Wife of Bath's Tale and the six tales following have been called 'The Marriage Group' by Professor Kittredge, who thought of them as dealing mainly with that subject in a continuous process of debate by story, with a few deliberate cross-references. Yet the tales of the Friar and the Summoner are in no sense about marriage; and though part of *The Squire's Tale* is about love, many other tales also include love in their subject matter. Yet Kittredge's distinction is useful at least in that it recognizes the importance of the subject to Chaucer, who is above all the poet of love, and moreover one who seems to see things more from the woman's point of view than from the man's.

The Wife of Bath

The Wife of Bath has often been regarded as Chaucer's most brilliant character creation. But, though she is the most vivid and original character among the pilgrims of *The Canterbury Tales*, she is not as subtly delineated, nor as revealing about the workings of a remarkable but apt and truthful psychology as Criseyde and Pandarus, two of the three main characters in Chaucer's masterpiece, *Troilus and Criseyde*. She may be potentially as interesting, but although she is the character who is given most space in *The Canterbury Tales*, her latency cannot develop and be fulfilled as can that of a character who is central to a long narrative work, and is constantly in dramatic action.

The 'good Wif of biside Bathe', who is described with penetrating economy in the *General Prologue*, in her own *Prologue* delivers a remarkable account and defence of her own love life, and then tells a graceful story which neatly expresses the main theme that emerges from her account of her life. The result is a dramatic evocation of a character of great force and originality, who is very much the heroine of her own life story, and performs as such with an exuberant frankness of self-revelation.

The world and the consciousness of the Wife of Bath are given shape by the medieval contention about the moral status of women, in which the attack on them is launched by the Church. The origin of the attack lies essentially in the account of the Fall in Genesis, in which Eve, who was seduced into sin by Satan, became responsible for the corruption first of Adam and, through him, of the whole of humankind. The defence lies in the citation of other parts of the Bible, favourable to women, as well as in pragmatic social, moral and biological observation of women's roles and the relations between the sexes, particularly in marriage. And the counter-attack on the bastions of male privilege and superiority takes the form of women's struggle for mastery within marriage. The Wife of Bath, like other Chaucerian characters caught up in this debate, is affected by it as a person. But at heart, as a kind of special representative of Chaucer in the matter, she believes in harmony between partners, however it is arrived at. This comes out clearly in and among the descriptions of the lurid life-style she embraces as a necessary riposte to the assumptions of a man-dominated social and moral system.

The thirty-two lines which describe Alisoun, the Wife of Bath, in the *General Prologue* are the merest sketch for the gargantuan dimensions of the portrait of character which is to follow. In the second line we are told that 'she was somdel deef' (deaf), and how she became deaf – buffeted on the ear by her fifth husband for tearing three pages out of the anti-feminist book he was reading at her and punching him so that he fell into the fire – becomes a central event in both her thesis and her emotional life. Her insistence on precedence in church, her bold face and red hair, and her wide hips, turn out to be due to Mars, planet of the aggressive god, which influenced her birth. But her broad-hatted, red-stockinged finery, and her openness and jollity in company, are attributed to her having been born under the sign of Venus, whose influence is proved in these two bald lines of the *General Prologue* which are later hugely expanded in detail and excitement:

> Housbondes at chirche dore she hadde fyve,
> Withouten[1] oother compaignye in youthe ...
>
> (III, 460–61)

That such a career is not fortuitous, but an effect of profound energy and complex amorousness, may be understood by Chaucer's interim summary judgement of her, before he goes on to consider the ideal religious figure of the poor Parson:

> Of remedies of love she knew per chaunce,
> For she koude[2] of that art the olde daunce.
>
> (III, 475–6)

(In line 475 there is an allusion to Ovid's *Remedia Amoris*, 'Cures of Love', see pp. 181–3.)

1. besides   2. knew about

The Wife of Bath's Prologue opens Fragment III of the manuscript without any preamble such as a request by the Host or conversational interplay among the pilgrims:

> Experience, though noon auctoritee
> Were in this world, is right ynough for me
> To speke of wo that is in mariage ...
>
> (III, 1–3)

This first pronouncement by the Wife of Bath, confident in its assertion, assures us that the debate on marriage and women is to start with a vigorous *con*, rather than a *pro* supported by the usual authorities, of the conventional position. 'Experience' – and what a woman's interpretation of it! – and not authority is to be the guide. The 'wo' to which she refers is not shared equally between spouses, but in her experience has mainly been inflicted by her upon successive husbands.

Her opening gambit is to use her remembered and duly instructive 'experience' to counter Church teaching about virginity. Why, she asks, since both women and men, and even Christ himself, have sexual organs which are designed not only for the passing of urine, should we defy creation and be chaste? If all were virgins, the supply of virgins would dry up. 'Virginitee is greet perfeccion', she admits while implying the opposite, and she asserts her life-intention by twisting the religious 'sentence' (meaning and interpretation) almost every time she quotes or refers to the Bible:

> In swich estaat as God hath cleped[3] us
> I wol persevere; I am nat precius.[4]
> In wyfhod I wol use myn instrument[5]
> As frely as my Makere hath it sent.
>
> (III, 147–50)

It should be noted that, although the Wife of Bath repeatedly refers to her pudendum, she uses various circumlocutions which are not technically obscene: 'belle chose', 'membre', 'thynge smale', 'instrument', 'harneys', 'quoniam', 'chaumbre of Venus', and 'queynte' (an adjective used absolutely, meaning 'ingenious thing'). Concerning the last, a doubtless erroneous etymology used at one time to explain it as an early form of the word 'cunt'. Alisoun exercises the same slight delicacy in choosing terms to describe sexual intercourse: Larry D. Benson in his Biennial Lecture to the New Chaucer Society in 1984, '"Queynte" Punnings of Chaucer's Critics', notes amusingly that the scribes of some

3. called   4. fastidious   5. i.e. sexual organ

of Chaucer's manuscripts showed even greater delicacy, and changed words of strong and possibly obscene meaning.

The peroration of the Wife's opening argument is:

> An housbonde I wol have, I wol nat lette,[6]
> Which shal be bothe my dettour and my thral[7]
>
> (III, 154–5)

– meaning that she will insist that her husband both pays the debt of marriage (i.e. by making love with her whenever she feels inclined) and yields her the mastery in the marriage relationship. This appals the epicene Pardoner, who interrupts to say that, until she spoke, he had been thinking of getting married (it is a joke in itself that such a person should contemplate marriage, see pp. 78–9); but when she implies that there is worse to come, he begs her to continue.

There follows the Wife's account of her five marriages. In justifying the number of her husbands, she coins the delicious word 'octogamy' to describe the condition a woman lives in when she has had eight husbands in succession. Though much of the material of her narration is drawn from diverse medieval and classical authors, from the Fathers of the Church and above all, in the passages which most acutely deal with the psychology of sex, from the *Roman de la Rose*, it is presented within the solid context of the life of a fourteenth-century English countrywoman of some pretension, and is vividly completed with domestic and kitchen references and popular proverbs.

Her first three husbands were 'goode men, and riche, and olde', over whom she established domination by demanding of them more activity in bed than they could well manage, and by so overruling them in their dotage that each of them in turn 'ful blisful was and fawe (eager)' to bring her 'gaye thynges fro the fayre' (220–21). She was still young when her fourth husband, a hard-drinking adulterer, came on the scene. She returned the jealousy he made her feel by, so she says, pretending to have lovers; it may well be that, since adultery was a grave offence at law for a woman, the Wife of Bath stopped short of admitting the act in sheer self-preservation despite her wish to perform memorably before her fellow-pilgrims. In Biblical terms, she certainly did commit adultery 'in her heart' with 'oure clerk', Jankyn, whose legs she admired when he was walking behind the coffin at her husband's funeral. When she married for the fifth time, Alisoun was forty and Jankyn twenty.

Jankyn was a violent husband who often beat her, but made her loving amends with his skill in bed – a commonplace of sexual psychology

6. be hindered   7. slave

culled from the *Roman de la Rose* (14472 ff.), which often reads like a modern sex manual. The passage in the *Roman*, not used by Chaucer, in which the Old Woman counsels the lover how to achieve simultaneous orgasm with his beloved (14293–303) is a case in point.

In the pairing of Alisoun and Jankyn the battle of the sexes, which had been fiercely but only implicitly waged before, emerged into the open. Jankyn, being learned, possessed in a single binding a formidable store of anti-feminist literature drawn from the classics and Church Fathers, and read to her continually from it. Not surprisingly, she could not stand for ever listening to such abusive descriptions of women as:

> . . . somme han slayn hir housbondes in hir bed,
> And lete hir lecchour dighte hire[8] al the nyght,
> Whan that the corps lay in the floor upright.[9]
>
> (III, 766–8)

So she attacked both him and the book, and took the buffet which left her partly deaf. Jankyn's remorse at having struck her was such that he burned his book and agreed that she should have the mastery; whereupon they swore to be true to one another, and then lived in peace and mutual trust.

The Wife of Bath's Prologue is a remarkable achievement. It could have dealt with the war between the sexes as an orderly debate, with every point clearly made; but Alisoun's narration is so rambling that until the last section it is not always easy to be sure which husband she is reminiscing about. She actually begins the sections on her fourth and fifth husbands twice. Her interpretation of the Bible passages that she quotes is never reliable, and everything she says, and the way in which she says it, adds to the richness of a genuine character, because it rings true to experience and is often funny at the same time. The mixture in her of resentment against masculine tyranny, joy in triumphing over it, fear of threatening old age, and delight in remembering the joys of happy love, makes a memorable poetry of human, and especially feminine, life. Here, touched off by her memory of youthful love exploits with her fourth husband, is her famous lament for her lost youth, which can stand beside the more extended treatments of the same traditional theme by the fifteenth-century French poet, François Villon, of which there are well-known translations by Rossetti and Swinburne:

> But, Lord Crist! whan that it remembreth me
> Upon my yowthe, and on my jolitee,
> It tikleth me aboute myn herte roote.

8. lover fornicate with her   9. prone

Unto this day it dooth myn herte boote[10]
That I have had my world as in my tyme.
But age, allas! that al wole envenyme,[11]
Hath me biraft my beautee and my pith.
Lat go, farewell! the devel go therwith!
The flour is goon, ther is namoore to telle;
The bren,[12] as I best kan, now moste I selle;
But yet to be right myrie wol I fonde.[13]
Now wol I tellen of my fourthe housbonde.

(III, 469–80)

Though she is now only bran, and no longer the 'flour' of youth – a farmyard comparison which holds her lament to earth, well below the poetic sky – she will look for a sixth husband to whom to sell herself, and enjoy life as best she can. An astrological determinist, in that she lays responsibility for her instincts and morals on Venus and Mars, whose influence she does not dream of resisting, she seals her defiance of accepted morality by explaining that, in a 'privee place', she has a mark of Mars, which would be a big and reddish-purple mole, and lamenting 'Allas! Allas! That ever love was synne!'. It seems a fair plea; but the Church taught that attention to its doctrine enabled virtuous people to resist errant astrological predeterminings.

Chaucer's source for the passage quoted above is in the *Roman de la Rose*, and is spoken by the Old Woman, whose warm worldly cynicism and shrewd evaluation of experience he constantly exploits in developing the character of the Wife of Bath, who is original not least because she achieves her particular idealization of love by resisting the woman's role allotted to her by society.

With unerring dramatic sense Chaucer, before loosing the Wife on the telling of her *Tale*, relocates her audience of pilgrims, and whets our appetite for the consequences of the sharp brush between the Friar and the Summoner which occurs at this point. The Friar comments on the length of the Wife's 'preamble' to her tale, and the Summoner picks him up, both for interfering and for using such a word.

The Wife of Bath's Tale is formally an Arthurian romance on the folk theme of the Loathly Hag, that is, the ugly old woman who tests a knight's chivalry, either by demanding a kiss or by forcing him into marriage with her and then asking whether he wants her fair by day and foul by night, or vice versa. In Chaucer, the question after marriage is whether he will have her ugly and faithful, or beautiful with the risk

10. good   11. poison   12. bran   13. try

('aventure') of her being unfaithful. For reasons which will appear later, he chivalrously leaves the choice to her, thus yielding her the mastery, whereupon she promises to be 'good and trewe/As evere was wyf', and turns into a beauty.

The Wife of Bath's hero is different from those of the analogues by reason of his sinful and desperate start. While out hunting, he rapes a country girl, and King Arthur hands him over to his queen for judgement. The queen promises the knight his life if in twelve months' time he can tell her what 'thyng is it that wommen moost desiren' (I I I, 905). On the last day of the year the knight meets the Loathly Hag, who says she will tell him the answer in return for a promise that he will do whatever she asks if the answer saves his life. Of course the answer is that women want sovereignty over their husbands, and when that is successfully communicated to the queen and her ladies, the hag demands that the knight marry her. The closing prayer at the end of the *Tale* takes a form specific to the Wife of Bath: the blessing is requested only for women; obedient men are ignored, and domineering, old and mean husbands are cursed:

> . . . Jhesu Crist us sende
> Housbondes meeke, yonge, and fresshe abedde,
> And grace t'overbyde [14] hem that we wedde;
> And eek I praye Jhesu shorte [15] hir lyves
> That wol nat be governed by hir wyves;
> And old and angry nygardes of dispence,
> God sende hem soone verray pestilence!

> (I I I, 1258–63)

That bald summary makes the main points without indicating the subtle variety and interest of the story. Structurally, it may be a romance, but like most of Chaucer's *Tales*, it is shot through with classical and Christian resonances, besides which it is full of the personality of its narrator, whose thematic drive against masculine domination, and muddled self-condemnation and romantic cast of mind are fully expressed. Her opening apology – for that is what it is – for offering a romance effectively puts down the noisy Friar who broke the spell she had woven in her *Prologue*: Friars, she maintains, with their busybodying round the country, blessing buildings of all kinds, have got rid of all the fairies who used to dance with the Elf-queen in the days of King Arthur.

Despite that opening, within forty lines her story is under way, and Arthur's queen has posed the problem to the guilty rapist. As he ponders the question, the knight goes over many circumstances and qualities

14. outlive   15. shorten

which women might most desire, nearly all of which are discreditable to women, and these the narrator admits as possibilities. One suggestion which comes to the mind of the knight is that women desire steadfast discretion above all. But the Wife herself dismisses that idea, citing the case of Midas's queen who, unable to keep to herself the knowledge that her husband had asses' ears, ran to a marsh and shouted it out. Some of Chaucer's listeners would know that in the classical myth it is Midas's barber, not his wife, who cannot keep the secret, and that by adjusting the detail as she does, the Wife is exposing yet another of her own vices. Then, sure enough, the Wife brings dancing fairies into her story; the knight meets them on the day of his dread return to Arthur's court to be given his doom. When they vanish – a sure sign of magical goings-on – the Loathly Hag is there to advise him.

The most surprising and significant thing in the *Tale* is the sermon delivered by the hag as she lies in bed with the knight, who is appalled at finding himself married to a woman of low birth who is both poor and old. It is an impeccably Christian advocacy of 'gentilesse' of attitude to low birth, poverty and old age, which draws on moral, and what we would now call democratic, ideas from Dante and from the ever-suggestive *Roman de la Rose*: 'he is gentil that dooth gentil dedis [deeds]' (III, 1170). In despair at his own inadequacy, the knight yields mastery to the magical hag and receives his reward, presumably because that is the result which fulfils the secret wishes of the story-teller – to have a handsome and young husband completely under her thumb. Arthur's queen, the dancing ladies, the hag and the beautiful and masterful bride that she becomes are all images of herself created by the Wife of Bath.

The Friar and the Summoner

Since these two exemplars of clerical vice work in oppositional tandem, each telling a tale against the other in even more vitriolic style than the other vociferous enemies, the Miller and the Reeve, it is convenient to treat them together. They illustrate vices which are observable almost whenever Chaucer satirizes servants of the Church, vices which arise in clerics too frail to observe the Church's prohibitions of two favourite activities of man: copulation and usury.

The Friar of the *General Prologue* is not to be thought of as typical. Yet a London judgement of 1387 of a friar-turned-Lollard who accused the mendicant orders of many crimes surprisingly went in the Lollard's favour (see Bowden, *A Commentary on the General Prologue to The Canterbury Tales*, p. 140); which seems to imply that a general odium was attached to friars. In depicting his Friar, Chaucer draws on anti-fraternal literature, and on sermons and tracts written within the Church which condemned friars' abuses of their power. Friar Hubert's vices are lechery and avarice, which he gratifies by abusing his spiritual power, both as a confessor and as a beggar on behalf of his Order. This power he could exercise as a 'limiter', that is, a friar licensed to work for his order in a limited area of the secular world. He seduces girls and marries them off, presumably when they become pregnant. With biting irony, Chaucer explodes him with a phallic pun: 'Unto his ordre he was a noble *post*' (my italics), a pun also used by Pandarus (*Troilus and Criseyde* I, 1000–1001) when he foresees that Troilus will be a credit to the God of Love. The Friar haunts taverns, avoiding the beggars and lepers who should have been his spiritual business, and conning pretty or prosperous women into giving him gifts, and sometimes their bodies as well, by greeting them as he crossed their thresholds, as convention had established, with the opening words of the Gospel according to St John, 'In principio' (In the beginning). Against the rule of poverty, he is well-dressed; he sings to his own fiddle accompaniment, and has a strong white neck – a physiognomical sign of lechery. Chaucer gives him a true philanderer's energy:

> And in his harpyng, whan that he hadde songe,
> His eyen twynkled in his heed aryght
> As doon the sterres in the frosty nyght.

(I, 266–8)

The Friar is modelled on an unpleasant character in the *Roman de la Rose*, False Seeming, the offspring of Fraud and Hypocrisy (see p. 193).

The Summoner of the *General Prologue*, another creature straight out of the literature of anti-clerical satire, is perhaps the most revolting of all the pilgrims, a scabby, lecherous, hard-drinking ignoramus who tyrannizes people in the name of God's justice. The job of a summoner was to bring charges against citizens who would then be tried in the lower ecclesiastical court of the diocese, which was presided over by the archdeacon. That explains why he says 'Purs is the ercedekenes helle' (III, 658); instead of going to hell, sinners pay money to the Summoner for transfer to the archdeacon. But as the Friar later says, the Summoner keeps back half the money for himself. The Summoner works through threats and bribery, and uses those over whom he has power as informers and bearers of false witness.

The prologues of the Friar and the Summoner contain such violent abuse, each of the other, that their ability to fulfil their story-telling seems threatened. Indeed, when the Friar says that no good can be said of summoners, the Host chides him for stooping below the standard of his 'estaat' (rank). But the Friar holds his peace when the Summoner, introducing his own *Tale*, asserts that friars inhabit Satan's arse in hell. Then, each is the villain-and-victim hero of the other's tale, and each, within fifty lines of the start, interrupts the other to protest against the calumny being developed, only to be squashed by the Host. Clearly the latter, as master of ceremonies, senses that the listening pilgrims wish to enjoy the battle, because he urges each of the pair in turn to spare no detail. Each villain accordingly describes the other in characteristically perfidious action as part of his story.

In *The Friar's Tale*, a Summoner on his way to lay a false charge against a poor widow meets a yeoman who, when asked where he lives, answers 'fer in the north contree' – the north being the traditional abode of Lucifer. When the Summoner discovers that he pursues the same occupation as his fellow-traveller, namely, extortion, he asks his new acquaintance his name. 'I am a feend; my dwellynge is in helle', comes the reply. Not at all put out, the Summoner questions him rather as Marlowe's Dr Faustus quizzes Mephistophilis, about the devil's power to change shape, and the constitution of his body. They agree to share their day's winnings.

They meet a carter whose cart is stuck in the mud, and who urges on his horse by wishing it to the devil. But when the Summoner tells the devil that he has won the horse, the devil replies that the carter did not mean it. He is proved right when, a moment later, the horse having pulled the cart free, the carter asks Christ to bless his horse. They arrive at the widow's house, where the Summoner summons her to the arch-deacon's court. She asks for legal help, and he replies that for twelve pence he will see that she is acquitted. But she has no money, and when he threatens to take her new pan in settlement of her debt to the court, she declares her innocence of all crimes, including that of cuckolding her husband, and wishes both him and her pan to the devil. The yeoman confirms that she really means that, and carries the Summoner off to hell. The Friar's closing prayer is unusually long, being a hellfire warning in which the Summoner is the dread exemplar who suffers the 'peynes of thilke cursed hous of helle' (III, 1652).

The Summoner's Tale is of a Friar who visits a sick man called Thomas in order to extort whatever he can. In the course of glorifying the work and power of friars, he treats the man's wife familiarly ('kiste hire swete'), demands to be fed, and asks for money. The sick man replies that he has never felt better as a result of giving friars money. Then, at suit of the wife, whose baby has died within the last fortnight, the Friar delivers to Thomas a long sermon warning against anger ('ire'). The result is of course to infuriate Thomas, who says he will contribute to the convent if the Friar will promise to share what he gives among all the friars. At Thomas's invitation, the pleased Friar puts his greedy hand down Thomas's back to extract from the bed what he hopes will be a rich picking. The contribution turns out to be a fart louder than any horse could let fly. The extremely ireful Friar is hounded out of the house by the sick man's servants, and goes to complain to the local lord. The latter's response is that, since Thomas asked that his fart, which was only reverberation of air, should be divided, he must be mad. But the lord's squire, who is carving meat at the next table, overhears and suggests how the fart may be shared among the twelve friars in the convent: if each friar puts his nose to the end of one of the spokes of a wheel, and the Friar places his nose at the nave, then if Thomas farts at the nave, all thirteen friars will effectively share the fart. The lord and his lady judge that the sick man cannot be mad after all, and the squire, whose name is Jankyn, is rewarded with a new gown for having provided the solution. With this extended lavatory story, upon which no pilgrim comments, Fragment I I I of the manuscript ends.

Fragment I V contains two richly contrasting tales concerned with the marriage debate, together with their linking material: *The Clerk's Tale* and *The Merchant's Tale.*

The Clerk

The Clerk of the *General Prologue* who, like 'hende Nicholas', the amorous and inventive scholar of *The Miller's Tale*, is 'of Oxenford', presents the modern reader with a translation problem, because he is not a clerk in the modern sense, nor is he a member of a specified profession within the Church. But since he is clearly preparing for a Church career, and prays for people who give him the wherewithal to continue studying, he might be defined as a theological student, probably one with his first degree behind him (he 'unto logyk hadde long ygo'). He is one of Chaucer's idealized characters: too unworldly to have competed for a 'benefyce', thin from underfeeding, shabbily dressed from poverty, sparing of speech, and covetous only of books which further his study. Best of all, he has a virtuously open attitude to education: 'gladly wolde he lerne and gladly teche' (I, 308). Chaucer makes only one joke at the expense of this sorrily mounted pilgrim, whose horse is as lean 'as is a rake': though he is a philosopher, he has not used his expertise to convert base metals into gold (see Chapter 15).

The Clerk's Prologue contains no reference to the Friar's or the Summoner's tales, but as the Clerk refers ironically to the extravagant values of the Wife of Bath at the end of his story, we should see him as taking up the mantle of a corrector of false views about matrimony, after the crude irruption of the Friar and the Summoner on this holy ground. It is a relief for the listener, particularly after hearing out the Summoner, once more to connect with lofty poetry – which is not to suggest that the dialectic of the punitive fart is anything but funny. In requesting a tale from the Clerk, the Host, with his usual clumsy courtesy, shows respect for the new prospective story-teller, but apprehensively expresses the hope that the learned man will not confuse the pilgrims with philosophy and rhetoric; he wants 'som murie thynge of aventures'. The Clerk acknowledges the hint and, true to his scholarly vocation, proposes a story by the famous Italian poet, Petrarch.

The Clerk's Tale was almost certainly written before the idea of *The Canterbury Tales* came to Chaucer, except for the last few stanzas, which are clearly of a later date. The story is taken from Petrarch, who made a lengthy Latin tale based on the very last story in Boccaccio's *Decameron*. This position of honour for the story was probably due to its popularity all over Europe. To judge by the number of manuscript copies in existence, it was the most popular of all Chaucer's poems, and almost certainly the most widely distributed.

The Clerk's Tale exhibits Chaucer's overwhelming preference, when writing for the religious or moral edification of his public, for his exemplar of virtue to be a beautiful woman. In this respect Griselda, the Clerk's heroine, is one with the Man of Law's Constance, the Second Nun's Cecilia, the Physician's Virginia, and Prudence of Chaucer's *Tale of Melibee*. In this saintly gallery, only the 'litel clergeon' of *The Prioress's Tale* does not meet the definition. The very mention of the well-known story of 'Patient Griselda' – 'patient', be it remembered, being derived from the Latin verb meaning 'to suffer' – conjures up a picture of an unimaginably long-suffering and obedient wife being cruelly tested by a calculating and perversely inventive husband. This Walter, a marquess, starts the story as a blithely pleasure-loving bachelor whose people love and fear him. As he has not thought of the succession, one of his wisest subjects is delegated to urge him to marry, with this result: he picks

Griselda, whose beauty and virtue he has often noticed while out hunting, out of the rural gutter, binds her by oaths of obedience which go far beyond the requirements of the marriage vow, and marries her. Then, over a period of twelve years, he submits her to four torturing tests, the effects of which are cumulative, since Griselda's passing of any one of the tests does not remove the grief occasioned by it.

Walter has first their baby daughter, and then their two-year-old son, taken away, ostensibly to be killed; next, he sends her back to her father and to poverty on the pretext that he wants to make a better marriage; and lastly, he brings her back, in her rags, to make his castle a fit place in which to receive his new bride. She stands these tests unflinchingly and without rancour, whereupon he restores her children and takes her back into a state of married honour. But the pilgrims are not meant to think of the *Tale* as the unusually dreadful *exemplum* that it appears to be: Chaucer follows his chief source, Petrarch, in asserting its real purpose:

> This storie is seyd, nat for that wyves sholde
> Folwen Grisilde as in humylitee,
> For it were inportable,[16] though they wolde;
> But for that every wight, in his degree,[17]
> Sholde be constant in adversitee
> As was Grisilde; therfore Petrak writeth
> This storie, which with heigh stile he enditeth.[18]
>
> For, sith a womman was so pacient
> Unto a mortal man, wel moore us oghte
> Receyven al in gree[19] that God us sent;
> For greet skile is, he preeve that he wroghte.[20]

> (VI, 1142–52)

That explanation, given near the end, points towards a kind of allegory in which the husband stands for God, and the wife for humanity, and even for the Son; and there are other religious indications in the story, though they exist primarily as factors in an extended human pathos of high artifice.

The measures Chaucer uses to achieve such a pathos are various. First and above all, he makes each stanza of his favourite 'solemn' metre, the rhyme royal, a smooth and stately regular unit of narrative, or dialogue, or commentary; most of the lines are end-stopped, and each fresh stanza begins a new unit of sense. Next, each element in the theme is spaciously deployed without digression or use of humour – two of Chaucer's staple

16. intolerable   17. according to his rank   18. writes   19. good will   20. for it is excellent practice to test what he created

resorts in other kinds of poetry. To fit this way of proceeding, the characters move and speak like figures in a masque, every gesture – kissing, embracing, glancing, kneeling, swooning – a step in a formal dance which carries its own explication, every speech precise and formally pointed, however long and courteously delivered. Until his surprise ending, the Clerk certainly obeys the Host in using 'termes . . . colours and . . . figures' with a restraint which, by leaving crucial expressions of thought and emotion unadorned, intensifies the power of the ruling pathos.

All this is done while Chaucer is sure-footedly developing his characters in this story as credible human beings; so that while reading, one may be caught off-guard accepting the unacceptable: the husband being tempted to test his wife's obedience by sending her home to her father, the wife submitting to having her children taken away to be killed.

Although Chaucer is more faithful to his revered author's version than to that of any other poet he 'translates' in verse, there are passages of his own invention, and these, characteristically, tend to be those in which the humanity of his heroine and the pathos of the tale are heightened. Here, for example, is Griselda's farewell to her baby girl as the sergeant sent by the marquess waits to take her away, and the Clerk's comment:

> And thus she seyde in hire benigne voys,
> 'Fareweel my child! I shal thee nevere see.
> But sith I thee have marked with the croys
> Of thilke Fader – blessed moote he be! –
> That for us deyde upon a croys of tree,[21]
> Thy soule, litel child, I hym bitake,[22]
> For this nyght shaltow dyen for my sake.'
>
> I trow that to a norice[23] in this cas
> It had been hard this reuthe[24] for to se;
> Wel myghte a mooder thanne han cryd 'allas!'
> But natheless so sad stidefast was she
> That she endured al adversitee,
> And to the sergeant mekely she sayde,
> 'Have heer agayn youre litel yonge mayde.'

(IV, 554–67)

The aura of humanity surrounding Griselda is not always sentimental, right though sentiment is in the above forlorn predicament. Griselda has a point of view to express besides abject compliance with Walter's wishes. Her request to the sergeant to give her children good burial, so that their

21. wooden cross   22. entrust to him   23. nurse   24. pity

corpses shall be safe from ravening beasts and birds, may be taken as routine, but quite different is her advice to her husband concerning the young bride who comes to take her place. She says in the presence of all before the marriage feast begins:

> 'O thyng biseke I yow,[25] and warne also,
> That ye ne prikke with no tormentynge
> This tendre mayden, as ye han doon mo;[26]
> For she is fostred in hire norissynge
> Moore tendrely, and, to my supposynge,
> She koude nat adversitee endure
> As koude a povre fostred creature.'[27]

(IV, 1037–43)

The guarded 'as ye han doon mo' is the nearest she goes to reproaching Walter directly. The link Griselda here establishes between poverty and the strength to bear suffering is germane to the whole story, and indeed to its religious meaning. This piece of advice marks the turning point of the *Tale*, the end of Griselda's tribulations, because it prompts Walter to relinquish his mania for testing her. He reveals that his new bride-to-be and her young brother are Griselda's children, and all ends happily.

The continuous but unobtrusive religious sense of the story alternates with observations of human conduct which are often sharp. For example, when Walter's subjects approve the young girl in whose favour Griselda has been jettisoned, the narrator, in a passage original to Chaucer, expostulates at their fickleness:

> 'O stormy peple! unsad[28] and evere untrewe!
> Ay undiscreet and chaungynge as a fane![29]
> Delitynge evere in rumbul[30] that is newe ...
> A ful greet fool is he that on yow leeveth.'[31]

(IV, 995–7, 1001)

That commonplace about the political behaviour of crowds, which transcends periods, is expressed in recognizably biblical language; less commonplace is the judgement on Walter when he falls to the temptation of taking away Griselda's son:

> But wedded men ne knowen no mesure,[32]
> Whan that they fynde a pacient creature.

(IV, 622–3)

The absence of 'mesure', which in medieval religion and philosophy was an important virtue, is further annotated:

25. one thing I beg of you   26. to another   27. creature brought up in poverty   28. unstable   29. weathercock   30. rumour   31. believes in you   32. moderation

> But ther been folk of swich condicion
> That whan they have a certein purpos take,
> They kan nat stynte of hire entencion,
> But, right as they were bounden to a stake,
> They wol nat of that firste purpos slake.

> (IV, 701–5)

The dominating image of the *Tale* is of Griselda's body, barely covered by a shift. Three times she is stripped (and the violent verb 'streeped' is used twice, 'despoillen' once). The first time is when, the wedding agreed upon, she is brought out of her father's house in her rags and in the open, 'right there', stripped naked so that she brings 'no thyng of hire olde geere' into the castle. The poverty and dirt of her old clothes are emphasized:

> . . . thise ladyes were nat right glad
> To handle hir clothes, wherinne she was clad.

> (IV, 375–6)

The second time she is stripped is when Walter sends her back to her father – with her dowry, which she defines as 'But feith, and nakednesse, and maydenhede' (866). She successfully begs to be allowed a shift to cover her nakedness as she leaves. The third time is at the reunion with her children and reinstatement of the marriage, when her rags are finally removed.

There remains the question of the palinodal ending, when the Clerk turns to the Wife of Bath with an ironical compliment to her alternative philosophy of marriage, in which the wife enjoys 'heigh maistrie'. His song, in six stanzas of a new and heavily rhymed metre, urges women to

> Beth nat bidaffed for[33] youre innocence,
> But sharply taak on yow the governaille.

> (VI, 1191–2)

This they should do, he says, by being quick-tongued and by cultivating good company, leaving their husbands to 'care, and wepe, and wrynge, and waille'. It is as if he refused to believe the obvious message of his own tale. Not surprisingly, the Host misses the irony of the ending as well as the religious message, and wishes his difficult wife could hear the story. The restoration of the thematic discussion to the society of the pilgrims is dramatically right, and should not be allowed to dull the impact of the severe majesty of Griselda's story. Derek Pearsall aptly characterizes the return from the world of the *Tale* to the world of the

33. fooled on account of

pilgrims as 'like blinking surprisedly awake in the sunlight after a harrowing dream' (*The Canterbury Tales*, p. 276). 'Sunlight'? . . . well.

The Merchant

The Merchant of the *General Prologue*, with his smart boots and Flemish beaver hat, is a prosperous business man who seems to be either a merchant adventurer or a member of the Wool Staple. As a regular importer of cloths from the Low Countries, who lives on credit, he wants the seaways between Holland and East Anglia kept free of pirates. Chaucer presents him as a substantial and dignified personage who deals illegally in currency exchange and whose conversation shows a preoccupation with profits in his business.

No pilgrim story-teller prefaces his tale with such an outburst of personal anguish as the Merchant, who reveals in his *Prologue* that his two-month-old marriage has brought him 'Wepyng and waylyng, care and oother sorwe'. No unmarried man, he says, could tell of such sorrow as he – which of course prompts the Host to invite him to tell a tale.

The Merchant's Tale is the masterpiece among the four fabliaux in *The Canterbury Tales*, and by far the longest. The theme, that of the *mal marié*, the old man who marries a young wife, is even older than Ovid. It is germane to the predicament of the Merchant, who develops it with savage irony and perverse use of learned reference. This theme, which necessarily involves the wife's adultery with a younger lover, comes to a climax in the last two hundred lines with Chaucer's blending of two common themes from popular folk story. One is the Fruit Tree Episode, in which a blind husband's sight returns in time for him to see his wife copulating up a tree, and the other is the Optical Illusion, in which a wife, when her husband catches her with a lover, persuades him that his sight is defective. Both folk themes are emblematic of components in the literature of sex: the first illustrates the determination of a young wife to have her lover in spite of ludicrous physical difficulty, and the virtual certainty that she will be found out; and the second illustrates the power of a wife to deceive her husband by persuasion.

That summary appears to place *The Merchant's Tale* as anti-feminist literature. Yet the chief target of the satire is the old husband, January, a knight, whose senile lust is presented with clinical accuracy and devastating bitterness; while the greedy lust of the wife, May, a person 'of smal degree' (little rank), is presented as a given factor which does not require equivalent analysis. If applied to the story-teller, this would mean that the Merchant is eaten up with self-hatred and unable to forgive himself for having married a young wife. Clearly the spirit of the Wife of Bath, who started the debate, still rules concerning the 'wo that is in mariage' (*Wife of Bath's Prologue*).

So at the outset we are presented with a sixty-year-old lecherous chevalier who, 'Were it for hoolynesse or dotage', decides to marry for the first time. He thinks a young wife, if made heir to his riches, will obey him, labour for him if he becomes poor and look after him when he is ill. January refutes Theophrastus (*circa* third century B.C.), whose *Golden Book of Marriage* was quoted approvingly by St Jerome as a warning against marriage (see Robert P. Miller (ed.) *Chaucer: Sources and Backgrounds*, Oxford 1977, pp. 411–16) and, since he looks forward to regular sexual satisfaction unencumbered with divine disapproval, declares that a wife is 'Goddes yifte' (IV, 1311).

January calls together his friends to announce his decision and declares that he won't marry anyone older than twenty. His filthy mind formulates his proposition thus: '... bet [better] than old boef is the tendre veel' (1420) and, asserting that he wants to procreate children lawfully for 'th'honour of God above', he boasts that his continued virility is not in doubt. His friends give him their advice, and the debate eventually centres on January's two brothers, Placebo (meaning 'I will please') and Justinus. The former flatteringly tells him to go ahead, but the latter advises caution, particularly in choosing a wife, since his own marriage is 'of alle blisses bare'. Justinus says that January will be able to satisfy his wife for three years at most; which outrages January, who explosively ends the consultative meeting.

Planning his wedding, January indulges in 'heigh fantasye and curious bisynesse' concerning his bride's virtues and sensual beauties. When next he sees his friends, he airs a religious scruple to them: if he is to enjoy earthly bliss through happy marriage, how will he afterwards get to heaven, which should be dearly bought with 'tribulacion and greet penaunce' (1649)? Justinus, hating his folly, sourly suggests, 'Paraunter (perhaps) she may be youre purgatorie!' – in which case January's soul will skip to heaven as fast as an arrow; and he approvingly cites common hostile views of marriage. But January, unenlightened and undeterred, has a marriage settlement drawn up in which he leaves all his land to May.

During the wedding festivities the old man continues his fantasies, and wonders whether he may not be sexually too strong for May: 'God forbede that I dide al my myght!' (1761). As he impatiently but politely

urges his guests to leave so that he may get the girl to bed, his squire
Damian, having carved before the happy pair (he is the third squire so to
operate a sharp knife on a joint in *The Canterbury Tales*, the other two
being the Squire of the *General Prologue* and the problem-solver of *The
Summoner's Tale*), falls in love with May and retires to bed shattered
with despair, as courtly lovers tend to do. January primes himself with
aphrodisiacs, including an Arab one brought to the West by an eleventh-
century monk who wrote *De Coitu*, and prefaces his pillow declaration
of love by kissing his bride:

> He lulleth hire, he kisseth hire ful ofte;
> With thikke brustles of his berd unsofte,
> Lyk to the skyn of houndfyssh,[34] sharp as brere –
> For he was shave al newe in his manere –
> He rubbeth hire aboute hire tendre face ...

> (IV, 1823–7)

Then he labours till dawn, celebrates with a drink and a song:

> The slakke skyn aboute his nekke shaketh
> Whil that he sang, so chaunteth he and craketh[35]

> (IV, 1849–50)

and goes to sleep. May's disgust, her first recorded reaction in six
hundred lines, is briefly indicated: 'She preyseth nat his pleyyng worth a
bene' (IV, 1854).

After Mass on the fourth day, January, noticing Damian's absence,
sends May to comfort him in his sickness. Damian secretly passes her a
letter declaring his love which she, an instantly avid conspirator, conceals, reads and gets rid of in the privy before returning to January.
Awakened by his own coughing, January asks her to 'strepen hire al
naked' because her clothes get in the way of the 'plesaunce' he proposes
to enjoy. In her secretly conveyed reply to Damian, she grants him her
grace, the effect of which is to make him quit his bed in health and
happiness.

When the old man is struck blind (in monkish lore, a possible effect of
over-indulging in sex) the opportunities of Damian and May to be together are even further restricted because the old man is so jealous that
he 'hadde an hand upon hire everemo' (2103). They communicate by
signs. Then May makes a wax imprint of the key to the high-walled
secret garden where January and his wife do 'thynges whiche that were
nat doon abedde' (2051), and gives it to Damian. On the 8th of June,

34. dogfish 35. sings like a corncrake

May eggs January on to visit their garden of love where Damian, having
used his second key, is sitting under a bush ready. The old man begs
May to be true, saying that he will make over to her the rest of his
property and explaining that he is jealous because he cannot bear to be
out of her company. She weeps at the slur on her fidelity, asking to be
put in a sack and drowned if she is proved false, 'and with that word' she
signals to Damian to climb into a pear-tree. Before anything happens,
we are brought into the company of Pluto, the 'kyng of Fayerye' and his
wife Proserpine who, we have previously been told, sometimes visit
January's garden to sing and dance round its well. These supernaturals
foresee that January is about to be cuckolded. Pluto says that he will
restore the old man's sight so that he will catch his wife in the act, and
Proserpine – a Wife of Bath figure in her style of speech and sexual
partisanship – caps that with, 'I shal yeven hire suffisant answere'. And
so it turns out. May pretends to be pregnant and to yearn for pears, and
stands on January's back to climb into the tree, where Damian 'Gan
pullen up the smok, and in he throng'. That is what the unblinded
January sees. Under May's sanguine double persuasion that she has just
cured his blindness, and that his sight will be faulty for a day or two,
January moves from certainty that he has seen May tupped to certainty
that she has cured his blindness and deserves even greater love than
before, the transition happening this fast:

> 'Strugle!' quod he, 'ye algate [36] in it wente!
> God yeve yow bothe on shames deth to dyen!
> He swyved thee, I saugh it with myne yen.' [37]
>
> (IV, 2376–8)

> 'But, by my fader soule, I wende han seyn [38]
> How that this Damyan hadde by thee leyn,
> And that thy smok hadde leyn upon his brest.'
>
> (IV, 2393–5)

> This Januarie, who is glad but he?
> He kisseth hire, and clippeth [39] hire ful ofte,
> And on hire wombe he stroketh hire ful softe,
> And to his palays hoom he hath hire lad.
>
> (IV, 2412–15)

As that summary indicates, the limited sympathy Chaucer grants
January, by reason of his kindness to the sick Damian and his generosity
to and total dependence on May, is offset by the ruthless analysis of his

36. nevertheless   37. eyes   38. I imagined I saw   39. hugs

arrogance, self-absorption and cold lasciviousness. On the grounds of his behaviour throughout he deserves a bride who is ready to gobble up alternative sexual experience and his wealth with equal unreflecting alacrity. And it all amounts to penetrating treatment of phenomena of human behaviour which are widespread. It could not be argued that this savagely funny fabliau has subject matter that is 'far out' or that its sharp focus on the details of activity and speech which are right for the characters is gratuitously obscene.

Much of the sophisticated fun of the poem lies in Chaucer's subversion of literary and religious values by employing them in bizarre circumstances. Thus, courtly love values are invoked several times; most notably when May responds to Damian's epistolatory advance. The traditional argument that a lady should not be cruel, and kill a suitor by refusing him, is used by May when she grants Damian 'hire grace', and Chaucer's Merchant actually credits her with the supreme courtly lady's virtue, pity, quoting, with reference to her, a line of high affirmation from *The Knight's Tale* (1761): 'Lo, pitee renneth soone in gentil herte!' (1986). As in *The Shipman's Tale,* conventional epithets from the courtly vocabulary, such as 'gentil' and 'noble' are freely applied to the inappropriate principals.

Even more outrageous in its context, and therefore especially funny, is January's speech of adoration to May when she entices him into the garden on the 8th of June, ostensibly to make love with him, but actually to copulate in his presence with Damian. It is full of phrases from the Song of Solomon, that poetical book of the Old Testament, in which earthly profane love is used figuratively to represent the love of the Church for Christ:

> 'Rys up, my wyf, my love, my lady free![40]
> The turtles voys is herd, my dowve[41] sweete;
> The wynter is goon with alle his reynes weete.[42]
> Com forth now, with thyne eyen columbyn![43]
> How fairer been thy brestes then is wyn!
> The garden is enclosed al aboute;
> Com forth, my white spouse! out of doute
> Thou hast me wounded in myn herte, O wyf!'
>
> (IV, 2138–45)

Subtler artifices abound. For example, at the planning stage January fantasizes about moulding a young wife 'Right as men may warm wex with handes plye [shape]' (1430), and it is the shaping of wax by May

40. noble   41. dove   42. wet rain   43. dove-like

which enables Damian to make the duplicate key to the garden where he puts his own 'clyket' (key) into May's own 'wyket' (gate). More important is the play with ideas about physical and metaphorical blindness which provides the structure upon which all elements of the poem are mounted towards the end. Metaphorically speaking January is blind, intellectually, spiritually, emotionally and erotically (see Peter Brown, 'An Optical Theme in the *Merchant's Tale*' in *Studies in the Age of Chaucer* No. 1, 1984, pp. 231–43). When the blind man jealously keeps his hand on May as she signals her eager randiness to Damian, the Merchant comments:

> . . . as good is blynd deceyved be
> As to be deceyved when a man may see.

(IV, 2109–10)

Physically, blindness is subject here to comic magical action and, as indicated above, ridiculous perversions of received truth about the science of optics enable this round of the war of the sexes to be won by a young acolyte of the Wife of Bath.

In the *Epilogue* to *The Merchant's Tale* the Host's eruptive comment, as so often, at the end of a tale, shows that he has missed the main point, which is the punishment of January's folly. His response to May's lurid behaviour is to apply it to his own wife, whom he has already described, in the *Prologue* to *The Monk's Tale*, as a termagant who eggs him on to violence. Here he admits that his wife is faithful, but says she has so many vices that he will not talk about them for fear that some female pilgrim – and that must mean the Wife of Bath – will report him to her. So ends Fragment IV.

The Squire

The Squire of the *General Prologue* is entirely conventional: every detail of his appearance, character and attainments is straight out of the approved courtly literature – so much so that the reader tends to take it all as gentle, sympathetic satire, which is at least a better response than to accept it with uncritical sentimentality. A strong lad with curly hair, he can do all that an aspirant to knighthood should do: fight bravely, ride well, behave humbly, sing, dance and play a musical instrument as well as compose, and wear fancy clothes. Above all, he dedicates everything he does to some lady on a pedestal whose grace he hopes to win, and on her account at night 'He sleep namoore than doth a nyghtyngale' (98). He is the Knight's son, and since his tale must be of the same romantic loftiness as his father's, even if it is to lack the

105

mastery and discipline of *The Knight's Tale*, Chaucer decently places it elsewhere. It appears as an indirect riposte to the scabrous tale of the Merchant, before the Franklin, who is a realist and idealist par excellence, resolves the marriage debate with his profound and most pretty tale.

The *Introduction* to the *Squire's Tale* begins Fragment V of the manuscript, the last continuous section of the so-called marriage debate. The Host asks for a story about love, because the Squire must know 'theron as muche as any man', and the Squire acquiesces, apologizing in advance for any shortcomings.

The Squire's Tale is in two parts, and threatens to be in three, but mercifully the third part is interrupted by the Franklin before it has well begun. Probably by design rather than accident, this story bears marks of the narrator's immaturity: his starry-eyed and unquestioning acceptance of romance conventions, his excessive dalliance with pathos in the second part, his frequent apologies for not getting on with his story though he acknowledges the need. For all that, *The Squire's Tale* is still good reading, and in a typically medieval way. Thus the first part catches the tone and subject matter of Arthurian romance, though the presiding royal figure is a Tartar king called Cambyuskan. At his court, as a formal feast reaches the third course, a 'strange knyght' appears, who reminds one at once of the Green Knight entering Arthur's feast at Camelot to terrify Guinevere and alarm the Round Table, in *Sir Gawain and the Green Knight*. He brings magical gifts from 'the kyng of Arabe and Inde': a brass horse which will fly its rider anywhere and can be made to disappear, a mirror and ring for the king's daughter Canacee, and a sword. The sword will cut through any armour and inflict wounds which can be cured only if they are stroked with the flat of its blade; the mirror will tell any lady if her lover is false; the ring will enable its wearer to understand the speech of birds and know the healing properties of all herbs. After speculation about the optic qualities of the mirror, it and the sword are put away safely and, after some courtly dancing led by the strange knight and Canacee, the company gather marvelling round the brass horse, which suddenly vanishes. The details of Part I, which now ends abruptly, resemble some in the Prester John stories, and the idea of the flying brass horse probably owes something to the ebony horse in the *Thousand and One Nights*.

Of the magical equipment produced by the ambassador from 'Arabe and Inde', only the ring operates in the narrative; perhaps if the Squire had been allowed to continue, he would have completed the kind of interlaced romance suggested by the four gifts. Part II is about Canacee who, unlike the rest of the court, which continued feasting until almost dawn, went to bed early. She rises with the dawn birdsong to walk in the park, wearing her new ring, and comes across a female falcon, perched in a dry tree and pecking herself in frantic grief. The bird is so near swooning that Canacee spreads her skirt to catch her should she fall, before asking her cause of grief. The falcon flutters swooning to the ground and then, safe in Canacee's lap, unfolds a story of the kind which occupied Chaucer throughout *The Legend of Good Women*. She plighted her troth to a tercelet, who seemed perfect in faith and all manly virtue but, being separated from her by Fortune, left her for a kite. However, the inconstant lover is persuaded by Canacee's brother to repent and fulfil his former vows. The true passion and fidelity of the falcon contrast nicely with the love values of *The Merchant's Tale*, which precedes it in many manuscripts. Perhaps such a sense of completeness explains why the Franklin interrupts just as the Squire starts Part III with another of the astrological date and time clues which the *Tale* contains; in any case, whether it is important or not, this tale suits its teller.

The Franklin

The Franklin of the *General Prologue* is the only pilgrim of social substance apart from the Knight whose pretensions Chaucer seems to spare. He rides in company with the Sergeant of the Law, has been sheriff and knight of the shire, and is so open and generous in hospitality that 'It snewed in his hous of mete and drynke'. The fishpond beside his big house breeds only big fish such as bream and pike. His character is defined as 'sangwyn' – the type which is generally jolly, healthy and good-tempered – and he is an Epicurean, that is, one dedicated to pleasurable life through the exercise of virtue. But, as he reveals when interrupting *The Squire's Tale*, he has to bear the sorrow of having a wastrel son, whose extravagance, gambling and love of low company contrast with the 'gentillesse' of the Squire, whom he compliments for speaking 'feelyngly' in his narration.

In his short *Prologue*, after the Host has poured contempt on his pretension to 'gentillesse', the Franklin announces that he will tell a Breton lay – a type of short narrative Romance poem associated with Marie de France, a poetess of the twelfth century who was possibly the half-sister of Henry II – in blunt and unliterary style.

*

In *The Franklin's Tale* Chaucer shows in moving and thrilling action a phenomenon of morals and behaviour the essence of which usually lies in stasis, because its true manifestations are devoid of interesting conflict; the phenomenon being a marriage based on absolute equality and mutual trust between the partners. If there is to be conflict involving the attrition of either quality, with ensuing resolution, then the catalyst, the factor that causes conflict, must come from outside. In *The Franklin's Tale* it comes from a threat to the security of the marriage to which neither party to the sacramental bond yields. The device, as in *The Merchant's Tale*, is a folk theme common to diverse cultures; this time, that of the Damsel's Rash Promise, which is so called because the promise governs a set of circumstances in which chastity is at stake.

Rash promises tend to be made out of a sense of total certainty or moral superiority, or both. In this poem Dorigen, the virtuous wife of the knight Arveragus, when propositioned during her husband's absence by a squire called Aurelius, is so sure of not even being tempted that 'in pleye' she agrees to show him mercy (that is, become his lover) if and when all the rocks on the coast of Brittany are removed.

Through the agency of a wizard, who creates an illusion ('apparence') that all the rocks have disappeared, Aurelius establishes the condition demanded by the promise. The appalled and sorrowing Dorigen explains all to her husband, who heroically accedes to the moral ineluctability of the situation:

> 'I hadde wel levere ystiked for to be[44]
> For[45] verray love which that I to yow have,
> But if ye sholde youre trouthe kepe and save.[46]
> Trouthe is the hyeste thyng that man may kepe' –
> But with that word he brast anon to wepe ...

> (V, 1476–80)

When Dorigen meets Aurelius to commit the sanctioned adultery, he is so moved by her lamentation that he releases her from her promise. This display of magnanimity is joined next by the wizard, who forgives Aurelius the huge debt incurred for the cost of the magic.

In Boccaccio, who tells a similar story in *Il Filocolo* as well as in the *Decameron*, the main interest lies in the question of love at the end: which of the three magnanimous men showed most generosity, the husband, the prospective lover or the magician? Chaucer's Franklin poses this question in a single line, leaves it hanging in the air and ends without even the customary blessing. His interest lies in the operation

44. rather be stabbed   45. on account of   46. if you do not guard and keep your good faith

under stress of a marriage founded on multiple mutual promises which are being kept.

These exchanged promises open the *Tale*. Two-way patience, tolerance and humility are covenanted between the pair, and the 'maistrie' traditionally exercised by woman during courtship and by man in marriage is specifically forsworn: Arveragus's only reservation concerns the face the marriage puts to the outside world:

> Save that the name of[47] soveraynetee
> That wolde he have for shame[48] of his degree.[49]
>
> (V, 751–2)

Accordingly 'Thus been they bothe in quiete and in reste' (760), which echoes the state of bliss between Troilus and Criseyde at the height of their love, and may therefore be thought of as Chaucer's ideal for lovers. This opening passage concludes with the Franklin extolling marriage in words very like those used ironically by the Merchant. It looks like a direct challenge to that previous story-teller:

> Who koude telle, but he hadde wedded be,
> The joye, the ese, and the prosperitee
> That is bitwixe an housbonde and his wyf?
>
> (V, 803–5)

Arveragus leaves home to seek honour by knightly exploits in England, leaving Dorigen sorrowing in her seaside castle with friends who try to comfort her. They walk the shore and Dorigen, looking out to sea and longing for her husband's ship to return, curses 'the grisly rokkes blake' upon which she imagines his ship being wrecked:

> But wolde God that alle thise rokkes blake
> Were sonken into helle for his sake!
>
> (V, 891–2)

When Aurelius offers love to her, it is her dread of these rocks that gives form to her rash promise – an ironical twist. Aurelius grieves at the impossibility of his task, and prays to Apollo and to Lucina 'that of the see is chief goddesse and queene' to help him.

Arveragus returns loaded with honour, and he and Dorigen resume their happy love relationship, while Aurelius languishes for two years. At length his brother puts him in touch with a wizard in Orleans who performs the required 'myracle'. When Dorigen is challenged to fulfil her promise, she launches into a long formal complaint to Fortune, citing

---

47. title pertaining to   48. 'shame' is the quality which guards personal honour   49. status

hosts of famous women who preferred death to the violation of their chastity. The long account of the doings of the brothers with the wizard, and this complaint of Dorigen's, slacken the forward thrust of the narrative, but perhaps the resulting rhythm gives greater prominence to the surprising triple dénouement.

Some critics have been bothered by what they regard as the unreality of Arveragus's instruction to Dorigen to fulfil her promise and commit adultery: Derek Pearsall goes so far as to write: 'There are many things that a decent and sensible man in his situation could have done, and this is not one of them' (*The Canterbury Tales*, p. 152). But the context, the frame of multiple promises within which the couple exist, make it the only thing that this decent and sensible man can do. It has the ring of emotional truth and the sanction of the logic by which the two live in trust. It is a transcendence of sharing, and immensely painful to both: Arveragus very nearly breaks as he instructs her how she may limit the damage:

> ... 'I yow forbede, up peyne of deeth,
> That nevere, whil thee lasteth lyf ne breeth,
> To no wight telle thou of this aventure, –
> As I may best, I wol my wo endure, –
> Ne make no contenance of hevynesse,
> That folk of yow may demen harm or gesse.'
>
> (V, 1481–86)

He actually has her escorted to the garden where she is to meet Aurelius, being instinctively buoyed up, in spite of all, by an innate trust in her which spills over on to fortune: 'It may be wel, paraventure, yet to day' (V, 1473). Arveragus weeps. Dorigen is beyond tears when Aurelius meets her and asks where she is going:

> And she answerde, half as she were mad,
> 'Unto the gardyn, as myn housbonde bad,
> My trouthe for to hold, allas! allas!'
>
> (V, 1511–13)

In such great moments of the poem, Chaucer's Franklin is given the unadorned style, without 'colours of rethoryk', that he modestly offered in his *Prologue*. Its down-to-earth strength is matched by such genuine and unclouded perceptions as those of Dorigen when she is first propositioned:

> By thilke God that yaf me soule and lyf,
> Ne shal I nevere been untrewe wyf

> In word ne werk, as fer as I have wit;
> I wol been his to whom that I am knyt.
>
> (V, 983–6)

and

> What deyntee⁵⁰ sholde a man han in his lyf
> For to go love another mannes wyf,
> That hath hir body whan so that hym liketh?
>
> (V, 1003–5)

Such stern and even prosy practicality is set in exotic foils: the attractive but conventional courtliness of Aurelius, the voluminously recorded processes of the miracle-making and of the classically-based complaint of Dorigen, and the sudden icy reminder of the season when Aurelius and the wizard journey to Brittany from Orleans. Phoebus the sun-god becomes old and

> ... now in Capricorn adoun he lighte,
> Where as he shoon ful pale, I dar wel seyn.
> The bitter frostes, with the sleet and reyn,
> Destroyed hath the grene in every yerd.
>
> (V, 1248–51)

In this conclusion to the part of the 'marriage debate' most pointedly argued among the pilgrims, Chaucer makes his case against courtly precept and social custom, as well as against the religious ideas about marriage expressed in the form of 'Solemnization of Matrimony' in the *Sarum Missal*, which was compiled in the thirteenth century and was in Church use for many centuries thereafter. The case he makes establishes his own highly civilized and indeed Epicurean idea of 'gentilesse' in marriage.

50. delight

Chapter 7. Tales of the Second Nun, the Canon's Yeoman, the Manciple and the Parson

The Second Nun

The Second Nun's Prologue opens Fragment VIII without links to the pilgrimage. The story-teller is the Prioress's 'chateleyne' of the *General Prologue*, where that is the only information about her. There is nothing in her *Prologue* or *Tale* to suggest that they were written for *The Canterbury Tales*, and it is generally agreed that both are early work which was probably written in the mid-1370s and allotted to the Second Nun without adaptation: there is one line in her *Prologue* indicating that the speaker is a man, an 'unworthy sone of Eve'. Her story, the legend of St Cecilia, is listed as Chaucer's work in the *Prologue* to *The Legend of Good Women*.

This prologue is a conventional preamble to a saint's legend, in four parts. It opens with an exhortation to avoid idleness, a sin with which the speaker contrasts her own 'feithful bisynesse' (VIII, 24), and proceeds to an invocation to the Virgin Mary which contains some fine poetry drawn from the same source that Chaucer used for the Prioress's *Prologue*, though the writing here is more diffuse: the prayer of St Bernard in Canto XXXIII of Dante's *Paradiso*. Next comes a short apology of the conventionally modest kind for the lack of subtlety in the story to follow, and last of all is a respectful but fanciful etymology of the name of the saint.

The Second Nun's Tale of the life of St Cecilia recounts, without going into character and motivation and without demanding emotional response from the readers or listener, a series of miraculous conversions and other events, and some cruel acts of persecution. This patron saint of music is colourless beside Constance or Griselda, but that is in the nature of the saint's legend, in which miracles and matters such as unargued dedications to holy virginity stand, simple and unadorned, as factors which reinforce or express faith.

Cecilia, who has been brought up in Rome as a Christian, wears a hair garment under her wedding gown, and asks her husband, Valerian, if she may remain a virgin after marriage, saying, 'I have an aungel which that loveth me' (VIII, 152). Not surprisingly, Valerian suspects that she has a lover, but she proves her case and so converts first him and then, with the help of the angel, his brother Tiburce. She explains the Trinity and the Passion, and sends Tiburce to be christened by Pope Urban, after which the grace he obtains enables him to see the angel every day. Soon after, the authorities require the brothers to worship the image of Jupiter. They refuse, and convert the official charged with their execution. Cecilia encourages them to persevere in their faith: 'Gooth to the corone [crown] of lif that may nat faille' (VIII, 388), she says. When required publicly to sacrifice to Jupiter, they kneel in Christian prayer 'And losten bothe hir hevedes [heads] in the place' (VIII, 398). Next, the newly converted executioner is whipped to death and buried beside the brothers at Cecilia's order. She herself is then required to give up her faith by the prefect Almachius, and in reply she lectures him about his powerlessness against her faith, and mocks him for worshipping a stone idol. He becomes angry and orders her to be burnt in a bath of red flames. But miraculously she does not even sweat with the heat, and so Almachius orders her execution. Even the third stroke does not sever her head, and she survives, preaching to fellow-Christians until she succumbs on the third day after. It is not one of Chaucer's most arresting tales.

The Canon's Yeoman

The Canon's Yeoman's Prologue brings a burst of action into the Links, which elsewhere consist almost entirely of comments on tales and tellers. 'At Boghtoun under Blee' (VIII, 556), which is near Ospring, a staging point less than ten miles from Canterbury, two riders appear who have galloped their horses into an un-Cecilia-like sweat in the effort to overtake the company and join their pilgrimage. One is a canon who wears a shabby black cloak over his white surplice, and perspires so much that he has a burdock leaf under his hood to soak up the sweat; to no avail, because his forehead drips like a still. The other is his yeoman, whom the Host proceeds to question, particularly about his master. It transpires that the Canon practises alchemy; he could, says the Yeoman, pave with silver and gold the road between them and Canterbury. But, as the Host has noticed, his clothes are threadbare and, as the Yeoman says, he lives in a suburb among dead ends where criminals lurk. Clearly the Canon misuses his 'overgreet' wit. And when the Host asks the Yeoman to account for his discoloured face, which is the result of close work at the alchemist's furnace, the man's disillusion with the master mingles with his hope that his experiments may yet succeed:

> Yet is it fals, but ay we han good hope
> It for to doon, and after it we grope.

(VIII, 678–9)

The Canon overhears, and when the Host, scenting an exciting story from a new pilgrim, eggs the Yeoman on to tell his tale, the failing alchemist rides away in shame, not wishing to hear the truth about himself and his art.

The Canon's Yeoman's Tale is in two parts. The first is an agonized personal confession about seven fruitless years spent in the Canon's service, which is full of lists of materials used and processes confusingly described. Ever longing for his master to succeed, cursing his failures, envying him the learning which goes into the practice, and above all suffering physically in the hot and smelly work, the Yeoman knows at heart's root that what he does is immoral, being based on avarice: 'Lo! which advantage is to multiplie!'¹ (VIII, 731). Though dealing with arcane processes, in this autobiographical statement by the Canon's Yeoman Chaucer shows unforgettable informed sympathy with the toiling drudge who is an underdog. Elsewhere his poetry contains no parallel account of, for example, the hardships of field work in winter, or seamanship, or coal-mining, or warfare. Blowing the fire till his heart faints, sickened by the explosions which signal the failure of successive attempts to make new gold or silver, and listening to his master's explanations of what went wrong in dread that the blame will fall on him, the Canon's Yeoman inhabits the gap between the materiality of the demanding minute-by-minute operation of a job he understands only dimly, and the spirituality of a system of eternal values that he instinctively recognizes. The close of Part I of his *Tale* is a cry of disillusion from his inmost heart:

> He that semeth the wiseste, by Jhesus!
> Is moost fool, whan it cometh to the preef;²
> And he that semeth trewest is a theef.
> That shul ye knowe, er that I from yow wend,³
> By that⁴ I of my tale have maad an ende.

(VIII, 967–71)

Part II of *The Canon's Yeoman's Tale* is a straightforward story about the gulling of a stupid and avaricious priest by an alchemist who is a canon – though the Yeoman insists that the villain of the story is not his own master. The story is straightforward because it lacks the element of surprise; from the start, we are told that the canon-alchemist is a rogue,

---

1. increase by transmuting base metals into precious ones 2. proof 3. go 4. by the time

and we see that his behaviour, like that of his gullible victim, is predictable. First, to establish confidence, the canon borrows money from the priest and honourably repays it; then, he twice performs alchemical experiments with base metal supplied by the priest, and surreptitiously adds extra metal to ensure the 'alchemy' works profitably; the third time he gets a goldsmith to confirm the value of the product. He has won the confidence of the priest, who agrees to pay him forty pounds for the secret silver-making process. The priest is left with a useless recipe, and the canon disappears.

The religious undertones provide the interest. The canon is indirectly called a 'feend' and a Judas, and later is abused as 'feendly', and the solemn conclusion to the *Tale*, after a lengthy moralization, is that the true secret of alchemy is so dear to Christ

> That he wol nat that it discovered bee,
> But where it liketh to his deitee
> Men for t'enspire, and eek [5] for to deffende
> Whom that hym liketh; lo, this is the ende.

(VIII, 148–71)

Consequently, says the Yeoman, anyone who

> ... maketh God his adversarie,
> As for to werken any thyng in contrarie
> Of his wil, certes, never shal he thryve,
> Thogh that he multiplie terme of his lyve.[6]

(VIII, 1476–9)

The religious reservation about alchemy is the main aspect of Chaucer's treatment of the subject which Ben Jonson, in his brilliantly funny play *The Alchemist*, does not seriously consider. Otherwise, both regard it as a false science practised only by charlatans, who gull the avaricious. But only Chaucer gives us the pain of the genuine doubter who feels that his soul's truth is impugned by involvement in the work.

The Manciple

The Manciple of the *The General Prologue*, whose *Prologue* and *Tale* constitute Fragment IX, is the last in Chaucer's gallery of corrupt professional manipulators of other people's cash. The twenty-line entry for this buyer of provisions for lawyers in the Temple concerns only his skill in handling purchases and obtaining credit, and ends with the judgement

5. also   6. i.e. practise alchemy for the rest of his life

that in such activities he can fool anyone. Chaucer makes the point with irony at the Creator's expense:

> Now is nat that of God a ful fair grace
> That swich a lewed mannes wit shall pace[7]
> The wisdom of an heep of lerned men?

(I, 573–5)

The Manciple's Prologue shows Chaucer further developing sophisticated ways of binding the *Tales* into the evolving experience of the pilgrims, though the tale the Manciple tells, however it may or may not suit him, is thought to have been composed earlier and then attached to this narrator. The particular technique Chaucer uses here is that of the quarrel between two pilgrims, of which there have already been three examples: the Reeve and the Miller, the Friar and the Summoner and, most recently, the Host and the Pardoner. Here it is between the Manciple and the Cook, two professionals who by the nature of their jobs must interact, since a cook turns into edible food what a manciple buys.

When the pilgrims reach Harbledown, which is near Canterbury, the Host for some unexplained reason turns on the Cook, who is snoozing drunk and swaying on his horse, and demands a story from him. The Manciple usurps the Host's function by offering to excuse the Cook from telling a tale, but suddenly turns censorious and abuses him for his stinking breath:

> Hold cloos thy mouth, man, by thy fader[8] kyn!
> The devel of helle sette his foot therin![9]
> Thy cursed breeth infecte wol us alle.

(IX, 37–9)

The Cook is so cross that he falls off his horse and has to be helped up with 'greet showvyng bothe to and fro', and the Host agrees that the Manciple may tell a tale. But he rebukes him for reproving the Cook, pointing out that the Cook in return could expose the Manciple's fiddling of accounts. The Manciple repents and gives the Cook wine from his own gourd, a peace offering for which the Host praises Bacchus.

The Manciple's Tale, on the folk theme of the Tell-tale Bird, is taken chiefly from Book II of Ovid's *Metamorphoses*. It sits more gracefully in that world, where classical deities and mortals pursue their loves, than it does in the degraded courtly milieu of the English medieval Thebes

7. outdo 8. father's 9. this suggests that a gaping mouth is the way in and out for the devil

where Chaucer's version is set. In plot, the *Tale* is the merest anecdote, and explains why crows are black. A bird starts the story as a talking white crow, a sweet-singing pet of Phoebus who watches his master's wife copulating with 'A man of litel reputacioun' and reports the fact. In rage, Phoebus kills his wife, but at once regrets the deed, cursing himself for rash anger and the crow for telling a 'false tale'. He pulls out all the bird's white feathers, turns him black, condemns him to cawing instead of singing, and throws him out. The Manciple's rather tedious closing moralization warns against the danger of rash speech:

> My sone, be war, and be noon auctour[10] newe
> Of tidynges, whether they been false or trewe.
> Whereso thou come, amonges hye or lowe,
> Kepe wel thy tonge, and thenk upon the crowe.

(IX, 359–62)

In Ovid, Apollo's lover Coronis, the prettiest girl in Thessaly, pulls her jealous husband's arrow out of her breast and pleads pathetically that his child whom she is carrying be allowed to live. Chaucer omits the child altogether, and gives a perfunctory two lines to the murder. Most other elements of the story are also debased in the retelling. Certainly Phoebus is first described as a conventionally fine courtly man, but there is nothing of 'fine amour' about his unnamed wife's adultery:

> And so bifel, whan Phebus was absent,
> His wyf anon[11] hath for hir lemman[12] sent

(IX, 203–4)

> Whan Phebus wyf had sent for hir lemman,
> Anon they wroghten al hire lust volage.[13]

(IX, 238–9)

The literal narration is preceded by three instances of beast behaviour, two of which apply very loosely to the bird, and one, more clearly, to the wife, all culled from the *Roman de la Rose*: the caged bird that prefers any hardship in the wild to pampered life in a cage, the cat which, however overfed, will still hunt mice, and the she-wolf which will take even 'the lewedeste wolf' for mate.

The Manciple – if the *Tale* is his in more than name – has one serious idea. Pondering the word 'lemman', he reflects on the injustice of using different terms for nobles and plebeians who do the same thing:

> But that the gentile,[14] in estaat above,
> She shal be cleped[15] his lady, as in love;
> And for[16] that oother is a povre womman,

10. author   11. at once   12. lover   13. wanton   14. noblewoman   15. called   16. because

> She shal be cleped his wenche[17] or his lemman.[18]
> And God it woot,[19] myn owene deere brother,
> Men leyn that oon as lowe as lith that oother.

(IX, 217–22)

Despite its context, this relates to a perennial theme of Chaucer's: that virtue may be found equally among rich and poor, high and low. But the rather low moral, in lines 359–62 quoted above, that the Manciple draws from his story can only be justified, it seems to me, by referring to the Manciple's own rash speaking, to the Cook, before he began his *Tale*.

The Parson

The Parson's Prologue is the most informative of all the prologues, epilogues and introductions which function as linking sections. We are given the time and date: it is four o'clock on 20th April, two days and six hours after the Man of Law began his tale of Constance. Chaucer clearly meant *The Parson's Tale* to be the last: it will be remembered that in his original plan, the Host proposed that each pilgrim should tell four tales, two on the way to Canterbury and two on the return journey to Southwark; but now, as he turns to the Parson, he says: 'Now lakketh us no tales mo than oon'[20] (X, 16). The suggestion that we are near the end and that that carries a religious consequence is plain: the pilgrims are 'at a thropes [village's] ende', and the Parson, rejecting fables as worthless, offers to show them

> ... the way, in this viage,
> Of thilke parfit glorious pilgrymage
> That highte[21] Jerusalem celestial.

(X, 49–51)

Evening, leaving a village, the Holy City in prospect. With a decided glint of ironic humour, the Parson excuses himself from contributing in verse. Since he cannot compose in alliterative verse as Northerners do – 'rum, ram, ruf' he calls it – and thinks rhyme but little better, he offers 'a myrie tale in prose'. Suspecting a long sermon, the Host urges him, 'Be fructuous [fruitful], and that in litel space'.

The Parson's Tale confirms the Host's fears because it is not a tale at all, and not even a sermon, though it begins as one. A sermon would at least

17. trollop   18. concubine   19. knows   20. we lack only one tale   21. is called

have entertained if it were as masterful as *The Pardoner's Prologue* and *Tale*; but this treatise on penitence is far longer than any other tale, and just over half of it describes the seven deadly sins and their remedies. The work draws on Macrobius and other conventional medieval sources and is liberally laced with quotations from the Bible and the Church Fathers. The whole treatise is presented as an answer to the unspoken question in Jeremiah VI, 16: 'Stand ye in the ways, and see, and ask for the old paths, where is the good way, and walk therein, and ye shall find (cool) rest for your souls.' The process of salvation is through penitence, confession and satisfaction. The latter is defined as two things: almsgiving, which includes forgiving and counselling people as well as sustaining the needy, and bodily pain, which means praying, fasting, wearing rough cloth next the skin, and scourging oneself, all in religiously appropriate gladness.

It used to be doubted that Chaucer wrote *The Parson's Tale*, but it is now generally agreed to be his, and to have been written early enough for him to quote from it in several other tales. But the material is traditionally Christian, and Chaucer could have made up his precise contents from the contemporary devotional literature of treatise and sermon with which, particularly in the latter part of his work, he shows himself to have been so familiar. Since the material is not original (though there is no known single source for the plan of the whole tale) and the work is in prose, it seems fair to consider whether the hand of a great poet may be seen in it. It may be argued that Chaucer's powers are subsumed in giving verisimilitude to the religious subject matter, and that the language and imagery carry the qualities and charisma of his source material rather than anything especially characteristic of him. Here is the poet-chameleon taking colour from a traditional description of contrition as the root of the tree of penitence:

The roote of this tree is Contricioun, that hideth hym in the herte of hym that is verray repentaunt, right as the roote of a tree hydeth hym in the erthe. Of the root of Contricioun spryngeth a stalke that bereth braunches and leves of Confessioun, and fruyt of Satisfaccioun.

(X, 112–13)

The Parson's treatise makes forbidding reading. 'Thou shalt not' is the hell-avoiding principle by which it proceeds, especially in its frequent railing against sexual activity. Lechery is the deadly sin treated at greatest length. The obsession requires sexual display to be a lurid target in the description of pride: people's 'horrible disordinat scantnesse of clothyng' does not cover

119

the shameful membres of man, to wikked entente. Allas! somme of hem shewen the boce [22] of hir shap, and the horrible swollen membres, that semeth lik the maladie of hirnia, in the wrappynge of hir hoses; and eek the buttokes of hem faren as it were the hyndre part of a she-ape in the fulle of the moone. And mooreover, the wrecched swollen membres that they shewe thurgh disgisynge, in departynge [23] of hire hoses in whit and reed [24], semeth that half hir shameful privee membres weren flayne [25].

(X, 421–4)

The key statement of the whole treatise is a denial of the Franklin's life-delighting Epicureanism: 'A man shal be verray repentaunt for alle his synnes that he hath doon in delit of his thoght; for delit is ful perilous' (X, 291). The Retraction appended to *The Parson's Tale* concludes the entire *Canterbury Tales*. It is summarized on pp. 197–8.

In its rejection of the broad humanity and the poetic values of the mass of Chaucer's poetry, it harmonizes exactly with what the Parson has said. Whether it has the reality or only the appearance of a deathbed repentance, we cannot say; we can do no more than point to it, and to the finality of its concluding prayer: '... graunte me grace of verray penitence, confessioun and satisfaccioun to doon in this present lyf ... so that I may been oon of hem at the day of doom that shulle be saved' (X, 1089, 1091).

22. bulge   23. dividing   24. red   25. had their skin flayed off

Part III: Chaucer's Narrative Masterpiece

Chapter 8. Troilus and Criseyde

As Chaucer's longest single complete poem, and one of the great love poems of the world, *Troilus and Criseyde* has been the subject of a huge volume of expository criticism. The varieties of emphasis and differences of interpretation in this body of criticism can be more daunting than exhilarating. So it will not be easy to offer a straightforward critical account of what is generally regarded as Chaucer's narrative masterpiece.

First, there is the matter of the sources, to which editors constantly give much attention. Study of them will reveal something about the making of the poem, but should not be pursued at the cost of failing to see the artefact as a unique whole, which it is. It is true that Eustache Deschamps, Chaucer's French contemporary, salutes Chaucer as 'grant translateur', and that in this poem Chaucer is ostensibly translating Boccaccio's *Filostrato* (which means 'he who is stricken by love', *circa* 1335), and repeatedly mentions 'myn auctour' (my author) as if he were faithfully following him. But the alchemy Chaucer exercises on his sources in the realization of his own poetic vision should lead us to think of 'translation' in his case as the kind of transformation envisaged in Quince's observation in *A Midsummer Night's Dream*: 'Bottom, thou art translated.' Just as Poussin borrowed, and then transmuted, two of the most important figures in his painting of the 'Lamentation over the Body of Christ', Chaucer borrows and transmutes; applying his own processes to characters, speeches, descriptions, ideas.

For direct source, both medieval poets drew not on classical Greek and Latin accounts of the Trojan War, in which Troilus is a minor figure whose love life is not mentioned, but on the *Roman de Troie* (*c.* 1170) of Benoît de Sainte-Maure, a tenth of which concerns Troilus's love for Briseida, the daughter of the traitor-priest Calchas, and on the Latin prose redaction of Benoît, *Historia Destructionis Troiae* (1287) by Guido del Columnis. Possibly a French translation of Boccaccio was also used by Chaucer, and as in much of his work, the philosophical aspects of the poem owe much more to Boethius than to any other single thinker. Chaucer also drew on other Italian poems, by Dante, Boccaccio and Petrarch, and on works in classical Latin and French, of which the poems of Ovid and the *Roman de la Rose* are the most important. The three main characters, Troilus, Criseyde and Pandarus, are respectively

123

the Lover, the Lady and the Friend of the French poem, duly transmuted.

Chaucer's poem is longer than Boccaccio's, is cast on an epic scale, though written in five books and not Boccaccio's twelve, and contains a wider range of material, including a more complex and subtle moral scheme and much profounder characterization, especially of Criseyde, and of Pandarus, the go-between in her love affair with Troilus. Pandarus is cousin to Criseida in Boccaccio, but uncle to Criseyde, with appropriate connotations, in Chaucer. Boccaccio's poem is a personal love offering, to a lady whom he calls 'Filomela' (nightingale), and ends with a plea to lovers to sympathize with Troilo and a trite recommendation to young men to go for mature women, who need love more, and are more constant and discreet, than young women like Criseida. Chaucer presents *Troilus and Criseyde* through a carefully constructed persona of an all-seeing analytical poet who is nevertheless compassionate, and achieves a virtual apotheosis of love as an indispensable universal power, even though the particular love relationship in the poem dissolves in quick treachery and prolonged pathos.

In essence, *Troilus and Criseyde* is a story of love and its betrayal remarkable for the simplicity of its narrative frame, and equally remarkable for its complexities of character portrayal, description and thought, which are conveyed in rhyme royal stanzas of easy fluency. Its variety and power are maintained by the regulated deployment of almost every kind of poetic rhetoric known in medieval literature. Whether a nightingale is singing outside Criseyde's window, or Troilus is twisting in anguish on his bed, or Pandarus is busily leaping on errands between the lovers, or the ruling stars are conjoining to determine human action and fate, the narrative force and its poetic mould hold their courses with a sophisticated decorum. The story is as follows.

Book I (1092 lines): During the siege of Troy by the Greeks, Troilus, a son of Priam the King of Troy falls in love with Criseyde, a young widow whose father, a prophet-priest called Calchas, has deserted to the Greek side because he has foreseen the eventual Greek victory. Troilus suffers secretly, in despair at being unable to attain her, until her uncle Pandarus worms the cause of his sorrow out of him and promises his help.

Book II (1157 lines): Pandarus persuades Criseyde to hear Troilus's suit, bears letters between them, and sets up their first meeting, in the house of Deiphebus.

Book III (1820 lines): Pandarus arranges the secret coming together in bed of the lovers, in his own house, and similarly arranges their subsequent love-making opportunities.

Book IV (1701 lines): In an exchange of prisoners between the warring Trojans and Greeks, it is decided that, in return for Antenor, a Trojan prisoner of the Greeks, Criseyde shall be sent to the Greek camp to be with her father. The lovers and Pandarus lament, and discuss what to do. Troilus and Criseyde enjoin each other to be faithful during their enforced separation, and Criseyde plans to return to Troy after ten days away.

Book V (1869 lines): Diomede, a Greek prince, fetches Criseyde, who soon accepts his advances. Troilus waits in vain for her to return, discovers her infidelity and aims to kill Diomede in battle, but after many heroic deeds against the Greeks is himself killed by Achilles. His soul ascends to the stars, from which vantage point he declares heavenly felicity better than the vanity of this wretched world.

So simple a plot, so extraordinary the length of the poem: no wonder that the interest lies not in what happens, but in how it happens and with what consequences for the three main characters, of whom Troilus is the central one. At the beginning of each Book, Chaucer tells us exactly what is to happen. At the start of Book I, as the vengeful Fury Tisiphone is invoked, we are told that we may

> ... the double sorwes[1] here[2]
> Of Troilus in lovynge of Criseyde,
> And how that she forsook hym er she deyde.[3]
>
> (I, 54–6)

At the start of Book II, as Clio the Muse of History is invoked, we are informed that its subject will be 'How Troilus com to his lady grace' (II, 32), Book III opens not surprisingly with an invocation to Venus:

> How I mot[4] tell anonright[5] the gladness
> Of Troilus, to Venus heryinge?[6]
> To which gladnesse, who needs hath, God hym brynge!
>
> (III, 47–9)

Book IV opens with a joint invocation of the three Furies and Mars the god of war, whose help Chaucer requests to enable him to tell how Fortune cast Troilus

1. sorrows   2. hear   3. died   4. may   5. at once   6. in praise of Venus

> ... clene out of his lady grace,
> And on hire whiel[7] she sette up Diomede ...

> (IV, 10–11)

– an action completed in Book V, which opens with an invocation to the three Fates, who will

> ... don execucioun;[8]
> For which Criseyde moste out of the town,
> And Troilus shal dwellen forth in pyne[9]
> Til Lachesis[10] his thred no lenger twyne.

> (V, 4–7)

For all its leisurely unfolding and profound amplitude, the poem opens with signal economic urgency. The first eight stanzas constitute the poet's Dantean dedication to his task, and his prayer to happy lovers to have pity on all who, like Troilus, suffer for love. He calls himself 'servant of the servants of the God of Love' as if he were a high priest, like the Pope, one of whose titles was 'servant of the servants of God'. The heroic tone becomes at once servant to the high pathos of a noble love. The narrative develops crisply, and within another seventy lines we are told that Calchas has defected to the Greek side, that Criseyde fears consequent disgrace and threats to her safety, and that Hector frees her of guilt and promises to protect her.

Then the heroine appears among the springtime worshippers at a temple, a small figure in black, solitary for fear of shame, but matchless in her beauty. It is not until Book V that we are told that her eyebrows meet in the middle – probably, in physiognomical lore, a sign of excessive passion. Next we are shown, in the same congregation, the 'fierse and proude knyght', Troilus, scoffing at love, which prompts Chaucer to moralize amusingly on such presumption; because Troilus suddenly sees Criseyde, and is smitten with love. The response of Criseyde, who is aware of his covert contemplation, is the first of many master-strokes of characterization:

> ... for she let falle
> Hire look a lite aside in swich manere,[11]
> Ascaunces,[12] 'What! may I nat stonden[13] here?'
> And after that hir lokynge gan she lighte,[14]
> That nevere thoughte hym seen so good a syghte.[15]

> (I, 290–94)

Such perfection in observing the realities of sexual attraction in particular

7. wheel   8. perform execution   9. live in misery   10. Lachesis is the Fate who at death cuts the thread of life   11. a little sidelong in such a way   12. as if to say   13. stand   14. expression became more animated   15. it seemed he had never seen anything so beautiful

people continues throughout the poem, threading the frame of discourse, which is mainly that of courtly love. For Troilus goes from that encounter pondering the suffering that may come of his love being scorned, resolving to keep the matter secret, and then, unlike a 'fierse and proude knyght' but very much like a conventional courtly lover, sitting at the foot of his bed sighing and groaning. Throughout the poem, that bed symbol is used more as the scene of helpless suffering than of ecstatic coupling. There follows Troilus's first Song, which Chaucer attributes to 'myn auctour called Lollius': the name of Boccaccio is never mentioned; it is just possible that Chaucer may have possessed a manuscript of *Filostrato* without knowing who the author was. The song contains Troilus's courtly love vow, made to the God of Love:

> But wheither goddesse or womman, iwis,[16]
> She be, I not,[17] which that ye do me[18] serve;
> But as hire man I wol ay lyve and sterve.[19]
>
> (I, 425–7)

Typically, Troilus becomes braver in battle as his love-misery increases, and he fears being mocked for falling in love.

At length his friend Pandarus, visiting him unheralded, hears him groaning and presses him to reveal the cause which, three hundred and twenty lines later (873), he does. In that long passage is demonstrated in full the wonderful character of Pandarus, which has given us, at a low level, the word 'pander'. He uses every means he can think of to get Troilus to tell him the cause of his misery. He appeals to their friendship, and promises to share all the unhappiness, but is shamelessly eager to be informed: 'Hid nat thi wo fro me, but telle it blyve.' [quickly] (I, 595). He bombards Troilus with popular wisdom. Troilus is like a blind man without a guide, a knife without a whetstone: 'Wo hym that is allone!' (694). Pandarus is himself a frustrated lover, he says, and is thus peculiarly suited to be the confidant of one similarly placed – but we never see his beloved or even hear anything of her. Troilus says that he prefers to die rather than to tell; but Pandarus has a new stratagem. He offers to convey a message to the girl, whoever she may be, asks what is the point of despair, and scornfully depicts the man who suffers love without revealing it:

> What! many a man hath love full deere ybought[20]
> Twenty wynter that[21] his lady wiste,[22]
> That nevere yet his lady mouth he kiste.
>
> (I, 810–12)

16. certainly 17. don't know 18. you make me 19. for ever live and die 20. dearly paid for being in love 21. who 22. knew

The poetic moment when Troilus weakens, physically shaken by the avidly curious Pandarus, is quintessentially Chaucerian – true to the mode of courtly love, but playfully amusing, compassionate and realistic at the same time:

> Ane with that word he gan hym for to shake,
> And seyde, 'Thef,[23] thow shalt hyre name telle.'
> But tho gan sely[24] Troilus for to quake[25]
> As though men sholde han led hym into helle,
> And seyde, 'Allas! of al my wo the welle,[26]
> Thanne is my swete fo[27] called Criseyde!'
> And wel neigh with the word for feere he deide.[28]

(I, 869–75)

Pandarus can now work to heal Troilus's love-wounds, because revelation of the name of Criseyde, who is his niece, has made action possible. He says that since she is virtuous, she must be capable of 'pity', the courtly love quality a lady displays when she accepts her wooer. So Pandarus chides Troilus for having in the past mocked 'Loves servantz', invites him formally to repent his sin in order to appease the god's wrath, and consoles him with the observation that

> 'Was nevere man or womman yet bigete[29]
> That was unapt[30] to suffren loves hete,[31]
> Celestial, or elles love of kynde.[32]

(I, 977–9)

Book I ends with Troilus full of hope, not only playing the lion on the battlefield against the Greeks, but behaving like a reformed character, who is gentle, friendly and generous, and not haughty and scoffing as before. He is a fully depicted conventional courtly lover, but apparently completely in the hands of an intelligent, amusing and determined conspirator who is amazingly skilled in the timing of his interventions. Pandarus operates without malice, and his guise of friendship with Troilus is not feigned; he wishes to be the successful heirophant of a distinguished love ritual in which his princely friend and beautiful niece are the active celebrants. But again and again throughout the poem the reader is made aware of the real but unacknowledged force which drives Pandarus: his voyeuristic pursuit of a private satisfaction which derives from parasitic enjoyment, in the closest possible physical and spiritual

23. thief   24. hapless   25. shudder   26. the well of all my misery   27. foe   28. died   29. begotten   30. incapable   31. the fire of love   32. either heavenly (of God) or natural (of humans)

connection, with the passions and love-making of two people, to both of whom he acts as confidant as well as being their go-between. It is a condition with which Chaucer shows vivid and peculiar sympathy, even while implicitly judging it.

As for the heroine of the poem, by the end of Book I she has been off-stage for nearly eight hundred lines.

Book II, which is almost as long as *Macbeth*, concerns, first, the awakening love of Criseyde for Troilus and her pondering the likely effect of her yielding to it; second, their first tentative contacts with each other from a distance; and third, the engineering of their first meeting, which does not actually take place until the beginning of Book III. Not much event, you may think, for the single Book of the poem which is most often prescribed as a set text. The Book is dominated by Pandarus, who is the active progenitor of the first and third concerns of the Book enumerated above, and whose worldly advice and wily suggestion underlie the second. And here a little mildly statistical evidence may be offered, to give a true idea of the whole poem. Altogether, Pandarus speaks about one-eighth more dialogue than Troilus – and I include Troilus's Songs and Letters in his tally – and more than half as much again as Criseyde. Yet critics seem to pay him too little attention. As far as Book II is concerned, Pandarus's actual words occupy a third of the lines – almost as much dramatic dialogue, and it surely is dramatic, as is spoken by Othello in his whole tragedy.

Pandarus's persuasion, with its by now usual brilliance of timing and choice of stratagem, mingles with the gradual tilting, according to the understood code, of Criseyde's mind and passion towards her mostly supine adorer; and in the process, which is sometimes tender, sometimes funny, and often merciless, the unique relationship between niece and uncle is steadily revealed. Pandarus, suffering from his own frustrated desire, forces himself out of bed, with the aid of a mournful nightingale's dawn song, to carry out his promise to Troilus – to try and get Criseyde's 'grace' and 'mercy' granted. Often in the poem, when uncle and niece meet, they laugh at some shared joke. This is the first time we see them together, and the joke is that, when he has promised her a happy fortune, he asks for her good news, and she replies, 'Your maistresse is nat here.' And they dissolve in a fit of laughter, which ends with his proposal that they dance a little to 'don to May som observaunce', and she pretends to be shocked, as a widow ought to be.

But Pandarus has planted in her the hope that he brings some especially good news, and her curiosity is aroused. He cleverly turns the conversation to the daily battle exploits against the Greeks of the royal brothers Hector and Troilus: Chaucer never lets us forget that the great love affair churns forward against the background of an even greater battle affair of the classical world, which he has already firmly told us is the business of other poets, from whom we surely know all about it. The business of battle is never primary, but always secondary to that of love. The seed of Troilus's valour truly planted, Pandarus offers to leave, but Criseyde has remembered his promise of good which appertains to her, dismisses her attendants, and asks him what it is. His response is again to invite her to dance, and to suggest she give up disfiguring herself in 'widewes habit'. She is by now longing to know what is in his mind, and his recourse, after asking her, 'What sholde I peynte or drawen it on lengthe?' (II, 262) is to declare that Troilus loves her – but only after a further sixty lines of moralizing banter.

Pandarus's declaration is delivered in dread of hearing a conventionally outraged response from his niece, which he guards against with a well-timed outburst of tears, saying that, unless her response is favourable, both he and Troilus will die. Before she can reply, he placates her Danger (an allegorical character in *The Romance of the Rose* representing a woman's responses to being propositioned, see pp. 192–3) by minimizing the risk of their being found out, and describing the sheer virtue of assuaging the woe of Troilus:

> 'But alwey, goode nece, to stynte his woo,[33]
> So lat youre daunger sucred ben a lite,[34]
> That of his deth ye be naught for to wite.'[35]

(II, 383–5)

This lofty patter he reinforces by warning her against withering on the stalk, derided by the King's Fool, and proudly withstanding opportunities for love 'Til crowes feet be growen under youre ye [eyes] . . .' (II, 403). Criseyde upbraids his dishonesty, which prompts a further exculpatory threat of death from her uncle, and at last Criseyde 'gan to rewe' (had pity). She takes Pandarus's threat of death seriously and agrees that, though she cannot love Troilus, she will 'ples hym fro day to day' provided she can keep her honour. She binds Pandarus to go no further, but her curiosity is such that she asks him to tell her how he found out that Troilus loved her. Pandarus gives a knowing little smile and tells her a series of romantic lies eighty lines long which ends with the unequivocal

> 'Whan ye be his al hool,[36] as he is youre:[37]
> Ther myghty God yet graunte us see that houre!'

(II, 587–8)

33. end his misery 34. be sugared somewhat 35. not to blame 36. entirely 37. yours

She expostulates at that, but forgives him as he leaves, his pulsating seed well planted. 'Somdel astoned in hire thought' (somewhat astounded), Criseyde retires to her closet to ponder the conversation in terms of courtly love doctrine. It brings the first deep revelation of Criseyde's character.

This passage, lines 596–924, is one of the finest in English medieval poetry, and I choose it for the kind of detailed discussion which, owing to space limitations, I cannot give to other parts of the poem.

Criseyde's first thought, as she sits, is the self-protective one that if a man loves a woman even to the point of bursting his heart, she is nevertheless free to accept or reject him. But ironically, at that very moment, there is a burst of din at the nearby city gate, and shouts proclaim that Troilus has routed the Greeks. Criseyde's attendants rush her to the window to see him entering in triumph, his horse bleeding, his arms and armour battered and pierced, but his beautiful body unblemished and his demeanour modestly shamefaced. 'Who yaf me drynke?' (who has given me a love-potion?) she exclaims, blushes violently, and draws back: he does not see her.

She considers all his good points, and the poet, interceding now to explain and excuse, gives the main reason for her falling in love at that point:

> But moost hir favour was, for his distresse
> Was al for hire, and thoughte it was a routhe
> To sleen swich oon, if that he mente trouthe.[38]

(II, 663–5)

Her motives are thus exactly right according to the canon of courtly love: in order to mean 'trouthe', a man had to follow the high code in respect of unswerving passion and fidelity, secrecy and unquestioning service, while continuing in the public sphere to excel as a knight. It is worth observing at this point that 'secrecy' provides the linchpin of the whole fateful apparatus of the poem: bring in the concept of marriage, a public affair which Criseyde soon mentions dismissively, and there is no poem, because Calchas's demand that his daughter, who would by such a marriage become a member of the royal family, be sent to the Greek camp would then not even be entertained. The frame of the whole poem, for this chief reason, stands on the code of courtly love.

The gently interceding poet mentioned above now tells us that the stars in their determining courses have nudged things in Troilus's favour because Venus, who had in any case stood favourable to Troilus at his

---

38. But above all she loved him because he was in distress for her sake, and she thought that it would be a pity to kill such a man if his intentions were honourable

birth, was in her seventh house, that is, propitiously just above the western horizon. Criseyde's self-questioning resumes, realistically concrete, progressively defining her predicament, and fascinatingly unfolding the particularity of her character – her sweetness, her timidity, her yearning and growing agitation, and her self-protective calculation. It would bring honour to her and health to him if she had dealings with him, but he's the King's son, and if she scorned him she might earn his hatred and so bring harm on herself. But she knows that he is virtuous, and so then fears that people might discover that he loves her. What then? After all, Troilus could have any woman in Troy; and Criseyde now feels power and pride in being loved by him:

> 'And yet his lif al lith now in my cure.[39]
> But swich is love, and ek myn aventure.[40]
>
> 'Ne me to love, a wonder is it nought;[41]
> For wel woot I[42] myself, so God me spede,
> Al wolde I that noon wiste of this thought,[43]
> I am oon the faireste, out of drede,[44]
> And goodlieste, whoso taketh hede,[45]
> And so men seyn, in al the town of Troie.
> What wonder is though he of me have joye?'

(II, 741–9)

She rejects the idea of being subject to a husband's whims and domination – suddenly anticipating the Wife of Bath in this – but the thought of being a lover fills her with fear; it is her constant and characteristic response to any new development. Shall she give up her freedom? Isn't love 'the mooste stormy lyf'? Aren't 'wikked tonges' to be dreaded? Don't men often betray?

This is not the meditation of a tragic heroine, nor of a particularly good or bad woman, but the expression of a brilliantly conceived and rather ordinary woman, with whose predicament we are beguiled into raw contact. Criseyde's meditation ends for the time being on the upward note of 'Nothing venture, nothing have', and still unresolved. 'Now hoot, now cold', she goes into her garden with a throng of her women. At a pause in their playing about, 'Antigone the shene' (the beautiful Antigone) sings a Trojan song of thanks to the God of Love for giving her a lover:

39. lies entirely in my care   40. also my fortune or lot   41. it's not strange to love me   42. I know   43. though I'd rather no one knew I thought it   44. one of the loveliest, certainly 45. most virtuous, whoever notices

> '. . . that is the welle of worthynesse,[46]
> Of trouthe grownd, mirrour of goodlihed,
> Of wit Apollo, stoon of sikernesse,[47]
> Of vertu roote, of lust [48] fynder and hed.'

>>> (II, 841–4)

The catalogue of courtly virtues includes his attentiveness 'To serven wel', and when the song ends, Criseyde asks the singer for an assurance that lovers do indeed have such bliss; which is given, with the rider, implied in the form of a proverb, that only those fitted for love can experience it. At this point Chaucer temporarily abandons the code (so called because within it, singing about passion is a conventional means of stimulating it) and lowers the tone with a mock-heroic description of dusk:

> The dayes honour, and the hevenes yë,[49]
> The nyghtes foo – al this clepe [50] I the sonne [51] –
> Gan westren faste, and downward for to wrye,[52]

>>> (II, 904–7)

and the women leave the garden and put Criseyde to bed. Thereupon 'A nyghtyngale, upon a cedir grene' sings happily in the moonlight outside, sending her into a blissful sleep, in which she dreams that a white eagle digs his long claws into her breast, takes out her heart and puts his own there instead, without her feeling any pain. The dream confirms the ending of Antigone's song about love: 'ther is no peril inne'.

It is hard to do justice to that passage. In it, Chaucer carries his doubt-fully heroic heroine through some of the chief courtly love conventions, observing all with a poetic conviction which yet allows imaginative participation to be playful as well as powerfully empathetic. We can go forward knowing Criseyde as a real person, and understanding the powers – the values of courtly love, astrological fate, social nexus, her own intelligence, emotions and limitations – which will determine her affairs.

Next, Pandarus bears between the lovers letters which he first suggests they should write and then helps them to compose, after which he en-gineers several deceits and intrigues in order to bring the lovers face to face for the first time; for the major and finally successful part of this process there is no direct analogue in the sources. Essential though it is to focus on these two passages of sly fun mixed with passionate out-pouring, I must be brief, and first discuss the exchange of love letters through a confidant – a conventional process in Romance, though

46. honour   47. stone of dependability   48. delight   49. eye   50. call   51. sun   52. turn

Pandarus as the intermediary will transform and perhaps satirize the convention.

After Criseyde's dream of the white eagle, Chaucer returns us to Troilus, resting in his chamber after the day's battle. He sends 'two or three' messengers for Pandarus, who 'com lepying in atones' (immediately) with news of Criseyde's discreet acceptance of Troilus's declaration of love. Even in this, his first moment of joy, Troilus depends utterly on Pandarus:

> 'How shal this longe tyme awey be dryven,
> Til that thow be ayein[53] at hire fro me?'

> (II, 983–4)

Pandarus urges him to write a letter, telling him, in a funny little lecture on the appropriate epistolary style, to blot it with tears; which Troilus does, wetting his ruby signet and applying it to the paper. Pandarus tells Troilus to ride past Criseyde's window at an agreed time, and returns to Criseyde, who again twits him for his lack of success in love. When he ruefully replies, 'I hoppe alwey byhynde!' she bursts out laughing, but at once he arouses her curiosity with a promise of war news and takes her into the garden to satisfy it. There he produces Troilus's letter. An exchange of words and actions follows which brilliantly encapsulates the nature of the two participants, and their relations with each other. When she tells him to take the letter back to Troilus unread, he

> ... hente[54] hire faste,
> And in hire bosom the lettre down he thraste.

> (II, 1154–5)

That 'down' emphasizes not only the décolletage of the woman, but the sexual excitement and familiarity of the letter-thruster; but Criseyde accepts the gambit with humorous equability, proposing to leave the letter where it is until there is no risk of her being caught reading it by anyone not in the know. It is all a great joke to her; she smiles, and says that Pandarus can answer the letter for her, which he agrees to do, provided that she does the actual writing. The splendid upshot is:

> Therewith she lough,[55] and seyde, 'Go we dyne.'
> And he gan at himself to jape faste.
> And seyde, 'Nece, I have so grete a pyne[56]
> For love, that everich other day I faste –'
> And gan his beste japes forth to caste,[57]

53. again 54. got hold of 55. laughed 56. such great suffering 57. threw out his best jokes

> And made hire so to laughe at his folye,[58]
> That she for laughter wende for to dye.[59]
>
> (II, 1163–9)

After dining, she reads the letter in private, writes and seals her cautious reply, and goes to the window to sit by her uncle, whereupon, as planned, Troilus rides past with his ten men, humbly salutes her and nods to Pandarus. Criseyde's 'routhe' (pity) increases, and the poet gloatingly exclaims:

> To God hope I, she hath now kaught a thorn,
> She shal nat pulle it out this nexte wyke.[60]
> God sende mo swich[61] thornes on to pike![62]
>
> (II, 1272–4)

Pandarus eggs her on, and begs her to lay aside her 'nyce shame' and 'folie', as he miscalls her Danger and Reason (see p. 130). But she replies timidly that she wants to reward Troilus with no more than just the sight of her. Pandarus inwardly disagrees, and shoots off to deliver her letter to Troilus, whom he finds in bed, in a trance between hope and despair. He first consoles him by showing that he understands the problem: Troilus believes that Nature may be urging Criseyde to have Pity on him, but that Danger is telling her to say to him, 'Nay, thow shalt me nevere wynne!' (II, 1376).

Then comes Pandarus's plot, the deceptions of which involve, rather surprisingly, our spotless hero. Ascertaining that Troilus loves Deiphebus best of his brothers, Pandarus visits Deiphebus to tell him that 'some men' are wrongfully after the possessions of Criseyde, and asks him to collect her supporters at his house. As Pandarus is informing Criseyde of the (non-existent, of course) threats against her, Deiphebus arrives, to ask Criseyde personally to attend, and to ask Pandarus to bring Troilus along. That achieved without anyone having directly mentioned Troilus in connection with Criseyde, Pandarus coaches Troilus in what to do at Deiphebus's house: that is, pretend to be ill and go to bed. When the company convenes, Pandarus makes great play of the smallness of the room and the danger to Troilus of more than two visiting him at one time. Before bringing in the first pair, Helen and Deiphebus, Pandarus rushes in ('in he lepte') to tell Troilus: 'God have thi soule, ibrought have I thi beere!'[63] (II, 1638), a joke into which Troilus enters with a smile, thus, surely, contaminating his mind with an

58. fooling 59. imagined she'd die 60. week 61. more 62. pick at 63. I've brought your coffin

attitude peculiar to Pandarus and also to Criseyde herself, when she is with her uncle. Helen and Deiphebus are guided by Pandarus out of Troilus's room by another door, into a garden where they are to discuss documents which Hector is supposed to have given Pandarus for onward transmission; so that when Pandarus goes to bring in Criseyde, the way will be clear for Troilus and her to speak of love without violating the secrecy enforced by their code. Pulling the reluctant woman in by a fold of her dress, Pandarus urges her to accept Troilus's love, and warns her of the consequence of his dying if she refuses.

By now we are in Book III, in which they consummate their love in Pandarus's house, after another series of deceptions, of which Criseyde is the victim. In face of her uncle's scheming, and her lover's high passion and evident fragility of spirit, she appears timid, helpless and thus pitiable. But her sense of calculation, her love of fun in her scarcely innocent relationship with Pandarus, and her complaisance towards the implications of each fresh situation, give her a solidity and allure which make us accept the genuine rhapsody of her fleshly fulfilment when it comes.

This third book, which concentrates on the supreme harmony of union which the lovers enjoy until Fate intervenes, opens with a paean to Venus, the goddess of love, which is majestic, heartfelt and philosophic. Love is saluted as the force which is the essence of God, and the sole quality which justifies all living things. The doctrine is derived here, as elsewhere in the poem, from Boethius:

> God loveth, and to love wol nought werne; [64]
> And in this world no lyves creature [65]
> Withouten love is worth, [66] or may endure.

> (III, 12–24)

Love appeases the wrath of war, promotes virtue, courtesy and amity, and makes people reject vice. Love explains everything and sets the law of the universe; Chaucer, again humbly assuming the Dantean mantle of the epic poet, begs to be given the power to express 'Some joye of that is felt in thi [Love's] servyse' (III, 42). In the eventual coming together of the lovers, Pandarus's shaping art is again predominant. Troilus remains dependent on his friend's initiatives, and often incapable of action, even of consciousness, owing to the intensity of his emotions; while Criseyde at each step guardedly surrenders ground and sees her allegorical ally from the *Roman de la Rose*, Danger, outwitted or outflanked, in which process she complies, half-astonished but willingly imbibing its welling

64. refuse   65. living creature   66. has value

excitements. At the end of the meeting in the house of Deiphebus, she promises to accept limited service from Troilus:

> 'A kynges sone[67] although ye be, ywys,[68]
> Ye shal namore han sovereignete
> Of me in love, than right in that cas is...'
>
> (III, 170–72)

> 'If I be she that may yow do gladnesse,
> For every wo ye shal recovere a blisse.'
> And hym in armes took, and gan hym kisse.
>
> (III, 180–82)

When all the guests have gone, Pandarus lies down beside Troilus, and an extraordinary discussion and exchange of vows takes place between the pair. Pandarus's several purposes in begging Troilus to keep everything secret are made plain: he wants to preserve his niece's reputation, and to prevent his own part in the affair being discovered and bringing him into disrepute. In warning Troilus of the consequences of being found out, he especially wishes his true motive for all his actions to be appreciated. This, he says, is his desire to bring his friend Troilus out of distress and into joy. It is a theme established in classical literature, and pervasive in English literature, especially in Elizabethan and neo-classical drama, right up to the Romantic period: in matters of honour, friendship between man and man takes precedence over love between man and woman, as far as morals and obligations are concerned. The problem of this particular example is that Pandarus, the self-advertised disinterested Friend, so often shows self-interest of a peculiar sexual kind in advancing the interest of his innocent protégé. Troilus signals his acceptance of Pandarus's good faith by making an offer which, seen in any other context, and perhaps in this context as well, appears corrupt:

> 'And, that thow knowe I thynke nought, ne werie,[69]
> That this servise a shame[70] be or jape,[71]
> I have my faire suster Polixene,
> Cassandre, Eleyne, or any of the frape,[72]
> Be she nevere so fair or wel yshape,[73]
> Telle me which thow wilt of everychone,[74]
> To han for thyn, and lat me thanne allone.'[75]
>
> (III, 407–13)

In their discussion the word 'bawd' is avoided, as it was not in Book II,

67. son   68. for sure   69. condemn   70. disgrace   71. joke   72. crowd   73. formed
74. which one of all you want   75. to have for yourself, and leave me to arrange it

when Pandarus, protesting his purity of motive to Criseyde, says that he is not Troilus's bawd, but her uncle (II, 353–5).

Pandarus's hope of bedding his friend and his niece together is reinforced by an extraordinary conjunction of the crescent moon, Saturn and Jupiter in the sign of Cancer, which brings heavy rain (III, 624–6). That such a conjunction of Saturn and Jupiter, which was held to have caused Noah's Flood in the Bible, actually took place in May 1385, has been used to help to date the poem. Pandarus relies on the downpour continuing to keep Criseyde in his house when she comes to supper, and having got her there, he practises two major deceptions on her. First, when she accepts his urgent invitation to stay the night, he declares that Troilus is out of town, though he is in fact concealed in an adjoining room; and second, before ushering him into her bedroom – having stopped her from dressing – he tells Troilus that he has a rival in Criseyde's love, the effect of which is to produce a painful confrontation between the lovers which intensifies their passion.

Throughout the preliminaries, the fragility of Troilus is marked. Before being led into Criseyde's room, he calls on so many gods for help that Pandarus mocks him,

> . . . 'Thow wrecched mouses herte,[76]
> Artow agast so that she wol the bite?'[77]

> (III, 736–7)

And when Criseyde offers to die if her good faith in denying the existence of a rival is not believed, he swoons. Pandarus has to throw him bodily into her bed, where he then strips him, for Criseyde to massage and kiss him again into consciousness. It is one of the extraordinary achievements of Chaucer that, in spite of the unmanly fragility and inanition in love matters of his hero, and the knowing fecklessness of his heroine, his paean to the beauty and universal worth of love is sustained, and never more convincingly than at the time of his lovers' fulfilment, bracketed as it is by humorous but revealingly human absurdities.

Thus their bed session begins when Pandarus leaves with an injunction to Troilus not to swoon again for fear of waking Criseyde's attendant ladies in the next room; and Troilus's next words are to urge Criseyde to yield, to which her reply, full of *sang froid*, is

> 'Ne hadde I er now, my swete herte deere,
> Ben yold, iwis, I were now nought heere!'[78]

> (III, 1210–11)

76. heart   77. Are you so terrified that she'll bite you?   78. If I hadn't yielded before, for sure I wouldn't be here now

A passage of sustained glamour and ideal sensuousness about their first rapturous love-making is followed by Troilus's song of thanksgiving to the trinity of love – Venus, Hymen and Cupid. Its central passage is modelled on the great final prayer in Dante's *Divine Comedy*, in which St Bernard prays successfully to the Virgin Mary that Dante may be granted grace to behold the Trinity and so experience the union of human and divine. It is a nice example of Chaucer's freedom in mingling the profane – courtly love achievement in bedding the lady, and the involvement of pagan holy patronage – with the sacred. Troilus renews his vows and Criseyde rhapsodically proclaims her complete fulfilment: 'Welcome, my knyght, my pees, my suffisaunce!' (1309). Chaucer then, in a characteristic authorial intrusion, apostrophizes 'blisful nyght', and expresses, to those of his listeners who have feeling for the art of love, the hope that his poetry does justice to his subject. As day approaches after their hours of loving satisfaction, each of the lovers delivers an aubade (see p. 190), and when each is alone after the inevitable parting, desire recurs with the wonderful memory of what has just happened.

But for Criseyde, Pandarus is at hand. He enters her room with the coarse suggestion that she could hardly have slept at all on account of the noise of the rain. She calls him a fox for having brought about the events of the night, and hides her head under the sheets in shame;

> And Pandarus gan under for to prie,
> And seyde, 'Nece, if that I shal be ded,
> Have here a swerd and smyteth of myn hed!'
> With that his arm al sodenly he thriste[79]
> Under hire nekke, and at the laste hire kyste.
>
> (III, 1571–5)

Upon that action of voyeuristic, parasitic satisfaction, Chaucer comments ambiguously,

> I passe al that which chargeth nought to seye.[80]
> What! God foryaf his deth,[81] and she al so
> Foryaf, and with her uncle gan to pleye,[82]
> For other cause was ther noon than so.[83]
>
> (III, 1576–9)

In that moment when Criseyde, lying deeply fulfilled in her princely lover's body-taint, dallies complaisantly with her gratified uncle's fondling, lie truths of character and relationship the unravelling of which is central to the whole poem. Chaucer's conclusion to the passage, before

79. thrust 80. need not be said 81. forgave Christ's death 82. joke or dally 83. no reason for anything else

he turns again to Troilus, untangles them blandly: 'And Pandarus hath fully his entente'[84] (III, 1582). There follows a scene of deep mutual thanksgiving between the two men, which is briefly darkened by Pandarus's warning of the difficulty of keeping happiness at its present ecstatic height. The rest of Book III celebrates the effect of the fruition of love on that perfect courtly lover, Troilus. He is brave in battle, generous and friendly towards people, and in times of truce he successfully hunts only the most noble and dangerous beasts. (Chaucer's Greeks and Trojans behave like medieval European nobles, treating war as a princely game which may be suspended at either side's convenience.) But above all he rhapsodizes about his beloved in the intervals between meetings, and in song extols the universal power and virtue of love:

> 'So wolde God, that auctour is of kynde,
> That with his bond Love of his vertu liste
> To cerclen hertes alle, and faste bynde,
> That from his bond no wight they wey out wiste...'[85]
>
> (III, 1765–8)

The value system of courtly love is at this point confirmed: the lovers, whose sole contact is by periodic rendez-vous in a narrow closet containing a bed in a safe house, are nevertheless 'in quyete and in reste' or, as the last lines of Book III have it, 'in lust [delight] and in quiete'. Troilus, upon whom the poet's main illumination falls, is uninterruptedly 'in suffisaunce [utter content], in blisse, and in singynges'.

In Book IV, which for the purposes of this study will be treated only briefly, the shadow lightly adumbrated at the beginning assumes the terror of bulk and substance. After a day of battle in which the Trojans lose many as prisoners, the Greeks allow them a truce. An exchange of prisoners is agreed by which Antenor, who later betrayed Troy, is to be returned in exchange for Criseyde, who is to go to her father, another traitor, in the Greek camp. At this news Troilus becomes like a leafless tree in winter, 'I bounden in the blake bark of care' (IV, 229), smashes himself about like a wild bull against the wall and floor of his room and, collapsing in tears, expostulates against Fortune. Pandarus soon joins him, and gives him the kind of advice that the goose offers to disappointed lovers, in *The Parliament of Fowls*: 'The town is ful of ladys al aboute'. Troilus should look for another lover.

In his lofty rebuke, Troilus says that he would rather die than be false

84. has done what he wanted to   85. God, the creator of Nature, so willed his bond of love, with its power, to encircle and fast bind all hearts, that none could discover a way out

to Criseyde – a promise he keeps; and when he considers Pandarus's next piece of advice, which is that he should publicly plead for her not to be exchanged, he rejects it on two honourable grounds: that he should neither put pressure on his father, a head of state who has given his word about the matter, nor slander Criseyde by revealing their love, which is still secret after three years. Pandarus reports to Criseyde, and when he returns, he finds Troilus sorrowing in a temple. Troilus's agonizing is cast in Boethian terms, attacking Providence ('purveyaunce') and lamenting his fate under 'destinee'. But his reasoning, which includes a supplicatory prayer to Jove, is cut off before Boethius's reservation in favour of free will is reached. Since this particular philosophical passage does not figure in all the manuscripts, it has been suggested that it represents a late addition. I further discuss it, and its importance in the poem, on pp. 201–2.

When the lovers meet in their misery, Criseyde swoons and, thinking her dead, Troilus prepares to kill himself. But she revives in time to make him sheath his sword and, embracing again in bed, they sadly find that 'Naught was it lik tho nyghtes here-byforn'[86] (IV, 1248). As they discuss what to do, Criseyde says that she will be able to return from the Greek camp, that she expects peace, and that in any case she will arouse her old father's covetousness by promising him favours which she will obtain from Priam. It is an extended plea driven by wish-fulfilment, which Troilus answers point by point, adding a new fear: that when in enemy hands she will be attracted by a Greek gallant. So he resurrects Pandarus's third plan for the pair, which was that they should elope. Criseyde rejects it as foolishly profitless; the strength of her language probably owes as much to her fear of the unknown as to her usual self-concern. But she concludes with a vow to stay faithful to him and a promise to return by the tenth day after her removal to the Greek camp. Dawn approaches, and Book IV closes with the focus on the suffering of Troilus:

> For mannes hed ymagynen ne kan,[87]
> N'entendement[88] considere, ne tonge telle
> The cruele peynes of this sorwful man,
> That passen[89] every torment down in helle.

(IV, 1695–8)

For all the interest in the superior characterization of Criseyde and Pandarus, Troilus remains the emotional centre of the poem. Earlier I noted that, of the three main characters, Pandarus *speaks* most. But

---

86. it was not like former nights   87. man's mind cannot imagine   88. perception
89. exceed

analysis of the narrative given to each, describing actions, thoughts and feelings, shows that little time is spent on Pandarus in his own right: Criseyde has more than three times as much at its centre, and more than six times as much, with emphasis at times of climax, resolution and other change, is given to Troilus.

Book V, the longest of all, is appropriately dominated by the heroic pathos of Troilus. Pandarus's cynical and self-exculpatory advice, which now reads like that of the False Friend from the *Roman de la Rose*, becomes otiose as well as detestable in face of the resolution Troilus finds in his despair at Criseyde's infidelity, and he is brushed aside before the end. The process of Criseyde's falling into the arms of Diomede, and of her painful and self-deluding reactions to her own lack of virtue, make as compelling reading as anything in the poem. The well-reasoned and craftily applied lust of the newcomer, Diomede, apt to win pickings of war such as the stricken and helpless woman he is charged to squire, contrasts beautifully with the eventual high resolve of the hero. In the burning despair of his love-faith Troilus learns to take the initiative, which he has previously left to Pandarus to take for him; after being sick almost to death in his prolonged doubt about Criseyde, he faces the truth when it comes; and, declaring that his love will never change and that he will look for death on the battlefield, he brings glory to the Trojans by his feats before falling to Achilles. In continuing to draw on conventions of the medieval romance such as the formal lament, the intercession of the Friend, the prayer to Cupid, the Lover's song of despair, the exchange of letters, and the initially wrong, and subsequently right, interpretation of a dream, Chaucer treats his subject with even greater realism, if that is possible, than in the four previous Books. In particular, the detail of scene and mood during the separation of the lovers and the failure of Criseyde to return to Troy shows extraordinary insight into the world of love, in the medieval or any other age.

Book V has five parts, the first and third of which relate chiefly to Criseyde and Diomede, and the second and fourth, which are longer, to Troilus; while the last, which begins at the moment when Troilus is certain Criseyde has deserted him, contains the climax and the poet's *apologia*.

First, there is the public handing over to the enemy, by Troilus, of his secret lover. In the interest of Criseyde's honour and secrecy, his demeanour is under control, and he even manages to welcome the returned Antenor with a formal congratulatory kiss; only the crafty Greek deputed to squire Criseyde to her father reads the truth in Troilus's pale face

(V, 85–90). On the ride back, Diomede asks Criseyde to treat him as her brother, and not to scorn his friendship. He even speaks of love, but the stunned Criseyde

> ... was with sorwe oppressed so
> That in effect, she naught his tales herde
> But her and ther, now here a word or two.

> (V, 177–9)

The first of the two long passages on the pathos of Troilus follows. He returns from the handing over of Criseyde, his bottled-up emotions bursting out of him all night in wakeful throes and nightmares. When Pandarus turns up next day, having been delayed on the king's business, Troilus asks him to see to his possessions and funeral at his impending death, and to send his ashes in a golden urn to Criseyde. The thought of having to wait ten days for her to return is unbearable. Pandarus tenders his last piece of sensible advice. Is Troilus the only man who has had to put up with a lover's absence? Since there are contrary opinions about the truth of dreams (a matter to which Chaucer constantly adverts, as at the beginning of *The House of Fame*), why worry about them? They should divert themselves during the ten days' wait, so what about the musical feast at Sarpedon's house? The first of these three consolations is presented with an insidious suggestion that Troilus's love is to be ranked with covert adultery:

> 'How don this folk[90] that seen hire loves wedded
> By frendes myght,[91] as it bitit[92] ful ofte,
> And sen hem in hire spouses bed ybedded?
> God woot,[93] they take it wisly, faire and softe,
> Forwhi[94] good hope halt up[95] hire herte o-lofte.'

> (V, 344–8)

The feasting and the music at Sarpedon's are out of key:

> For she, that of his herte berth the keye,
> Was absent, lo, this was his fantasie,
> That no wight sholde maken melodie.[96]

> (V, 460–62)

When he is alone, he exclaims on Criseyde, and re-reads her letters; and on the fourth day, although they had been invited to stay for a week, he wishes to leave. When they do leave on the seventh day, Troilus imagines

90. how do people manage 91. power 92. happens 93. knows 94. because 95. keeps up 96. because she who carries the key to his heart was absent, he had the notion that nobody should make music

143

that he will find Criseyde waiting for him, an impulse Pandarus inwardly scoffs at, though outwardly declaring she will return as soon as she can.

The next day Troilus proposes a visit to Criseyde's house, which they find locked and barred. It is a timeless lovers' desolation that Troilus expresses in an apostrophe to the 'paleys empty and disconsolat', which he compares with a ring out of which the ruby has fallen. (Chaucer mentions hardly any other precious stone: the ruby, with its virtues, occurs time and again in his poetry.)

Everywhere he rides touches an endearing and passionate memory of his Criseyde:

> 'Lo, yonder saugh ich last my lady daunce;
> And in that temple, with hire eyen cleere,
> Me kaughte[97] first my righte lady dere.
>
> 'And yonder have I herd ful lustyly[98]
> My dere herte laugh; and yonder pleye[99]
> Saugh ich hire ones ek ful blissfully.
> And yond so goodly gan she me biholde,
> That to the deth myn herte is to hire holde.
>
> 'And at that corner, in the yonder hous,
> Herde I myn alderlevest[100] lady deere
> So wommanly, with vois melodious,
> Syngen so wel, so goodly, and so clere,
> That in my soule yet me thynketh ich here[101]
> The blissful sown, and in that yonder place
> My lady first me took unto hire grace.'

(V, 565–81)

Only such lengthy quotation can do justice to the sustained lyricism of this whole section. Troilus's memories of his lover's perfect allure, as represented conventionally by her dancing and singing – a convention Shakespeare follows in the portrayal of such heroines as Desdemona and Cleopatra – and by her laughter, which we were hearing throughout the first three Books of the poem, are followed by a black contrast. He cannot stop himself riding to the city gate, where he re-lives his parting from her. Interspersed with these powerful memories are two self-contained lyric apostrophes: one to Cupid, complaining of his fate and begging the love-god to return Criseyde to him, and the other to Criseyde, foreseeing his immediate death if she does not return on the tenth day. This second part of Book V ends with Troilus

97. i.e. she caught me 98. heartily 99. disport herself 100. most beloved 101. it seems I hear

walking the city walls and gazing towards the Greek tents, voicing the pretty conceit that the sweet wind he feels on his face is the sighing of Criseyde, as she breathes, 'Allas! whi twynned[102] be we tweyne?'[103] (V, 679).

The third part of Book V opens with Criseyde lamenting that her father will not agree to her returning to Troy, and fearing that if she steals away, she might be caught and ill-treated. She has nobody to confide in, and regrets that she and Troilus did not elope, as he had suggested. But she concludes with a resolution to flee to Troy notwithstanding; but Diomede arrives, and the opportunity – if indeed she could have taken it! – passes. Before his arrival is recounted, Chaucer, as if finally to shape up the three contestants in his triangular love conflict, presents each in a short character sketch, describing their physical, moral and spiritual qualities in a style following Theophrastus (fourth century B.C.), a disciple of the philosopher Aristotle: it is a strange interlude (V, 799–847) which disturbs the narrative.

Diomede develops his love plea to Criseyde with the kind of wily pragmatic argument which, on the evidence of her character as so far seen, she is scarcely equipped to withstand. He doesn't know why she has appeared sorrowful ever since her arrival in the Greek camp, he says, but if the reason is that she has left a lover in Troy, then the just cause of the Greeks – their determination to avenge the rape of Helen – and the prophecy of Criseyde's father that Troy will be destroyed, will ensure that any hope she has of resuming her love is certain to be frustrated. In any case, he says, she can find a better lover among the Greeks, and he modestly offers himself, a person of royal birth who should rightfully now be king. She lies to him that, being a widow, she is neither in love nor likely to be; but on leaving, he takes her glove.

Left alone, Criseyde expresses her fundamental weakness. She goes over

> ... in hire soule ay up and down
> The wordes of this sodeyn[104] Diomede,
> His grete estat,[105] and perel of the town,[106]
> And that she was allone and hadde nede
> Of frendes help.
>
> (V, 1023–7)

For a virtuous person, possessing inner strength, such considerations would apply without any of them affecting her constancy of purpose; but for Criseyde they are decisive, and she yields almost at once,

102. separated   103. two   104. peremptory   105. high rank   106. peril (to Troy)

lamenting that she will accordingly have a reputation for falsehood until the end of the world, though she promises to remain friendly to Troilus. Chaucer, intervening at this point with his poet's *persona*, at greater length than usual, blames her dereliction of faith on his sources, and exculpates himself from originating such a slur on women: 'Men seyn – I not – that she yaf[107] hym hire herte' (V, 1050). He confers his pity, rather than any harsh judgement, upon her:

> Ne me ne list this sely womman chyde[108]
> Forther than the storye wol devyse.
> Hire name, allas! is punysshed so wide,
> That for hire gilt it oughte ynough suffise.
> And if I myghte excuse hire any wise,[109]
> For[110] she so sory was for hire untrouthe,[111]
> Iwis,[112] I wolde excuse hire yet for routhe.[113]

(V, 1093–9)

Thus, Chaucer's rhetorical reticence highlights the ease and finality with which Criseyde betrays Troilus. In the next stanza, the first of the fourth part of Book V, the speed of her fall is emphasized, for we are told that it is only the eve of the tenth day since she left Troy.

From dawn till midday, and again till nightfall, Troilus waits at the city gate with Pandarus, agonizingly finding excuses for Criseyde's delay. But Pandarus laughs secretly at the unlikelihood of her returning: 'Ye, fare wel al the snow of ferne yere!'[114] (V, 1176). Troilus thinks he may have miscounted by one day, but as he walks the walls on each of the six following days, hope ebbs, and he becomes jealous and expects to die. He cannot hide his decline from his parents, and needs a crutch to walk. He dreams of a huge boar with great tusks lying beside Criseyde and kissing her, a dream that Pandarus comfortingly misinterprets, and at Pandarus's suggestion he writes her a long letter. They have now been separated for two months: since a courtly lover must not reproach his beloved whatever she does, he writes with great delicacy, his single complaint almost crowded out by the expression of prolonged grief and desire. The letter is an extraordinary poetic achievement by Chaucer, who exploits a convention which goes back at least as far as Ovid with a great effect of emotional realism.

In Criseyde's short reply she protests that she will return when she can, but Troilus is not satisfied and, still haunted by the boar of his dream, he goes to his sister, Cassandra, a prophetess, for an interpreta-

---

107. gave   108. I don't wish to rebuke this hapless woman   109. in any way   110. because
111. infidelity   112. certainly   113. pity   114. last year

tion. Chaucer turns to advantage the well-known myth about Cassandra: this is that the god Apollo gave her prophetic power in order to win her to his bed, and when she would not fulfil her part of the bargain, he added a rider that though her prophecies would always be correct, they would never be believed. Cassandra rightly interprets the boar as Diomede, and Troilus, refusing to believe her, leaves in anger. But fate slowly grinds forward; Hector is killed in battle, and Troilus's frequent letters to Criseyde eventually draw from her a reply which leaves him no alternative but to question her good faith. In it she suggests that he may be tricking her – a common tactic of faithless lovers. Confirmation of his suspicion comes when Deiphebus returns from battle with a trophy won from Diomede, a coat-armour which had pinned to it a brooch Troilus had given Criseyde. Throughout the separation of the lovers, Troilus and Diomede have met in battle from time to time, and on one occasion Troilus had wounded Diomede, which had caused Criseyde, newly dependent on her new man, to weep 'many a teere'. But now that Troilus is bent on personal revenge, and deliberately seeking out Diomede in battle, fate does not allow either warrior to die at his rival's hand.

So Chaucer does not offer a grand climax of bloody revenge, but applies an artistic stasis at this moment of extreme pathos and frustrated despair in the spirit of Troilus. He then commends what he calls 'litel myn tragedye' to posterity among the works of his masters, Virgil, Ovid, Homer, Lucan and Statius. Having done that, he reverts briefly to his hero. Troilus in his battle-rage distinguishes himself as never before, until he is killed by Achilles. Chaucer's conclusion is to invite his listeners to ponder the agonies of Troilus in this world in the light of eternity and the consolation of heaven, and to commend to them – and especially to 'yonge, fresshe folkes' – the love of God as preferable to worldly human love and its vanities and suffering. It is of course conventional for a medieval writer concluding a work to present it as a moral lesson and to bind it into a plea for divine grace. But the poetic power in this apparent retraction of the values of passionate human life which animate the poem forbids one to doubt Chaucer's intense seriousness about his ending. It is written in stately verse, solemn, humble and reverent, and ends with this majestic prayer, the first three lines of which are exactly translated from Dante's *Paradiso*. Chaucer follows the great Italian in intertwining the mystic significance of number with the rhythmic force of poetic incantation:

> Thow oon, and two, and thre, eterne on lyve,
> That regnest ay in thre, and two, an oon,
> Uncircumscript, and al maist circumscrive,

> Us from visible and invisible foon
> Defende, and to thy mercy, everichon,
> So make us, Jesus, for thi mercy digne,
> For love of mayde and moder thyn benigne.[115] Amen.
>
> (V, 1863–9)

Medieval literature gave to the Western world three or four great love stories which still live in the general imagination: Abelard and Heloïse (real, not fictitious characters), Tristan and Isolde, and Lancelot and Guinevere might be instanced besides Chaucer's poem. *Troilus and Criseyde* had two distinguished sequels. The fifteenth-century Scots poet Henryson wrote *The Testament of Cresseid* in Chaucer's metre, describing the retribution that fell on the heroine. Diomede tires of her, and she becomes a prostitute, a development which C. S. Lewis considers feasible. The gods punish her in various ways, and then the Moon strikes her with such hideous deformity that she is cast out, and joins a group of lepers. There is one moment which especially distinguishes the poem: as she sits beside the road with her cup and clapper – the lid which lepers rattled on their dish to warn of their approach – Troilus rides by from the battle, gives her alms, and is reminded of her without actually recognizing her. Henryson's poem used to figure in old editions of Chaucer as Book VI. The other great work is of course Shakespeare's play, the frame of which is derived from Chaucer though its spirit is closer to that of Henryson. In it Troilus has a serious political role in the part of the play in which satire of the heroes of old soldiers and statesmen balances the dark view of the love affair. Cressida appears as wanton from the start, and lacks the ambiguity of Chaucer's richly pathetic figure. Pandarus is a cruder and older-seeming man than he is in Chaucer, whose pen can nevertheless be seen to lie remotely behind his words as he ushers the lovers to bed for the first time:

'If ever you prove false one to another, since I have taken such pains to bring you together, let all pitiful goers-between be called to the world's end after my name: call them all Pandars; let all constant men be Troiluses, all false women Cressids, and all brokers-between Pandars. Say "Amen".'

(Arden edition, III. ii. 197–203)

And they both do.

To call *Troilus and Criseyde* 'the first psychological novel' is to suggest that subtle psychology which is displayed in many a medieval romance is

115. Thou One, and Two, and Three (i.e. Father, Son and Holy Ghost), eternally living, that reignest for ever in Three, and Two, and One, limitless, and canst encompass everything, defend us from enemies visible and invisible (i.e. earthly and hellish); and in thy mercy make each one of us worthy of thy mercy, for love of thy gracious Virgin Mother.

chiefly proper to the novel, and hence to raise the novel, as a kind, to dubious eminence. To call it 'a philosophical romance' is to nudge study of it towards source material drawn from religious moralists of old, and away from the perpetual pulse of the poem, the heart of which beats with the raptures and agonies of romantic love, treated with committed relish or quizzical detachment as poetic occasion demands. If a generic title is demanded, it might be 'a tragi-comic romance', which seems to me both more accurate and more open – except that the usual order of the tragic and comic elements in tragi-comedy is reversed. The ending is true tragedy, in so far as any work ending in Christian thought can be tragic; if the spirit is to live eternally in heavenly consolation, that must be considered a blessing.

Part IV: The Narrative and Other Poems

Chapter 9. The Love Visions: The Book of the Duchess, The House of Fame and The Parliament of Fowls

The Book of the Duchess (c. 1369), *The House of Fame* (c. 1375) and *The Parliament of Fowls* (c. 1381) are the first three major works of the poet that we know; since the first was written when he was between twenty-five and thirty, and the last when he was nearly forty, none of them should be thought of as apprentice work. It is the absolute distinction of *Troilus and Criseyde* and *The Canterbury Tales*, together with the strangeness of the dream vision as a literary convention, which accounts for the contemporary under-valuation of these three great poems.

These love visions – for they are all, at least ostensibly, dream visions about love – bring to the poet-dreamer experiences and insights which, when he wakes, he regards as significant for himself and the world of his audience. They all work broadly as follows. The Dreamer falls asleep, having shown by reason of being a disappointed lover, or of having been reading a bedtime book which relates in some way to love, that he is ready or yearning to make a discovery about love. Thus the state of mind in which he falls asleep helps to determine the nature of his dream. When the dream begins, the Dreamer finds himself in an emblematic setting, which the audience would either understand as being conventional in courtly love and romance, or accept because it was taken from a recognizable literary authority. In either case, it establishes a thematic harmony with the main material of the poem which is to follow. And the setting of that main material is also emblematic, not realistic. The Dreamer's journey from the first setting to the main one involves strange experiences which further distance the reader from reality, as Chaucer takes him into the country of each particular dream.

Thus, in *The Book of the Duchess*, the Dreamer goes from reading in his bedtime book the sad story of Ceyx and Alcyone, which is drawn from Ovid, to dreaming that his room is full of birdsong. He proceeds from there to a hunt with the Emperor Octavian, and then, crucially, is led by a puppy through a flowering forest of gigantic trees to an oak, against which sits a sorrowing 'man in blak'. In *The House of Fame*, he falls asleep pondering the nature and meaning of dreams, and finds himself at once in a gold-pillared temple containing pictures of naked Venus and the Fall of Troy. Almost imperceptibly, the story of Venus's son, the Trojan prince Aeneas, chief refugee from the burning city, becomes the story of Dido, the Queen of Carthage whom Aeneas loved and then abandoned, and of other constant women deserted by faithless and ambitious men. At this point the Dreamer leaves the temple by a wicket-gate, and looking up at the sky from the empty waste in which he finds himself, sees an enormous golden eagle gliding down towards him. The main dream, and Book II of this extraordinary poem, have begun. In *The Parliament of Fowls*, the Dreamer's bedtime reading is a fragment of Cicero known as 'The Dream of Scipio', which had been preserved and made the subject of a Neoplatonist exposition by a fifth century pagan, Macrobius. In it, Scipio the Younger, the Roman conqueror of Carthage, meets the spirit of his grandfather, Scipio Africanus, who tells him in a lofty discourse delivered from among the stars, that those who pursue the common good on earth will have eternal life in heaven. Chaucer's Dreamer – a first person narrator who regrets his inexperience in love and yet marvels at its power – falls asleep pondering Cicero's message and dreams that he in turn is met by Scipio Africanus, who leads him into a flowering forest which Chaucer's listeners would instantly recognize as a garden of love. The main dream has begun, and after some important preliminaries, Nature will judge a love debate among birds of different kinds whose attitudes harmonize with their positions in the hierarchy of their species.

The Book of the Duchess is an elegy which celebrates the wooing and virtues of a deceased lady and the grief of her lover. It is generally accepted, on evidence within the poem, that it was written for John of Gaunt after the death from the plague of his first wife Blanche in 1369. The dead lady in the poem is named, in line 948, as 'goode faire White' (*blanche* is French for white), and at the end the 'man in blak' rides off to a 'long castel [which might conceal Lancaster, Gaunt's family name] with walles white' (possibly Blanche again). Direct identification of Gaunt with the mourning 'man in blak' is not necessary; as that character tells the questioning Dreamer of his ideal wooing and happy marriage, and describes the beauty of 'faire White' and her virtues, its poetic *persona* has a role in the poet's double offering to his ducal patron. The poem's chief aim, the first part of the offering, is to console the duke for the loss of his wife, and indirectly to counsel him against immoderate grief – a sin condemned by the Church almost as a matter of routine; and the second part of his offering is to give an idealized portrait of the dead duchess. Much of the poem is inspired by French sources, the chief of which is Machaut's *Le Jugement dou Roy de Behaingne*, a debate poem in which the king of Bohemia is asked to judge which of a knight and a lady suffers more for love. The king says the man does, and as a result Machaut had to write a companion poem in which he corrected what some had regarded as an injustice, and made the lady the winner of a corresponding debate. The long idealized description of 'faire White' (815–1041) follows the technique and organization, and even to some extent the linguistic conventions, of Machaut. *The Book of the Duchess* is the work of an English poet in the French style, full of lofty dialogue and sentiment, and is at least as good as many of its models. Chaucer was to take its qualities onwards, subtly absorbing and transmuting them, into his mature and less French style.

Apart from the originality of its subtle processes, which bring it to a conclusive realization of the beauty of the lady and of her love relationship with the 'man in blak', the poem uses many standard properties and effects of courtly love poetry: the confession of the lover that he began in youth and idleness before being struck by serious love; the hunt and chess as metaphors for love activity; the telling of another tale near the beginning (that of Ceyx and Alcyone) to establish a theme; the seasonal apparatus of love, with birdsong in Maytime; the portrait of the fickle goddess Fortune; the suffering in love before the declaration of it; that eventual declaration in terms of humble and faithful service, followed by years of unrewarded constancy, before the lady grants her 'mercy'. Besides being an elegy, *The Book of the Duchess* is one of the few poems of Chaucer's in which an ideal courteous love, here presented as most acceptable to a noble patron in mourning, is celebrated without irony or other adulteration. The glints of humour conduce instead to sympathetic understanding. The poem is written in flowing octosyllabic couplets, the standard metre of French romance, which Chaucer was later to discard in favour of rhymed iambic pentameters.

The House of Fame, as Chaucer named it in the *Prologue* to *The Legend of Good Women*, or *The Book of Fame*, as he named it later in his Retraction at the end of *The Parson's Tale*, has as hero the poet himself, whose experiences in the dream constitute a kind of poetic autobiography. Thus, in Book I, in the Temple of Venus, the poet re-lives the grand pathos of Virgil's *Aeneid*, with special emphasis on the love of Dido and Aeneas, and the desolation of deserted Dido: a suitable vision for a poet of love. Book II starts with the eagle seizing Chaucer in its talons and taking him up into the sky, there to accuse him of writing about love without having been a successful lover, and of drawing on books rather than experience in his poetry. To remedy this, the eagle proposes to take him to the House of Fame to hear 'tydynges' of love and lovers, and on the way lectures him on the properties of sound and motion. The elevation of the poet to his rightful element, above the earth, takes place at the same time as his necessary scientific education, you might say. In Book III, which is more than half the whole poem, Chaucer first enters the House of Fame, where among statues of the famous he sees those of the classical poets. There he watches the goddess Fame wantonly and crudely granting or denying fame to various groups of petitioners. Then, still with the help of the eagle, he squeezes through a window into the Hall of Rumour, a construction of creaking twigs sixty miles long, where truth and lies, together with their exaggerations and distortions, fight to escape into the air. The authority figure who appears at this final scrimmage, apparently to explain everything, is abandoned in mid-line, before he can speak, as the poem ends. The dilemma of the poet in his quest for the power to observe and record truth has been represented by a complex comic image.

From that selective summary it can be seen that, although the poem is ostensibly a love vision, in spirit it breaks the medieval French mould and shows that its main concern is with the role of the poet rather than with love. In this, and in the many images which reflect his close reading of Dante's *Divine Comedy*, Chaucer demonstrates his further distancing from French models. *The House of Fame* has even been seen as a parody of the *Divine Comedy*, but its Chaucerian qualities mark it as just as different from the Italian poem as *The Book of the Duchess* is from the French *Le Jugement dou Roy de Behaingne*. So it is with reservation that people should think of Chaucer as going through, first, a French period, and then an Italian period; though some of his cultural borrowings come in that order.

In *The House of Fame* Chaucer confronts his own predicament of being a poet surrounded by conventional cultural touchstones, who is yet driven to find and express his unique self. He does it by representing the touchstones with alternate irony and sympathy, and by exploiting, sometimes in earnest and sometimes in parody, the literary conventions of the day. His difficulties, including the problems of definition which face him at many points, are treated in a spirit of amused yet penetrating inquiry, but at the end the reader has an impression of a *tour de force* of fantastic invention, conceived in exuberance, proceeding at high speed, and written with the confidence of a secure master of the imagination. The irony is not destructive, because Chaucer's elusive, compassionate seriousness is never far away.

The entertaining preamble to the poem presents a comically confusing discussion of the different kinds of dream and a mock-serious invocation of Morpheus the god of Sleep, with promise of a joyful future for those who hear his dream and curses for those who misinterpret it. The pathos and glory of the *Aeneid*, the summary of which follows immediately, prompts awed wonder:

> 'A, Lord!' thoughte I, 'that madest us,
> Yet sawgh I never such noblesse
> Of ymages, ne such richesse,
> As I saugh graven in this chirche;[1]
> But not wot I whoo did hem wirche,[2]
> Ne where I am, ne in what contree.'
>
> (II. 470–75)

That close conjunction of ironic humour and serious reflection – both conducted in a dream-like spirit appropriate to the poetic form – is typical, but as the poem develops, so does the element of fantasy and even nightmare. The description of the goddess Fame, whose emblematic qualities fit her wayward function, is a good example:

> Me thoughte that she was so lyte[3]
> That the lengthe of a cubite
> Was lengere than she semed be.[4]
> But thus sone,[5] in a whyle, she
> Hir tho[6] so wonderliche streighte[7]
> That with hir fet she erthe reighte,[8]
> And with hir hed she touched hevene . . .
>
> (II. 1369–75)

But this goddess, when she delivers judgement, slangs her petitioners like a fishwife; Chaucer is perhaps following the Romance tradition, in which, it has been observed, the speech of women, even noble ones, tends to be more unadorned and colloquial than that of men. Here is Fame refusing to grant renown to doers of good deeds:

> 'I werne[9] yow it,' quod she anon;[10]
> 'Ye gete of me good fame non,
>   Be God! and therefore goo your wey.'
>
> (II. 1559–61)

It is at the end of this funny scene that Chaucer (whom the eagle addresses as Geoffrey), when asked by a friendly by-stander if he is going to plead for fame with the rest, firmly rejects the idea and expresses confidence in his own estimate of himself:

1. church, meaning temple 2. I know not who made them 3. small 4. seemed to be
5. soon 6. then 7. extended herself 8. touched 9. deny 10. she quickly said

> 'Sufficeth me, as[11] I were ded,
> That no wight[12] have my name in honde.[13]
> I wot[14] myself best how y stonde;[15]
> For what I drye,[16] or what I thynke,
> I wil myselven al hyt drynke,[17]
> Certeyn,[18] for the more[19] part,
> As fer forth as I kan[20] myn art.'

(II. 1876–82)

The chief comic achievement of the poem is the garrulous Eagle, who dominates Book I I. He is pompous and self-admiring, and is the first of many pedantic or vain characters to attract Chaucer's power to portray and strip them without destroying them. Critics have wondered why Chaucer left unfinished a poem so clearly almost rounded off, at the arrival in the last line of 'A man of gret auctorite'. I don't think it absurd to suggest that, since the problems raised in the poem cannot be deftly solved, Chaucer deliberately stopped his sentence in mid-air – and that would stimulate a burst of understanding laughter. We must remember the pictorial evidence which shows Chaucer reading his poems aloud to an audience; it is unlikely to have been simply emblematic.

The Parliament of Fowls is a dream vision poem which really is about love: three kinds of love, which may be broadly defined, in order, as the love of social benevolence, which leads people to work for the common profit; possessive lustful obsession, which leads to misery and disaster; and natural sexual love, which leads to harmonious and honourable mating. It is a compact and graceful poem of 699 lines in rhyme royal in which, during the process of the Dreamer's experience, each kind of love has its exactly defined emblematic setting, presiding figures and participators. It is full of wisdom, wit and beauty. It is a small masterpiece, and the core and longest part of the poem is, as the title suggests, cast in the form of a bird debate, which takes place on St Valentine's Day.

The poem opens with a short appreciation of the power and mystery of love, followed by one of Chaucer's amusing and barely credible disclaimers to experience in the field. His awe is derived from reading about love, and sure enough, the bedtime reading upon which he then embarks is 'The Dream of Scipio', which has already been mentioned. The advice of Scipio goes beyond promising immortality to those who work for the common profit – itself a useful piece of pagan advice that Christians could accept – in assuring law-breakers, and especially lechers, that in

11. if   12. person   13. hand   14. know   15. stand   16. suffer   17. i.e. keep to myself
18. secure   19. most   20. practise

the hereafter they 'Shul whirle about th'erthe alwey in peyne' (80). And it is an emblematic environment of lechery to which, when the Dreamer falls asleep, Scipio conducts him. In the paradisal park through the gate of which Scipio pushes him, he sees Cupid, together with many of the allegorical characters associated with love pursuits in the *Romance of the Rose*. In a brass temple he sees Priapus standing 'in sovereyn [chief] place', 'with hys sceptre in honde' (an indirect reference to the big erect phallus which was the usual attribute of this god of fertility), and nearby 'in a prive corner', the goddess Venus herself. The allegorical characters, the prominence of the priapic deity, and the obscure siting of Venus coupled with the fact that she is guarded by a porter called 'Richesse', indicate that the Dreamer, despite having invoked Venus earlier as 'thow blysful lady swete', is in an abode of lust, no temple of ideal passionate love. A catalogue of earthly lovers, all of whom loved disastrously and died miserably, emphasizes the point, which prompts the Dreamer to escape back into the paradisal park.

At once he sees there, upon a hill of flowers, the 'noble goddesse Nature', preparing to preside over the mating decisions of all the birds, who are classified, in some semblance of human class divisions, as birds of prey, seed-fowl, worm-fowl and water-fowl.

This presentation of human problems through beast substitutes was a standard resort in the Middle Ages. Every animal, bird and fish had emblematic value, as the borders of illuminations of sacred texts abundantly show. T. H. White's *Book of Beasts* is probably the most accessible text for those interested in this aspect of medieval art. But we should not regard as a mere oddity a literary convention with which so distinguished a fabulist as Aesop has enriched readers' moral and practical sensibilities through the ages. With his bird debate, Chaucer follows an English tradition already established by such poems as the early thirteenth-century poem, *The Owl and the Nightingale*,[21] a master work in which the representation of human drives in bird form gains strength from the inevitable distancing from individual human character. *The Parliament of Fowls* may be thought of as a Chaucerian development continued, with more hilarity and only slightly less depth, in Chauntecleer and Pertelote, the cock and hen protagonists of *The Nun's Priest's Tale*.

The centre of the bird debate before the goddess Nature is a contest among three aristocratic suitors – eagles, of course – for the hand of a female eagle, a 'formel'. The terms of the suitors' protestations are those of

---

21. available in modern verse translation: Brian Stone, *The Owl and the Nightingale, Cleanness, St Erkenwald*, Penguin, second edition, 1987.

courtly love, and not surprisingly, the birds of lower origin express impatience, because their mates cannot be assigned until the business of the aristocrats is done. The water-birds, represented by the goose, recommend that any male rejected by the formel should seek a different mate. The turtle-dove, representing the seed-bird (though every listener would know she was a bird of Venus, emblematic of true love), is shocked at this utilitarian inconstancy, and the cuckoo, speaking for the birds that feed on worms, destructively advises that if the eagles cannot agree, they should be left single all their lives. The presiding goddess, whose role is to promote justice, harmony and good morality – Nature being the agent of God's purposes in the medieval scheme of things – leaves the choice to the formel herself. She decides that she is not ready to make a decision:

> 'I wol nat serve Venus ne Cupide,
> Forsothe as yit, by no manere weye.'

(II. 652–3)

Accordingly, Nature orders the three suitors to wait a year, and gives all the other birds their chosen mates. Before flying off in pairs, they sing a beautiful roundel in anticipation of the end of winter and the coming of summer, thus confirming the part of happily expressed mating in the seasonal processes of the universe. Through their activity and song, Chaucer celebrates open love, as opposed to secret, courtly love, in a just society as an essential element in cosmic harmony and creativity. The din of their singing of course wakes the Dreamer, just as the bell from the 'long castel with walles white' woke the Dreamer in *The Book of the Duchess*.

After composing these three poems, Chaucer returned to the love vision as a frame for a poem only once more, if the English translation of a part of *The Romance of the Rose* is excluded. This was when he wrote the *Prologue* to *The Legend of Good Women*, the second version of which is conjecturally dated 1394 (see next chapter).

Chapter 10. The Legend of Good Women

This poem appears to have been composed, and then abandoned, soon after Chaucer wrote *Troilus and Criseyde*. It consists of a dream-vision *Prologue* and nine short verse stories about women of antiquity who were faithful in love, most of whom were foully treated by lecherous or violent men. It is thus directly palinodal to *Troilus and Criseyde*, in which the woman is faithless and the man faithful till death. This connection is established towards the end of Book V of *Troilus and Criseyde*, when Chaucer, apologizing for writing about Criseyde's 'untrouthe', offers to atone by writing about pure women, the second of whom in this couplet is the central figure of the *Prologue* to *The Legend of Good Women*:

> And gladlier I wol write, if youw leste,[1]
> Penelopeës trouthe and good Alceste.
> *(Troilus and Criseyde*, V, 1777–8)

The poem thus stands in some relation to the medieval debate about women, in which Christian doctrine provided the fixed point for writers to react to. Much simplified, this doctrine was that women were inferior, partly because Eve had fallen to Satan's temptation in the Garden of Eden and was thus responsible for human sin and loss of innocence, and partly because the religious system reflected the larger social system anyway. Even the Virgin Mary, whose prominence in medieval worship reflected the impulse to soften such weird rigidity of attitude, acted for humans only as intercessor with the higher, male powers of God and Jesus Christ. So it is important to know that the *Legend* was given a different title in the catalogue of Chaucer's poems named by the Man of Law in his *Introduction*. There it is called *The Seintes Legends of Cupid*, which is a good title, because it makes the useful connection between Christianity – one form of Christian literature being the saint's legend – and the pseudo-religion of courtly love, or 'fine amour', as the French called it.

The Legend of Good Women has a number of features of special interest, some of which can be used to argue that it is in some way a transitional achievement, standing between *Troilus and Criseyde* and *The Canterbury*

1. if it please you

161

Tales. The *Legend* is a collection of stories which hang together on the frame of a common subject, the origination of which is made clear in the *Prologue.* They are all told by one person, a poet who, though less obtrusive as a narrator than he was in *The House of Fame* and *Troilus and Criseyde,* is a more or less continuous presence. So, as a collection, and one of two such in Chaucer's work, it stands superficial comparison with *The Canterbury Tales,* a collection of stories of many different kinds told from the saddle, including a sermon and a moral debate, the narrators of which are vividly delineated. The *Legend* is written in the metre Chaucer used for most of *The Canterbury Tales,* iambic pentameter rhymed in couplets.

The *Prologue* to the *Legend* is Chaucer's last, and probably his best, contribution to the genre of the dream vision, and is such a beautiful, tender and sophisticated example that one would expect the subsequent stories dreamt by the poet to follow it in mode or mood, just as the main material of his earlier three Love Visions followed their openings in spirit. But not a bit of it. The Legends of these good women are tales of disaster, drawn mostly from Ovid but also from Virgil, into which the ritualistic ideas and behaviour of courtly love rarely intrude. They are about cynical seduction and abandonment, suicide, rape and torture, narrated with concentration on the suffering of the women. The process of concentration can be judged by comparing them with the well-known source stories; Chaucer omits anything in these which is not relevant to his purpose. So, since his heroines have, above all, to demonstrate faithfulness in love, they are all presented simply as lovers or wives, and anything in their original stories which suggests that they could even think beyond secure mating, or that having lost that, they could conceive of such a thing as revenge, is ignored. Fidelity alone characterizes his ten heroines (one of the legends has two), and where the source story offers the lady consolation, as it does to Ariadne in the shape of a god for mate, or the chance of dramatic revenge, as it does to Medea and Philomela, Chaucer cuts off the tale before it arrives at that point.

Although the formal frame of the collection requires praise for the lady's virtue and sympathy for her suffering, as well as outraged condemnation of the gentleman, Chaucer applies these criteria in different ways. His ladies can appear absurdly prosy and calculating, as in the tower-top conversation between Ariadne and Phaedra, and his gentlemen can behave like conspiratorial comedians, as Hercules and Jason do. In legends like these, the literature of love and pathos requires wider definition than usual, and sainthood acquires a new meaning. As for the classical heritage, Chaucer turns its giants and giantesses into pygmies, and the characteristic secular literary form of his own age, Romance, he parodies. But with equal facility, he can offer almost straight (a daring word to use to describe any poem by Chaucer) tales of sentiment full of delicate feeling, such as the legends of Dido, Lucrece and Philomela. Variety within the required and superficially narrow frame is what Chaucer achieves: variety of character, story, tone and feeling.

The Prologue

This exists in two versions, which are usually printed as parallel texts on account of their differences and their slightly differing excellences. Although there is still some disagreement concerning which is Chaucer's definitive version, critics accord priority of composition to what is called the 'F version', and regard the 'G version' (from which I mainly quote) as a revision undertaken some years later. Probably 'F', which refers with compliment to Richard II's queen, Anne of Bohemia, was written in about 1386; it could not have been written before her marriage to Richard in 1382, and is unlikely to have been written before *Troilus and Criseyde* was completed, since in both versions the God of Love accuses Chaucer of the crime of translating this poem about a false woman. The references to Anne would have been inappropriate after her death in 1394, which is therefore agreed to be the earliest at which 'G' is likely to have been written.

The dream vision of which the *Prologue* consists is about the poet's own problem of choice of subject. It opens with a declaration of the worth of old books, from which the poet can be drawn away only by the show of spring in May – except, of course, if it happens to be a holy day. Spring brings the daisy, which Chaucer describes in loving detail, and this leads him to disclaim his power and any present intention to write about courtly love. He declares his neutrality between followers of the Flower, who bloom beautifully and briefly in love, and those of the Leaf, who remain sober and chaste in steadfastness; he is concerned, rather, with stories in old books written before 'swich stryf was begonne', that is, stories of classical Greece and Rome which were written before the conventions of Romance applied. But when he goes to sleep, having had his servants scatter flowers on his bed, the dream into which he slips takes him straight to the usual Garden of Love, full of flowers and birdsong. We are invited to construe that world as a standing temptation to him as a poet.

Soon a lark warns of the approach of the God of Love, but it is not he whom Chaucer first describes; it is the queen he is leading forth by the hand. It transpires that she is Alceste, the legendary queen who, when death came for her husband, went to die instead, but was rescued by Hercules. Alceste is a female human daisy, quite possibly portrayed in virtue and floral beauty as a tribute to Anne of Bohemia:

> ... a quene
> Clothed in real habyt [2] al of grene.
> A fret of goold [3] she hadde next hyre her, [4]
> And upon that a whit corone [5] she ber
> With many floures, and I shall nat lye;
> For al the world, ryght as the dayesye
> Ycorouned is with white leves [6] lite, [7]
> Swiche [8] were the floures of hire coroune white.
> For of o perle fyn [9] and oryental
> Hyre white coroun was ymaked al;
> For which the white coroun above the grene
> Made hire lyk a dayesye for to sene, [10]
> Considered ek [11] the fret of gold above.

> (G, 145–57)

The God of Love and his consort are followed by nineteen ladies in royal garments, and a numberless host of women who were true in love. They dance round Alceste singing a ballade exalting her above a whole catalogue of famous women of classical antiquity, and then the company settles down for the God of Love to hold court. He at once spots the poet lurking by a hillside, attacks him for traducing women in his poetry, and promises vengeance. He reels off the names of a string of classical and post-classical authors, including Ovid, who wrote about 'clene maydenes', 'trewe wyves' and 'stedefaste widewes' as examples of what Chaucer should write about.

Alceste speaks up in defence of the poet. He is only a translator, she says, following his original author, and it would be tyrannical to persecute him for that. The God of Love should be like the gentle lion, who disdains to take revenge on a fly that bites him, and allow the poet to plead his case. Then she names works of Chaucer in which women appear in the required favourable light – *The Book of the Duchess, The Parliament of Fowls,* and two stories which were evidently written before the idea of *The Canterbury Tales* came to Chaucer: Palamon and Arcite, which became *The Knight's Tale,* and the life of St Cecilia, which became *The Second Nun's Tale.* Alceste also mentions Chaucer's prose translation of Boethius, and two other devout works which have not survived.

2. royal dress   3. golden net   4. hair   5. white crown   6. petals   7. little   8. such   9. a single unflawed pearl   10. like a daisy to look at   11. considering also

The God of Love's response to his queen follows courtly practice: he defers to her and gives her the right of judgement. The poet kneels to her, pleading that his aim in writing about Criseyde was 'to forthere trouthe in love', teaching by example of contrary. Alceste then gives him his penance, which is that in future he must spend most of his time

> In makynge of a gloryous legende
> Of goode women, maydenes and wyves,
> That were trewe in lovynge al here [12] lyves;
> And telle of false men that hem [13] betrayen,
> That al here lyf ne don nat but assayen [14]
> How manye wemen they may don a shame;
> For in youre world that is now holden game. [15]

> (G, 473-9)

The God of Love praises her for making such a kind judgement, and compliments her on her beauty, which draws a modest blush from her. He then instructs the poet to include her among the virtuous women he will write about; but he must begin with Cleopatra.

So in spite of being based on the convention of the dream vision and its invitation to the world of romance and courtly love, the *Prologue* states a preference for books above daisies, and especially old books free of courtly convention. The irony of this is that Chaucer gets the tyrannical deity of courtly love to propose a poetic policy antagonistic to his own interests – because Chaucer, by concentrating on the 'real truths' of the virtuous lives of Greek and Roman women, will have to ignore the literary conventions upon which the power of the God of Love depends.

Even from this bald summary of the *Prologue*, the reader can see that Chaucer, although one part of his creative mind remains addicted to the glamour of the Garden, is enjoying his prospective freedom from it by satirizing it: that scattering of flowers on his bed, that immoderate praise of the daisy as if it were a beloved woman, that citing of idiotic lion-lore! In the stories, some idea of which I now give, this instinct for satire, which is not only directed at courtly love and romance as literary forms, but engages intermittently in the war between the sexes, remains humourously busy, even while Chaucer is exercising what is perhaps his greatest power – communicating his tragi-comic vision through the spectrum of a many-coloured pathos.

---

12. their   13. them   14. did nothing but try   15. regarded as a sport

The Legends

Cleopatra[16]

Cleopatra, an odd choice for the God of Love to insist on as the first of Cupid's saints, but a lady whose place in English literature is henceforward assured, is a noble queen who never murdered her dynastic rivals, never thought of betraying Antony to the beardless Caesar. She does take part in a fierce sea-fight, recounted in a boisterous alliterative style reminiscent of a different school of poets, but is not instrumental in Antony's defeat there. The whole point of the new story is to hurry her to a death which demonstrates utter fidelity to the dead hero. Not content with embalming him and filling his tomb with jewels, she applies no tiny asp to either of her royal breasts, but leaps stark naked into a pit full of snakes.

Thisbe

Like Cleopatra, *Thisbe* was taken by Shakespeare into a new story. Chaucer's legend is a pretty tale of pathetic young love, frustrated initially by 'wrechede jelos fadres' and destroyed eventually by a roaming lioness. Like Antony, Pyramus, the man in the case, is no heartless traitor, and the concluding point that Chaucer is at pains to make is

> Here may ye se, what lovere so he be,[17]
> A woman dar and can[18] as wel as he.

(G, 922–3)

Dido

Like Thisbe, Dido is the heroine of a narrative of sentiment. Chaucer draws selectively on the fourth Book of Virgil's *Aeneid*, but the long passage in which Dido is described falling in love with Aeneas and heaping upon him hospitality and love is richly medieval. She dandles the young son of Aeneas, confides her love to her sister Anne, and has in her mind already yielded to him before she and the whole court go hunting in sumptuous style. So that, when the pair are isolated in a cave to shelter from a thunderstorm (an occasion celebrated wonderfully by Berlioz in his opera, *The Trojans*), it is satisfyingly appropriate that there Aeneas kneels to her, swears eternal love-faith to her, and possesses her. But

16. In making these summaries, I have drawn on those in Chaucer's *Love Visions*, Penguin, 1983, pp. 155–9 17. whatever sort of lover a man is 18. dares and can achieve

there the courtly love ends. Everyone knows that they were alone in the cave. A neighbouring king's wooing procedures are spiked, and Aeneas publicly revels in his good fortune. In Virgil, Aeneas is a princely and fate-dominated refugee from Troy who leaves Dido because the god Mercury commands him in a dream to sail away and found Rome, but Chaucer follows Ovid in stripping him of heroic charisma and leaving him as a more or less casual lying lecher. His dream about Mercury is presented as the false excuse of a man who, in Alceste's word, makes a 'game' of seducing women. He leaves behind his sword, with which Dido, leaping upon a sacrificial fire, pierces herself to the heart.

Hypsipyle and Medea

Both are treated as consecutive victims of Jason. In telling the legend of Hypsipyle, Chaucer sometimes approaches the knockabout style in which, in several of *The Canterbury Tales,* he rejoices in fabliau-type seduction. The legend starts loftily, with the island queen succouring the sea-battered heroes, Jason and Hercules; but soon (1520 ff.) she falls to a conspiracy in which Hercules acts as pander, and one is reminded of the plotting of John and Aleyn, the two poor scholars who succeed in having the Miller's wife and daughter. Jason stays long enough to father two children on Hypsipyle, and pillage her possessions, before sailing away. Like Dido, Medea, Ariadne and Phyllis, Hypsipyle writes her treacherous deceiver a letter of reproach based on Ovid's *Epistolae Heroidum* (*Letters of Heroic Ladies*).

The promiscuousness of Jason is further celebrated – indeed, this fourth legend has one hero rather than two heroines – in the short account of his seduction and abandonment of Medea, whose titanic classical propensities for magic and revenge receive virtually no mention. Chaucer begins with a short prologue, in which he inveighs against Jason as a fox-like chicken thief. To have this farmyard villain pleading in courtly style with mysterious heroines from classical legend, who then proceed to give him their worldly goods as well as their bodies, no doubt diverted Chaucer's noble audiences in a none too lofty manner.

Lucrece

Lucrece's legend is a pretty one, prettier even that that of Thisbe, and both are delicate, unlike the legends of Hypsipyle and Medea. Here the shamefaced perfection of the heroine, inarticulate at her two terrible moments, the one of being raped and the other of committing suicide on account of that dishonour, is starkly but gently conveyed. Probably Chaucer's audience would know that Lucrece's suicide would rank as a cardinal sin in the Church, since she did not consent in any way to her ravishment by Tarquin, the brutal explicitness of whose crime contrasts eloquently with her helplessness. Nowhere else in this poem, or in any of the love visions, is Venus's third power, the incitement to lust, as sharply evinced as in Tarquin's imaginings (1745–74). After such real horror, Chaucer's audience would experience civilized amusement at the sainted lady's concern, as she falls dying, to cover her naked feet and other parts. Lucrece takes her place securely among the other bearers of Chaucer's message of female pathos: Constance from *The Man of Law's Tale*, Griselda from *The Clerk's Tale*, Virginia from *The Physician's Tale*, and Dido and Philomela, companion saints of Cupid in this legend.

Ariadne

With this legend, Chaucer offers a comic sophistication on the theme of heroic love, as remote as can be imagined from the world of the Rape of Lucrece. The story is the well-known one about Theseus, a prince of Athens, who goes with fellow-citizens as annual tribute to the King of Crete. The fate that awaits them is to be fed one by one to the Minotaur, a monster half human and half bull, offspring of a bull's service to a queen's lust, which is kept in a maze. The King of Crete's two daughters take pity on Theseus, and help him to thwart the Minotaur, which he kills, and to escape from the island of Crete. After a largely irrelevant opening about the siege of Megara, we are taken to the dungeon where Theseus is waiting to be fed to the Minotaur, while up above Ariadne and her sister Phaedra are mooning. Beneath them, a privy vent connects them with the sorrowing prisoner, whose lamentation they overhear. The word 'foreyne' does seem to mean 'privy', which makes the moonlight conversation of the two sisters, on the walls above, pleasantly ridiculous. Next comes Phaedra's suggestion that the Minotaur's teeth can be gummed up and so made harmless if Theseus throws balls of tow into his gaping maw. Practical women, these ancient Cretans, so practical that when Theseus, learning of their determination to save his life, professes courtly humility and service, Ariadne at once proposes to him (2089), and suggests titles for herself and her sister when they arrive safely in Athens. Theseus replies, almost in burlesque style, that he has in fact been in love with her for years, though it is clear that they have never met before. The coincidences pile up, and Theseus's sudden preference for Phaedra, which makes him abandon Ariadne on the island of Naxos, sees this martyr of love, practical to the last, tying her headscarf to a pole and waving it at Theseus's receding ship. The whole story is told in a relaxed way, and whenever there is danger of the atmosphere of true romance being established, Chaucer explodes it by dwelling on a funny or incongruous detail.

Philomela

Philomela (which means lover of song, hence nightingale) is the heroine of perhaps the grisliest of classical myths in which rape figures and, significantly for the mechanism of courtly love, the lady whose agony is represented whenever the nightingale sings. The story runs that Procne, after five years of marriage to Tereus, King of Thrace, longs to see her sister Philomela. Tereus sails to fetch her from her loving father, King Pandion of Athens, and on the way back hides her in a cave, where he rapes her, cutting out her tongue to prevent her reporting it. He tells Procne that he found her sister dead when he arrived in Athens; but Philomela in captivity weaves a tapestry with the news of her fate on it, and sends it to Procne. Chaucer stops his version with the sisters united in grief, and does not proceed to the well-known ending, in which the sisters kill the child of Tereus and serve him, cooked in a pie, to his father. The ghastly tale is suffused with the pathetically shared family feeling of King Pandion and his two daughters; Philomela calls desolately on her father and sister as she is raped. The only humour is in the closing abuse of cruel men.

Phyllis

Phyllis is another coastal queen who, like Dido and Hypsipyle, succours a storm-tossed philanderer. Demophon, son of the lecherous Theseus, possesses her, proposes to her, and then sails away on the pretext of having to prepare for their wedding. When he does not return, she writes him a reproachful letter, which Robert Worth Frank, Jr in *Chaucer and the Legend of Good Women* (1972), calls 'a handbook for lechers', and then strangles herself 'with a corde'. In this tale Chaucer draws much from Ovid's *Heroides*: he gives Phyllis's pathetic letter of censure at some length, but does not include the long pathos of the Ovidian scene of Demophon's departure.

Hypermnestra

Hypermnestra, the last of love's martyrs in this legendary, is bound by astrological predetermination and dream prophecy. The latter persuades her father that he can avoid assassination by a nephew – his son-in-law in prospect – only by making his daughter kill her husband in the bridal bed. The former gives her a character which makes it impossible for her to wield a knife in anger. The whole story is intensely dramatic, beginning with the dire interview between father and daughter, in which he swears to kill her if she does not murder her husband, and ending with the heroine sitting in despair to await her father's vengeance because she cannot run fast enough to accompany her cravenly fleeing husband, whom she had warned of the danger. A line or two of the conclusion is missing, and since this is the last of the legends, it can only be surmised that Chaucer left the whole work unfinished.

The Legend of Good Women is a teasing work, in which Chaucer can be seen fulfilling his penance to the God of Love with a wavering rather than constant good faith. This is because, although he is ostensibly concerned with the saintliness of his pure and steadfast heroines, he time and again emphasizes their gullibility. Dido, Hypsipyle, Medea, Ariadne and Phyllis all receive indirect censure for failing to see through beauty, rank and warrior glamour to the rottenness within the man. But underlying that, a certain covert admiration for such bounders as Jason and Theseus can be detected. In view of the teasing changeability of tone throughout, it would be unsafe to use this poem as evidence that Chaucer had radical views about women.

Chapter 11. Anelida and Arcite, and Short Poems

Anelida and Arcite

Of Chaucer's several incomplete works, *Anelida and Arcite* is the most interestingly flawed, because it opens in one mode, continues in another, and dries up altogether after one stanza of attempted renewal of the first mode. In a high style without leavening of Chaucerian humour, both modes are prosecuted with some elaboration, the first in language and the second in metre.

The first part of the poem (210 lines) begins with a three-stanza invocation to Mars and Polyhymnia, the Muse of lyric poetry, and then, by way of setting the scene for the story to follow, tells of the return of Theseus from his triumph over the Amazons and capture of their Queen, Hippolyta – familiar matter to readers of *The Knight's Tale* and *A Midsummer Night's Dream* – and then of Creon's pacification after the Theban Wars – the subject of Aeschylus's play, *Seven Against Thebes*. At line 71 the narrative of the Armenian Queen Anelida is introduced, and her love for the 'fals Arcite' is described, not shown. Like the many luckless heroines of *The Legend of Good Women*, she gives too much: 'Al was his that she hath' (107). Arcite, chasing a 'newe lady' who is not named, accuses Anelida of infidelity, and before this first narrative section ends we are told that the 'newe lady', without granting him grace, sends Arcite on repeated quests, 'now to londe, now to shippe'. The perspective has dwindled from epic consideration of great wars to close focus on boudoir agonies. The interfusion of such disparate elements is hard to manage, but Chaucer was to do it successfully in *Troilus and Criseyde*. The first part of *Anelida and Arcite* is based on Boccaccio's *Teseida*, as is the whole of *The Knight's Tale*, and Chaucer also used Statius's *Thebaid* and Dante's *Paradiso*; but for the second part he turned to Ovid.

The elaborate 'Compleynt of feire Anelida upon the fals Arcite' – the subtitle of the whole poem – which constitutes lines 211–341 often echoes Ovid's *Heroides*: Ariadne, Medea, Phyllis and Dido, among the heroines treated in *The Legend of Good Women*, are quoted here. Like some of them, Anelida sends a letter of reproach to her faithless man.

Besides the tentative play with epic style at the beginning, and the conventional and harmonious play with the genre of Complaint in the second half, Chaucer's indulgence in metrical excess in the Complaint is worth remarking. Though tightness of poetic form is often conducive to intensity of expression, as factors such as repetition, hypnotic quasi-musical rhythms and sounds, and heavy rhyming, spellbind the reader or listener, one almost certain effect is to constrain originality of thought or verbal content. Like the *Harley Lyrics*, which are metrically the most elaborate in the language, parts of 'Anelida's Complaint' sing simply and in set ways. For example, the sixth stanza of both strophe and antistrophe has nine lines of iambic pentameter in which only two rhyme sounds occur; and in addition, there is internal rhyming of the second and fourth feet in each five-foot line. Here is the conclusion of the strophe, with all rhymes italicized:

> My sweté *foo*, why do ye *so*, for sh*ame*?
> And thenké *ye* that furthered *be* your n*ame*
> To love a *newe*, and ben un*trewé*? N*ay*!
> And putté *yow* in sclaunder *now* and bl*ame*,
> And do to *me* adversi*tee* and gr*ame*,[1]
> That love yow *most* – God, wel thou *wost*[2] – alw*ay*?
> Yet come a*yein*, and yet be *pleyn* som d*ay*,
> And than shal *this*, that now is *mys*,[3] be g*ame*,[4]
> And al for*yive*, while that I liv*é* m*ay*.

(272–80)

The poem is a useful early experiment. Perhaps Chaucer learned from it that if originality, flexibility, depth and continuity are to be achieved in narrative poetry, elaborate metres must give way to, for example, iambic pentameter lines which are not necessarily end-stopped, and are rhymed in couplets – the chosen metre of the late masterpieces of *The Canterbury Tales*.

Short Poems

It is surprising that so few short poems of a poet as prolific as Chaucer have survived. Robinson's title for the part of *The Works of Geoffrey Chaucer* in which they figure eschews the term 'lyric' because modern readers expect something personal and emotional from such a description. But most of the twenty poems in the section are either conventional on the subject of love, or philosophic, and hence not lyrics in the sense that we understand. The poems about love, eleven in number, are Complaints or Ballades, and though they are conventional, at least three of them are amusing in part. The five 'Boethian ballades' – 'The Former

1. harm 2. knowest 3. wrong 4. sport

Age', 'Fortune', 'Truth', 'Gentilesse' and 'Lak of Stedfastnesse' – earnestly advocate the values of Boethius (see Chapter 14), and three of them conclude with *envois* addressed to prominent people: 'Lak of Stedfastnesse' to King Richard, and 'Truth' probably to Sir Philip de Vache. There remain the early religious poem translated from the French of Deguileville, 'An ABC', which may have been written for John of Gaunt's duchess, two *envois* to friends which are amusing about love, and the single rhyme royal stanza of rebuke to his scrivener Adam for incorrectly copying out his poems.

These minor poems reinforce the impression gained of the poet from his major narrative works: his urbanity, his power to lift the level of discourse to Dantesque eloquent seriousness, or collapse it into fun, his open-textured and precise language, his judicious transformation of other writers' material, and his mastery and development of the metres and poetic forms he chooses. And the Boethian ballades reinforce the values of such poems as *Troilus and Criseyde* and *The Franklin's Tale*. I propose to discuss one complaint, one Boethian ballade, one *envoi* and the triple roundel (derived from the French 'rondeau'), 'Merciles Beaute'.

Since 'The Complaint unto Pity' and 'The Complaint to his Lady' are conventional, and 'The Complaint of Venus' is a liberal translation of three ballades by the poet Otes de Granson (a knight of Savoy who fought for England and was killed in a duel in 1397), I take 'The Complaint of Chaucer to his Purse' for its special Chaucerian quality. Technically, a Complaint was exactly what it sounds like: a poem complaining to a person or force holding something back from the poet who desires it; characteristically, in medieval and Renaissance times, to a woman who denies her love to a suitor, or to the goddess Fortune when she deals unfairly with the poet. Chaucer turns the well-used model into another genre which was also common in a period when all sorts of people depended on favour or patronage for their livelihood: the begging poem. This one is only twenty-six lines long, and comprises three stanzas of rhyme royal and a concluding *envoi* asking the king to 'have mynde upon' his 'supplicacion'. The joke of treating the purse as the beloved who won't deliver works from the opening lines:

> To yow, my purse, and to noon other wight
> Complayne I, for ye be my lady dere!

His plea to her is not to love him, but 'Beth hevy ageyn, or elles mot I dye!'. That is the refrain line which concludes each stanza: it conjures up the lively absurdity of a man wanting his beloved to be weighty, instead of light and slender, as the traditional heroines of love always were.

That complaint is in strict ballade form, though it happens to be called a complaint on account of its content. The ballade is not to be confused with the ballad, the dramatic song which, whatever the circumstances of its composition, celebrates crucial events, especially tragic ones, in the popular culture of many countries. The ballade was the dominant form of courtly French poem in the fourteenth and fifteenth centuries; and it consisted of three stanzas of either seven or eight lines, followed by an *envoi* of four to six lines. The form which came to Chaucer from a French poet and composer whom he both admired and imitated, Guillaume de Machaut (?1300–77), was three stanzas of iambic pentameter of seven lines each, rhyming a b a b b c c, which Chaucer follows with an *envoi* in the same metre. The stanza is in fact rhyme royal or, as it has been called because of the fact that *Troilus and Criseyde* was the first substantial English work in it, the 'Troilus stanza'. So I think it is fair to say that Chaucer got his most famous stanza form from Machaut; but whether he ever envisaged the same musical requirements as his French master is, so far as I am aware, not known.

This musical form was a a b: that is to say, the tune of the first and second lines was repeated for the third and fourth, and a new melodic element, or development of 'a', made up the 'b', the tune for the last three lines. It is important to recognize the musical element in medieval verse forms, especially those forms which are complex and heavily rhymed, because for us, poetry and music have become largely separated. In the period with which we are concerned, the historical interfusion of poetry, song, dance and instrumental music, which had already gone from narrative poetry, was beginning to break up in lyrical poetry too, owing to the spread of literacy. By the early seventeenth century, a poet could begin a sonnet, 'If music and sweet poetry agree'; perhaps the last major English poet-composer was Thomas Campion (1567–1620).

The ballade 'Gentilesse' takes up the Boethian theme of nobility of spirit, defining it with the help of material from the *Roman de la Rose* and Dante's *Convivio*, both of which contain the phrase that Chaucer represents in English in the last two words of the third stanza, 'Vyce may wel be heir to old richesse', in which 'richesse' should be thought of as the spiritual richness of nobility rather than temporal wealth. The line reflects the essence of the poem, which is that 'gentilesse' (untranslatable by any single word, but it implies noble elegance and graciousness of spirit and morals) cannot be assumed to be inherited, but has to be earned by every person who aspires to it, by right conduct. Only God, 'the firste fader in magestee' – and the word 'fader' stresses the idea of bequeathing qualities – shows 'gentilesse' from the start and eternally.

The poem lacks an *envoi*. It is twice quoted in full, once by Henry Scogan (?1361–1407), who is thought to be the man addressed in 'Lenvoy de Chaucer a Scogan', in which Chaucer amusingly chides his friend for some failure in the conduct of a love affair.

In poetry, *envoi* defines the action of sending forth a poem, and hence, by usage, it became the closing stanza to the ballade which pithily summed up the content of the poem and was addressed to the dedicatee, most commonly in the vocative, 'prince'. Chaucer's two surviving *envois* preserve the original sense. In his 'Lenvoy de Chaucer a Bukton', his friend is facetiously warned against the perils of his forthcoming marriage. Why should he be like Satan, gnawing on his chain for ever? The line 'The sorwe and wo that is in mariage' brings to mind not only the fates of the several cuckolds of *The Canterbury Tales*, but the Wife of Bath herself, and sure enough, this poem ends with advice to the prospective groom to read her:

> The Wyf of Bathe I pray yowe that ye rede
> Of this matere that we have on honde.
> God graunte yow your lyf frely to lede
> In fredam; for ful hard is to be bonde.

The triple roundel, 'Merciles Beaute', is discussed in Chapter 13. I return to it in delight at the way Chaucer manages its strict form and turns a conventional Complaint theme, the intractability of his lady, into a rueful joke against himself, which is contained in two of the three repeated lines of the third roundel:

> Sin I fro Love escaped am so fat,
> I never thenk to ben in his prison lene . . .

The form of the roundel which, like the ballade, ought always to be thought of in terms of its music, is that of a poem of thirteen lines, in which the first three lines are repeated at the end; in addition, the first two lines recur as lines six and seven; and there are only two rhyme sounds in the whole poem. Having referred earlier to the 'serious' complaint of the first two roundels, I now give the whole of the third as conclusion to this chapter – at which point I should emphasize that many of the felicities mentioned, including this joke in a slightly different form, appear elsewhere. Whether Chaucer or the Duc de Berry invented it, or both used a previous model, is not known.

> Sin I fro Love escaped am so fat,
> I never thenk to ben in his prison lene;
> Sin I am free, I counte him not a bene.[5]

5. not worth a bean

He may answere, and seye this and that;
I do no fors,[6] I speke right as I mene.
  Sin I fro Love escaped am so fat,
  I never thenk to ben in his prison lene.

Love hath my name ystrike out of his sclat,[7]
And he is strike out of my bokes clene
For evermo; ther is non other mene.[8]
  Sin I fro Love escaped am so fat,
  I never thenk to ben in his prison lene;
  Sin I am free, I counte him not a bene.

Part V: Chaucer's Cultural Resources

Chapter 12. Classical Literature

To this day, knowledge of the classical world of antiquity is indispensable for the understanding and enjoyment of European literature of all periods, though perhaps the requirement is less pressing in regard to some arts of the twentieth century. For educated medieval people, the literature, history, philosophy and religion of Greece and Rome, which they knew about through classical Latin, medieval Latin (a simpler, less inflected form) and vernacular translation from these languages, provided substantial elements of their inherited culture. The heroes and heroines of classical myth and story, whether divine or human, carried the power, mystery and complexity of an idealized past, which medieval artists and thinkers used to enrich their own artistic, intellectual and religious present. Appeal to the past was an orthodox practice in all cultural contexts, partly owing to the Christian obligation to be guided and inspired by the original books of the faith and their acknowledged interpreters.

This backward-looking impulse, which was specifically ordained in religion, is a general phenomenon in the development of peoples and societies. Since the beginning of history, references back to, invocations of, and reinterpretations of so-called 'heroic' or 'golden' ages of this or that race have been made with the intention of creating or strengthening a living tradition. 'There were giants in the earth in those days' (Genesis VI. 4) expresses the impulse simply and well, and I suppose the most vivid example from the English Middle Ages was the frequent use in the arts of the myth that Britain was founded by Brutus, a descendant of the Trojans who fled from Troy after the Greeks had sacked the city. That Trojan War and its aftermath were the subject of three of the greatest poems of antiquity, Homer's *Iliad* and *Odyssey*, and Virgil's *Aeneid*. Mention of Troy carried as much cultural charisma to the medieval mind as mention of Rome or Athens has brought to the consciousness of any succeeding age, and Chaucer turned to 'the matter of Troy' time and again; most notably in *Troilus and Criseyde, The House of Fame* and *The Legend of Good Women*. The early and medieval Christian church, in following this impulse, created a problem for itself: Latin was the vehicle of all learning, including religion, and its classical form had to be mastered by every educated person; but the religion read about in classical Latin was pre-Christian and pagan, and the subject matter of the literature, though underpinned by the values of a pagan religion,

179

expressed a secularity and diverse morality which could rarely be reconciled with Christian values. But many attempts were made to reconcile the two systems, and the strategy used was recourse to the standard medieval device of allegorization: the deities of the classical pantheon, and the events in which they figured in myth, were moralized in such a way as to enrich Christian teaching.

All the gods, including Jupiter or Jove who, as presiding deity of Olympus, was often allegorized as God, were safe subjects for the treatment once the general threat of paganism retreated under the attack of Christianity. Thus, as Brewer amusingly describes (*An Introduction to Chaucer*, 1974, pp. 101–2), Venus, the naked goddess of profane love, becomes 'a classical representation of the Blessed Virgin Mary, Empress of Heaven and Earth and Hell'. According to Fulgentius, the sixth-century Christian mythographer, whose interpretations and style of interpreting set the pattern for medieval allegorizers of classical myth, Venus's nakedness moralized the crime of lust. She was naked 'either because she sends away naked those who are addicted to her, or because the crime of lust cannot be concealed, or because it is only suitable to the naked. She has roses because they are red, and sting, like lust, the red coming from shame, the sting from sin. As roses please for a while then fade, so lust pleases for a moment then always departs ... They paint her floating in the sea because lust in the end suffers shipwreck'. This mode was so powerful that even eight centuries after Fulgentius, Boccaccio, the near-contemporary of Chaucer upon whose early secular works in Italian Chaucer particularly drew for *The Knight's Tale* and *Troilus and Criseyde*, wrote in his devout latter years a long Latin treatise on the genealogy of the classical gods and goddesses (*De Genealogia Deorum*), Christianizing his material.

Though Chaucer had little to do with such esoteric interpretation in his poetry, that does not affect the general orthodoxy of his Christian position, which should be considered in the analysis of particular works when it is relevant. His response to the medieval classical legacy was to take its full force into his creative imagination, and to select from it according to his particular predilection at the time of composition. For example, in concentrating on feminine pathos in *The Legend of Good Women*, he omits the gory horror of the cannibalistic revenge of Procne and Philomela upon Tereus. But Chaucer's Venus, who presides over the activity of love – which, taking his works all in all, interests him above other subjects – is never diminished to a moral precept, but remains enigmatically inflaming, queen of the venereal impulse:

> Hyre gilte heres with a golden thred
> Ibounded were, untressed as she lay,
> And naked from the brest unto the hed
> Men myghte hire sen;[1] and, sothly for to say,
> The remenaunt was wel kevered[2] to my pay,[3]
> Ryght with a subtyl coverchef of Valence –
> Ther nas no thikkere cloth of no defense.
>
> > (*The Parliament of Fowls*, 267–73)

And as a counter to the last suggestion of Fulgentius, quoted above, there is Chaucer's delicate vision of the temple of Venus, the first thing the sleeping poet of *The House of Fame* dreams of:

> Hyt was of Venus redely,
> The temple; for in portreyture,
> I sawgh anoon-ryght hir figure
> Naked fletynge[4] in a see.
> And also on hir hed, pardee,[5]
> Hir rose garlond whit and red,
> And hir comb to kembe hyr hed,
> Hir dowves,[6] and daun[7] Cupido,
> Hir blynde sone, and Vulcano,
> That in his face was ful broun.
>
> > (*The House of Fame*, 130–39)

It must always be borne in mind that Chaucer, like his contemporaries in England, France and Italy, drew on the classical material as it appeared not only in the original Latin texts, but also in medieval Latin and vernacular accommodations of the material; re-telling, with or without embellishment, was the norm, and the modern idea that 'copying' is disreputable was simply not current in literature. But, though Chaucer drew heavily on Virgil and other Latin poets, on Dante and Boccaccio from Italy, and on a number of poets writing in French, there is one poet on whom he drew most heavily of all, and with whom he shows a close affinity in subject treatment and method.

This poet was Ovid (43 B.C. – A.D. 17) and the importance of the meeting across fourteen centuries of the two poets' minds may first be indicated by Dryden's slightly excessive perception: '... both of them were well-bred, well-natured, amorous, and libertine, at least in their writings, it may be also in their lives' (Preface to *Fables*, 1700). Today, few would go so far as to describe Chaucer's attitude in his poetry as libertine, though of course he wrote bawdy verse tales; and still fewer

1. see   2. covered   3. satisfaction   4. floating   5. by God   6. doves   7. Sir

would join Dryden in his speculation about Chaucer's private morals. The chief works of Ovid which are reflected in Chaucer's poetry are: *Amores, Ars Amatoria, Remedia Amoris* and *Heroides,* and above all *Metamorphoses.* In *Amores,* which is three books of love poems, Ovid self-deprecatingly apologizes for being dominated by love, which he half-seriously justifies as a heroic activity. *Ars Amatoria* is a mock treatise on seduction and sexual intrigue, which wittily and often cynically portrays Roman high society. *Remedia Amoris* is a mock recantation of the burthen of the *Ars,* as John M. Fyler writes in *Chaucer and Ovid* (pp. 11–12):

The *Ars* advocates self-deceptions that assist the libido, while the *Remedia* prescribes self-deception to resist a passion gone out of control; their comic opposition is made obvious in directly contradictory teachings.

Heroides are epistolary poems, the letters purporting to have been written by legendary women to their absent or faithless lovers or husbands. They read as passionate monologues in which the characters of the women are brilliantly delineated; Chaucer used material from *Heroides* for five of the nine stories about 'Cupid's saints' in *The Legend of Good Women. Metamorphoses,* an epic poem in fifteen books, was Ovid's most influential poem, a veritable mine which was quarried by medieval and indeed Renaissance European writers, including Shakespeare. It is a collection of stories culled from classical and Near-Eastern legend, which is given some unity by the ruling idea that every story contains a metamorphosis or transformation, and some sense of development through time in that it begins with the metamorphosis from chaos to order at the creation, and ends with the metamorphosis of the man Julius Caesar into a god at his death. The reasons for its enduring popularity may be read into Fyler's introductory summary (*Chaucer and Ovid,* p. 1):

The *Metamorphoses* offers a particularly handy collection of stories and the most wide-ranging if not most systematic compendium of information about the gods and heroes. Its central concern, the pathos and comedy of love, is the avowed topic of the elegiac poems. Through them Ovid becomes the Freud of the Middle Ages: the *Ars Amatoria, Remedia Amoris, Amores* and *Heroides* provide the most elaborate and memorable terminology for describing the uncertain stability of the lover's mind.

The fruitful paradox, 'uncertain stability', though conjured by Fyler to interpret Ovid, seems to me to provide a vital way into Chaucer's writing about love. Like Ovid, Chaucer pursues sympathetically and unflinchingly the ever-alluring and often treacherous courses of sexual passion, accommodating with equal equanimity and poetic insight the vagaries of lofty passion and natural desire, and placing them both within the scale of common humanity. An instance of lofty passion not being sentimentally reverenced lies in the amusing circumstances of the eventual bedroom conjunction of Troilus and Criseyde, which insist on the absurdity of sexual intrigue without diminishing the impact of the lover's rapture; and that, I think, is the essential Chaucer being true to life.

But there are differences between Ovid and Chaucer: the cynicism and occasional crudity of the Roman poet in the *Ars Amatoria* and *Remedia Amoris* have no strict counterparts in Chaucer, in whose poetry, when they appear, they figure mostly as expressions of created characters, such as Pandarus in *Troilus and Criseyde*, or the Wife of Bath, or the Shipman, rather than of the poet speaking as himself. But the worldly-wise and compassionate eye of Ovid, the outlook on sexual and other matters which accepts without overtly judging, and which observes passion at work in life without trying to provide either a rational or a moral framework, is often paralleled in Chaucer. Sometimes that quasi-Ovidian attitude appears in a surrogate authorial *persona* within the poem, such as Theseus in *The Knight's Tale*, or Pandarus.

Chaucer often de-mythologized the Ovidian material. For example, when he based stories of tragic love on their original versions in *Metamorphoses*, he did not follow Ovid in providing the compensating metamorphosis which consoled the lovers after death. In *The Book of the Duchess*, his Ceyx and Alcyone (a form of 'halcyon', a fabled bird) are left desolate in their separation by the death of King Ceyx, and not re-united as happily mating birds. And his Pyramus and Thisbe, in *The Legend of Good Women*, do not mingle their bloods after death, to share in providing juices for the mulberry tree.

In general in his classical references, Chaucer can be either Virgilian, that is, representing the gods and goddesses as cosmic forces presiding over the destinies of somewhat larger-than-life humans, or Ovidian, that is, showing them as capricious characters who have magic powers with which they bring misfortune to human beings – and, indeed, to other divinities with different powers. The descriptions in *The Knight's Tale* of the temples of Venus, Mars and Diana (1893–2088) show something of the Virgilian impulse, in spite of the catalogues of thoroughly human activities that they dominate. Such references are much less frequent than the Ovidian ones, in which gods and goddesses seem often to be playing a kind of heavenly one-upmanship. A nice example is the intervention at the end of *The Merchant's Tale* of Pluto, king of the underworld, and his queen, Proserpine. The male divinity uses his magic to reveal to the blind dotard January his wife's adultery, whereupon the female divinity responds by using her magic to grant the wife success in explaining away her extra-marital copulation up a tree. It was classicism's most famous extra-marital copulation, that of Venus, in defiance of her husband Vulcan, with Mars, which produced what is perhaps Chaucer's most elegantly witty use of classical myth derived from Ovid. Ovid gives little but the essential detail upon which Chaucer builds his fancy:

The Sun's loves we will relate. This god was first, 'tis said, to see the shame of Mars and Venus; this god sees all things first. Shocked at the sight, he revealed her sin to the goddess' husband, Vulcan, Juno's son, and where it was committed.

(*Ovid in Six Volumes*, translated by Frank Justus Miller, Vol. III, p. 191)

The Chaucerian response, which does not proceed to the classical denouement so uproariously treated in the *Ars Amatoria* – Vulcan's forging of a metal net in which the lovers are snared while the gods look on and laugh at them – is a poem of 298 lines known as *The Complaint of Mars*. Like *The Parliament of Fowls*, it is a poem for St Valentine's Day, the special day in all the year for mating propositions, when Venus, aided by probably specious astrological considerations, smartly gets the hefty god of war into bed. When Phoebus the sun god, as in Ovid, lights up their abode of bliss, Mars has to vacate it, though too late to frustrate discovery:

> He throweth on his helm of huge wyghte,[8]
> And girt him with his swerd, and in his hond
> His myghty spere, as he was wont to fyghte,
> He shaketh so that almost hit towond.[9]
> Ful hevy was he to walken over lond;
> He may not holde with Venus companye,
> But bad her fleen,[10] lest Phebus her espye.

(99–105)

The fact that Chaucer does not mention the sequel, concerning Vulcan's very public revenge, but leaves the idea of it to foment in the minds of listeners or readers, assuming that they would know it, is one of many indications that his poems were written for an astonishingly sophisticated audience.

Most of the rest of the poem is the actual Complaint, which Mars delivers according to the conventions of courtly love. We have the absurd

8. weight   9. broke in pieces   10. flee

spectacle of the Roman god of war behaving as a medieval knightly lover should, that is, according to Thomas Usk, a contemporary of Chaucer who wrote *The Testament of Love*, as 'a lion in the field and a lamb in the chamber'.

Chapter 13. Courtly Matters

If the chroniclers and poets are to be trusted, a nobleman reared according to the courtly ideal entertained a twofold ideal: to fight bravely and often, and to win women's love by obeying them. Before considering courtly love itself – a term which, by the way, was not in use in the Middle Ages – we must look at that sector of medieval society from which Chaucer drew the heroes and heroines of his major love poems. These characters are all of royal or aristocratic stock except, perhaps, for a few of the merchant class who have pretensions to courtly behaviour and, since pretension is a folly and therefore a funny subject, tend to appear in fabliaux. A further exception must be made of churchmen of various ranks and functions who tread on the forbidden ground of sex in Chaucer's tales. I write here especially of knights, and of the ideals of chivalry.

To begin with, modern readers must take on board the universal medieval idea that hierarchy was inherent in the scheme of things which was continuously produced by Nature under God's rule. Human beings, like angels or animals, and even trees, existed in ranked order, in which their particular fixed status gave them an allocation of precedence or inferiority in all matters, and conditioned their propensity to virtue or vice. In medieval Christian society there were three main categories of people, or estates:

The clergy, whose business is with prayer and with pastoral ministration to society's spiritual needs; the warriors, whose business it is with their swords to uphold justice, protect the weak, and defend the Church; and the labourers, by whose toil the land is tilled and whose work provides for the physical needs both of themselves and of the other two estates.

(Maurice Keen, *Chivalry*, 1984, p. 3)

Typically a Christian warrior, when knighted at the end of his training as a squire, swore to avoid false judgement, commit no treason, honour and help all women, attend Mass, and fast every Friday in remembrance of Christ's Passion. The ceremony of dubbing a knight included symbolic attestations to such virtues as chastity and humility, loyalty and courtesy, and the two particularly knightly virtues of prowess and largesse. Prowess referred to courage and all the skills of fighting, including those of leadership, and largesse meant generosity of spirit, including magnanimity and charity. A thirteenth-century poetic treatise on chivalry exhorts knights to 'prize honour before all, and eschew pride, false-swearing, idleness, lechery, and especially treason' (Keen, *Chivalry*, p. 10). According to a slightly earlier formulation, the three worst treasons were to kill one's lord, to lie with his wife, and to surrender his castle. Chaucer's Knight seems to be of this antique type, though when he tells his tale, it is one which faithfully replicates the conventions of 'courtly love' in its dialogue and action. But his Squire has a more delicate, up-to-date and love-orientated sensibility, which reflects the further knightly precepts which are important in Chaucer: knights were enjoined to learn singing and dancing, and to keep fit. They practised martial arts in the controlled conditions of various kinds of tournament, and are usually portrayed at this dangerous exercise adoringly overlooked by balconied ladies. It was considered good for knights to be 'in love', because that made them keener and braver in tournament and battle, since they were then motivated to win honour for their ladies as well as for themselves. But the highest virtue in a knight was to perform glorious deeds, and then to give all the credit for them to God.

Chaucer's most important knights, the Knight of *The Canterbury Tales*, the warriors in *The Knight's Tale*, Troilus, and the 'man in blak' in *The Book of the Duchess* (who is generally thought to be a poetic evocation of John of Gaunt mourning his dead duchess) show all the above qualities except the last-mentioned. However, *The Knight's Tale* is the only major work of Chaucer's to deal at any length with knightly valour, and even there, as in *Troilus and Criseyde*, the dramatic context is sexual passion of great intensity. Accordingly it seems fair to observe that the poet has little interest in the essence or operation of chivalry and its conventions, apart from their relevance to the theme of love.

This brings us to courtly love itself, concerning the origins of which there has been much speculation but little firm agreement. What agreement exists centres on the opinion that, round about the twelfth century in Europe, the subject of love began to be treated in literature and other arts in a new way which can be accounted for only minimally by examining either the classical heritage or early medieval Christianity. The former treated attraction between the sexes comparatively frankly, and in the latter the idea of 'love', though not sexual love, was central to the conception of the relationship between people and God, and between people. It has been suggested that an oriental impulse entered Southern Europe with the Moors, bringing Arab and Jewish elements into the expression of love in songs and lyric poems. And the new way of writing about love has been located in the south of France: as C. S. Lewis puts it in *The Allegory of Love* (1936, p. 2), 'Everyone has heard of courtly love, and every one knows that it appears quite suddenly at the end of the eleventh century in Languedoc.' But his view of it as a mode separate from other modes of writing about love is not held by all, and D. W. Robertson, Jr., one of the most distinguished of North American Chaucerian scholars, has always been at pains to place the whole mode in the broad context of the classical heritage and the thought and practice of European Christianity. With regard to the assertion that the troubadours, the court poets in the south of France who flourished between 1100 and 1350, were the first to celebrate it, and that their position at centres of power and communication ensured the spreading of the 'doctrine', Robertson remarks, 'the troubadours included men of very diverse types whose treatment of love was by no means uniform' (*A Preface to Chaucer*, 1962, p. 392). So it is wise to approach the matter with caution and not to romanticize excessively about what is, however you look at it, an extremely romantic business.

The foundation of the spirit of 'courtly love' is the belief that woman is a lofty creature to whom service is due, and who ennobles the man whose love she possesses, whether she rewards him with her love or not. The lover's service must be total, as that of vassal to lord: his lady, like the lord in the feudal system, and God in the Christian religion, is perfect and must not be adversely criticized. The quasi-religious aspect of the convention is recognized in the arts. There are, for instance, parallel poems, one of a pair being addressed to the earthly loved one and the other to the Virgin Mary; the metre, imagery and expressions of adoration hardly differ. And the Church adapted secular love-song melodies to plainsong or anthem. It is hardly surprising that it was in the fourteenth century that angels, who had been thought of as masculine in Jewish and early Christian lore, could now be thought of as feminine.

Such a way of regarding women and love was essentially different from the classical attitude to them, which was to see passionate love as a humanly attractive but destructive aberration that placed its participants at odds with fate, and probably with society as well. And though Greece and Rome allotted women an inferior place in law, marriage and society generally, in their arts they submitted them to neither degradation nor idealization; their bodies and souls had as real and open an existence as those of men. As for medieval Christian doctrine, it saw sexual love as, at best, an unavoidable necessity, and an essentially selfish one because it detracted from the love of the individual soul for God. Even when the passion was between married partners, it was frowned on, and the sexual act was thought justifiable only when its purpose was procreation.

Courtly love doctrine was different even from that which was expressed in the conventions and practices of secular society, in which a noblewoman's role was to bring her lord power and riches through marriage, and to support him as ruler and fighter. In all these systems, extramarital love was an offence against society, and in the last two it was an offence against God as well. In courtly love, by contrast, love had an absolute value, independent of marital or social considerations, which made the pursuit and satisfaction of it self-evidently desirable and justifiable; added to which, women were accorded a novel and extraordinary priority. These two characteristics have had permanent effects on European culture, as they still to some extent affect relations between the sexes and some social conventions. But the essence of medieval courtly love is no longer strong. This essence was courtesy, a studied and formal kind of aristocratic behaviour featuring elegance, graceful politeness and generous sensitivity.

This formal and aristocratic person, the courtly lover, must now be described as he figures in the literature of Romance, the dominant medieval poetic form. He acts secretly, and is humble before his lady, both before and after consummation. He shows total fidelity in act and thought. He champions her when she needs an advocate. He undergoes any test that she prescribes for him, whether it engages valour, or fidelity, or honour, or humility, or some other virtue. In pleading for her favour, he expresses his fervour in love; he appeals to her grace, or pity, typically asking for her mercy as if she were a goddess, and may specify his own worth as long as that does not infringe the important virtue of humility. She may grant him two kinds of grace, the first of which may or may not lead to the granting of the second. The first is to allow the knight to serve her as vassal, which makes him her faithful warrior to whom she has allowed this personal recognition; it carries no sexual rights, and may therefore with decency be granted to a knight by, say, a queen. The second grace, which concerns the granting of love by the lady, posits the secret fulfilment of a passionate sex relationship, with all that that involves. A lady usually so grants her 'mercy' because the knight's pleading and demonstration of his fervour and his suffering, his personal worth and fidelity, have aroused in her the important emotion of pity. So 'mercy' and 'pity', which are goddess-like virtues, usher in 'desire'.

The narrative Romance, whether in verse or prose, is the characteristic form for the literary expression of courtly love. Shorter characteristic forms, all of which have classical antecedents, and may appear as separate poems or as elements within narrative poems, are the Complaint, in which the lover laments the unresponsiveness of the lady to his advances;

the Aubade, or dawn song, in which the lover, in bed with his lady, regrets the arrival of the light which must separate them if secrecy is to be preserved; and the Song, a lyrical outpouring in which the lover, or indeed any person who is in love or wishes to be in love, celebrates the power and beauty of that passion. In Chaucer's frequent use of them may be discerned something of his debt to his French contemporary, the composer and poet Guillaume de Machaut.

All the facets of courtly love so far mentioned are met in Chaucer, and above all in *The Knight's Tale* and *Troilus and Criseyde*. They also receive extended expression in *The Book of the Duchess* and *The Parliament of Fowls*, and frequently figure in both serious and amusing form in a number of *The Canterbury Tales*.

So far in this discussion of courtly love, the phenomenon has been seen from the man's point of view. But the woman's side is much more interesting, partly because of the exceptional rights granted her – though any reasonable feminist would observe that a person put on a pedestal has only limited freedom of action – but much more because medieval literary convention provided such a full mechanism for describing processes which resulted in her withholding or granting her 'mercy'; feminine psychology in short. This mechanism is demonstrated at the extraordinary length of about 22,000 lines in the great French allegorical poem of the thirteenth century, *Le Roman de la Rose* (*The Romance of the Rose*). Like most of his European fellow-poets, Chaucer knew it well, and he referred to it, or quoted it directly, hundreds of times.

The *Romance* is a two-part allegory narrated by the Lover about his pursuit of the Rose, which symbolizes the love of the Lady who, in the last few lines of the poem, allows him to lie with her. The first 4000 lines are by Guillaume de Loris, and tell of the planting of love in the lover by the god of Love, and of his attempts to pluck the Rose. He has to contend with allegorical personages, a few of whom help him, but the most important of them are those which represent aspects of the lady's character. The lover gets as far as kissing the Rose before her main defences, Shame, Danger, Fear and Foul Mouth (who is, broadly speaking, Gossip and Slander rolled into one) prevent further progress. Chaucer's *The Romaunt of the Rose* is largely a translation of this part of the poem, but does include about two thousand lines from the second and larger part.

This is the 18,000 lines written by Jean de Meun, which begins precisely as a continuation of De Loris's poem, but rapidly develops into something of grander scale and less pure allegory. In the process of bringing the lover to his goal, De Meun gives us ten long digressions which, because of their independent interest and length, tend at times to make the allegorical love contest seem remote. They consist of extended debates, realistic and romantic narrative, satire, and voluminous annotations and discussions of different aspects of love, including cynical observations about conduct in love matters which remind one of Ovid – who was indeed a much-used source of De Meun. The first digression is of special importance, being a 3000-line argument between Reason and the lover in which the latter rejects Reason's advice to discontinue his pursuit of the Rose. At the end of the poem the lover's triumph over the virginity of the lady – his plucking of the Rose – is recorded in transparent metaphor; Venus had begun the assault on the castle of the Rose by shooting a burning brand into a nether aperture between the pillars – the lady's legs, of course:

By this path, narrow and small, where I sought passage, I broke down the paling with my staff and gained a place in the aperture. But I did not enter halfway; I was vexed at going no farther, but I hadn't the power to go on. But I would have relaxed for nothing until the entire staff had entered, so I pressed it through with no delay. But the sack, with its pounding hammers, remained hanging outside; the passage was so narrow that I became greatly distressed, for I had not freed any wide space. Indeed, if I knew the state of the passage, no one had ever passed there; I was absolutely the first.

(ll. 21635–56, translated by Charles Dahlberg, 1971, p. 352)

No such short description of *The Romance of the Rose* can do justice to its expansive and almost comprehensive treatment of love as it figures in medieval literature both lofty and low, as it appears in an actual society as a realistically inclined poet-observer saw it, and as it figured in the moral system prescribed by the religion of the day. Its importance to readers of Chaucer's poetry must now be made clear, and the chief question to be answered is, 'Why, if as all commentators agree, Chaucer wrote hardly any pure allegory – that is, a work in which personified abstractions representing qualities engage either in action or debate or both – is some knowledge of *The Romance of the Rose* desirable?' The short answer is that most of the allegorical qualities, classical deities and further abstractions who are characters in the *Romance* appear in more realistic guise in Chaucer with their values still recognizable, altered though they may sometimes be, and that the mechanism and content of the French poem are evidently assumed by Chaucer to have been known by his readers or listeners. Furthermore, the structure of the poem seems to have provided bases for the structures of such major Chaucerian works as *The Book of the Duchess, Troilus and Criseyde* and *The Knight's Tale.*

Two instances, the first obvious and the second not, must suffice at this point. Near the end of *The Book of the Duchess*, the 'man in blak' tells the dreaming poet that when he first wished to propose to his lady, he was so overcome by 'pure drede and shame' that he could speak only the single word, 'mercy!' (1219). Then, in *Troilus and Criseyde*, there is the crucial and long-deferred moment in Book II (449–50) when Criseyde's uncle first reveals to her that Troilus is in love with her:

> Criseyde, which that wel neigh starf for feere,[1]
> So as she was the ferfulleste wight . . .[2]

That 'feere' is exactly the quality shown by the Rose at the assault which led to the kiss at the end of De Loris's part of the *Romance*, and which had to be assuaged in De Meun's before the lover's assault on her castle could succeed. This fear includes many aspects: instinct for self-preservation in the face of male attack; and for maintaining her individuality and independence, as well as her morality, and her terror of the unknown. All these can be removed only if all her other reservations, including those about her honour, reputation and safety, and her certainty that the lover is burning with love and not lust, have been answered; if she is satisfied as to the lover's prowess, largesse, humility and beauty; and if, above all, Venus has shot that carefully directed arrow of fire into her womb.

An attribute of the Lady in the *Romance* which requires brief discussion is Danger, a word which also occurs often in Chaucer in its ordinary modern sense, as well as in the medieval and Renaissance sense of 'power' – the Summoner had 'the yonge girles of the diocise . . . In daunger . . . at his owene gise'. Courtly love Danger is different: one translator calls it 'resistance', and another 'offishness', which I rather like. C. S. Lewis, in a long note in *The Allegory of Love* (pp. 364–6), writes that manuscripts of the *Romance* vary, apparently not distinguishing between Danger and Disdain; which warrants the assumption that the two terms are interchangeable. He also gives examples to show that pride, distance and excessive dignity are associated with the lady's spirit of Danger. Danger appears in straightforward allegory, together with Pity and Mercy, in the second roundel of Chaucer's 'Merciles Beaute', a poem which is a fine example of his special quality of juxtaposing the serious and the comic: the first two roundels are addressed to the lady in the form of conventional love complaint, but the third is a comic expres-

1. died of fear 2. person

sion of his relief that he doesn't have to bother with love any more because he has grown so fat. The serious allegorical lines I refer to are:

> So hath your beautee fro your herte chaced
> Pityee, that me ne availeth not to pleyne;[3]
> For Daunger halt your mercy in his cheyne.

In the *Romance*, Danger is a huge and hairy churl, which I suppose signifies the response he produces in the lover.

Three further qualities of the woman which appear as allegorical characters in the *Romance*, and in realistic action in Chaucer, are Fair Welcome, Franchise and Shame. Fair Welcome is the aristocratic gentility and openness which requires a noble lady to give anyone a fair hearing. As C. S. Lewis points out, 'he is a false friend to a maidenhead' (*The Allegory of Love*, p. 23). Franchise, the quality of the freeborn (derived from the name of those medieval conquerors, the Franks), connotes confidence and is related to Fair Welcome. Shame, a curious compound of repression, fear for reputation, and an exaggerated sense of honour owing much to Christian prudery and urgent guardianship of privacy, is related to Danger.

Some other important characters, allegorical and other, who appear in *The Romance of the Rose*, may now be briefly indicated. First, there are those who seem to be partly expressions of the personality of the Rose, and partly exterior forces: Jealousy, Foul Mouth, Old Woman (Vekke in Chaucer), Friend, Genius (the instinct for love) and Nature. Then there are those who seem to belong to the company of the god of Love and Venus, such as Sweet Looks (who carries Cupid's bow and arrows for him). These following characters obey the god of Love's summons to his parliament; but the last two are not welcome:

Lady Idleness, the keeper of the garden, came with the largest banner. Nobility of Heart came, Wealth, Openness, Pity, and Generosity; Boldness, Honour, Courtesy, Delight, Simplicity, and Company; Security, Diversion and Joy; Gaiety, Beauty, Youth, Humility and Patience; Skillful Concealment; and Constrained Abstinence, who led False Seeming with her – without him she could hardly come; all these came with all their followers. Each one of them had a noble heart, but not Constrained Abstinence and False Seeming with his face of pretense.

(ll. 10449–65, trans. Dahlberg, p. 186)

We learn a few lines later that False Seeming is the child of Fraud and Hypocrisy.

Without some idea of *The Romance of the Rose* and the system which for convenience is called 'courtly love', appreciation of such poems as

3. complain

The Book of the Duchess, the *Prologue* to *The Legend of Good Women*, *Troilus and Criseyde*, the tales of the Knight, the Franklin, the Merchant and the Wife of Bath (together with her *Prologue*) is likely to fall short of full understanding.

In considering the relation between such poems and the *Romance*, one should judge the extent to which the *Romance* supports or contradicts medieval religious teaching about love. The progress of a lover from initial sight of his lady to successful assault of her sexual castle clearly represents, in the Church's eyes, 'cupidinous love', a selfish passion to win delight through possession. To commit such a sin, that of lechery, a man was supposed to go through three stages. The first was the arousing of the senses, which was achieved by Satan; the second was delight of the heart, which was the effect of Eve, and hence, in early Christian writing and iconography, the representation of lechery as a woman; and the third was the consent of the perverted Reason. A more widespread, and secular, tradition which is also found, though incidentally, in religious writing, is that concerning the five steps in love. The first step is seeing the loved one, which gave rise to the late classical and medieval idea that people fall in love 'at first sight', as do Chaucer's 'man in blak' in *The Book of the Duchess*, Troilus, Criseyde, and the rival cousins Palamon and Arcite in *The Knight's Tale*. The four following steps are talking with, touching, kissing and bedding the loved one. Both these processes, that of the three stages and that of the five steps, are followed in the *Romance*. Critics are not agreed on the extent to which the poem vindicates Christian morality about sex. Does it portray a vicious process as a warning, or defiantly celebrate delight? Perhaps these lines near the end are equivocal:

... I rendered thanks, among the delicious kisses, ten or twenty times, first to the God of Love and to Venus, who had aided me more than anyone, then to all the barons of the host [i.e. people like Fair Welcome – B.S.], whose help I pray God never to take away from pure lovers. But I didn't remember Reason, who gave me a lot of trouble for nothing.

(Dahlberg, p. 354)

Chaucer does not use the conventions of courtly love described above as a philosopher uses a school of thought, within which he may develop his own ideas; or as a priest uses his religion when writing, in order to develop a treatise within a scheme of accepted belief. Chaucer can indeed write entirely within courtly love conventions, and may seem when so doing to be comparable with my posited philosopher or priest. But almost always he is simultaneously writing within and outside them,

implicitly distancing himself from them as he delineates the people in
action in his created world. Some of his most important created characters believe that they operate by the rules of courtly love, but usually
they interact with other characters who are less convinced, and have
their own conventions and other kinds of morality and wisdom. Some
indeed confront the ideas of courtly love with opposition and even derision. And always at hand is the gently ironic authorial figure of Chaucer
himself, commenting, juxtaposing, questioning and, in each work in
which courtly love figures, providing a synthesis which fulfils the requirement of his particular subject matter. For Chaucer, who can treat
opportunistic copulation and refined marriage relationship with equal
conviction – I think at this moment of *The Reeve's Tale* and *The
Franklin's Tale* – the conventions of courtly love, like the realism of folk
story or the morality of a society which, at least formally, was Christian,
provide just one means, though a vitally important one, through which
he can communicate his poetic visions of the all-important subject of
human love in its variety, ambiguity and depth.

Chapter 14. Christian Belief and Practice

Chaucer's work as a whole reflects a continuous and profound interest in matters philosophical and religious. The philosophical aspects concern the moral philosophy of classical Rome which Chaucer learned from his reading and which, like the Church Fathers before him, he took into his system of religion, transmuting it as necessary. The result is something of a hybrid, as I hope to show. The special interest for readers of all Chaucer's work lies in the observation that, as his career proceeds, he reflects classical moral and philosophical ideas less and less and medieval Christian ideas more and more. The latter figure pervasively in *The Canterbury Tales*, where they are expressed in complexity and great variety of debate. The debate may be among characters in individual tales and their prologues and epilogues, or be represented by the juxtaposition of separate tales in which different standpoints are taken. This has been so much remarked that attempts have been made to represent the main structure of *The Canterbury Tales*, unfinished though the grand design is, as an edifice of Christian themes which is concluded, and in some sense fulfilled, in the last tale, the sermon-like treatise delivered by the Parson. It is therefore essential for readers of Chaucer to know something about fourteenth-century English Christianity.

Today we think of the Church chiefly in terms of its primary functions of relating humankind to God and saving souls, but in Chaucer's England, besides aiming to fulfil these, the Church was something like a state within a larger state in terms of its powers, rights and duties, and its organization. As property-owner, tithe-collector (the 'tithe' being the tenth of produce which was taken by the Church) and potential or actual employer, it bore on every citizen. As law administrator of its own people, it operated to a large extent outside the common law, and in addition, many of its dogmas and tenets were embodied in that common law. As moral and educational mentor of both the individual soul and the body politic, its beliefs, knowledge and ways of thinking dominated almost every forum, whatever subject was being discussed and in whatever field policy or action was being considered – international policy including war, home government, law, education and the operation of society in all its detail. Matters relating to the classes, trades, crafts, industry, agriculture and all occupations, together with their organs of administration and expression, came or were liable to come under

Church influence. Accordingly, the Church bore heavily on the arts, through its near-control of literacy and its ever-active twofold purpose: the promotion of works of art, literature and music for the glory of God and the salvation of souls, and the restriction or proscription of works which presented the Christian religion or its functionaries in an unfavourable light.

Of course there were literate lay men and women, and there was no general obstruction to the writing and performing of secular works – though, from our point of view, six hundred years later, we can say with certainty that much of the secular literature of the Middle Ages failed to survive because the manuscripts were not kept in the libraries of religious houses; and those that were so housed would later be at risk during the Dissolution of the Monasteries under Henry VIII in 1536–9.

So the large body of surviving literature, in poetry and prose, is shot through with Christianity and observations upon it even when it is not overtly religious in bearing; literary works of most kinds conventionally ended in prayer. The accounts of personal and social life in both fact and fiction show the age as deeply permeated by concerns of religious thought and practice. Perhaps the most significant literary monument to the religious spirit of the age is the drama, all the surviving texts of which are religious, consisting of finely crafted verse plays which make precise biblical or doctrinal points. The drama presented, in cycles of many short plays, the whole religious history of humankind, from the Creation to the Last Judgement, and mounting a performance of a cycle would occupy a whole community for weeks at a time. Besides the cycles of plays, of which four have survived in manuscript, there are individual plays from cycles which have disappeared, and single plays on such subjects as the lives and miracles of the saints.

In considering how the religion of such an England is represented, and with what effects in the poetry, it may be useful at the outset to juxtapose examples of opposite tendencies in Chaucer, both of which are authorial statements in important works. One of them expresses committed personal orthodox devotion; the other, comic and outrageous blasphemy.

The first is Chaucer's well-known Retraction, which is appended to the last of *The Canterbury Tales*, the long sermon given by the Parson. It is Chaucer's farewell to the writing of poetry and translations, being superscribed: 'Heere taketh the makere of this book his leve'. In it, Chaucer protests that his purpose in writing has been 'for our doctrine' (instruction), and asks his readers to thank Christ for what has pleased them, and to pray to Christ that he may be forgiven for what has not pleased them. He then lists his 'translacions and enditynges of worldly

197

vanitees', that is, his whole output of secular poetry, including those of his 'tales of Caunterbury that sownen into [tend towards] synne', all of which he retracts before God. Then he thanks Christ and the Virgin Mary for his 'translacion of Boece [Boethius] de Consolacione, and othere bookes of legendes of seintes, and omelies [homilies], and moralitee, and devocioun'. The whole Retraction constitutes a prayer that on Doomsday Chaucer's soul may be saved through the grace and mercy of Jesus Christ.

The example of blasphemy that I cite is in *Troilus and Criseyde* (III, 1577–8), where Chaucer compares Criseyde's forgiveness of her uncle for tricking her into bed with Troilus with God's forgiveness of humankind for crucifying Jesus: there is no mistaking the meaning.

Faced with such immediate contraries, the student may well abandon as unprofitable, and probably as useless in terms of literary criticism, the search for the answer to the question, 'How Christian was Chaucer (at any particular stage of his writing career)?' Better to inquire into the varying permeation of works of different kinds with medieval religious thought and practice, and the comments on them, and to study Chaucer's mastery of different kinds of religious writing in their particular contexts.

Whether writing in his own declared voice or giving life and individuality to the many characters he created, Chaucer expressed orthodox devotion in its many forms – such as prayer, homily, *exemplum*, saint's legend, theological and moral debate, sermon and even, in *The Parson's Tale*, a treatise on the Seven Deadly Sins; he rejoiced in an extraordinary variety of comment on, and discussion of, religious and moral matters. Whether he is writing of the life he saw around him, or of the life he created out of his classical and early medieval heritage, or indeed out of the Continental literature of his own time, readers should always take account of the subject and tone of his poetic discourse. This holds good whether his subject is overtly religious, as in the tales of the Pardoner, the Prioress, the Second Nun and the Parson, together with a few of his shorter poems, or secular with a moral or philosophical slant, as in most of his poetry. Such a process renders less important the obligation to distinguish between 'devotional' and 'moral-philosophical' threads in Chaucer's poetry, which has been a perennial critical concern.

The most important single source of religious ideas used by Chaucer, the *De Consolatione Philosophiae* (*The Consolation of Philosophy*) of Boethius, was both religious and philosophical. Boethius (?470–524) had been sole consul of Rome under Theodoric, the Ostrogothic ruler of Rome, until he was strongly suspected of plotting an Italian restoration.

His work, which was written in prison, where he was eventually put to death, was Boethius's response to his unjust fate. Though it is cast as a dialogue in the classical style between Boethius and a feminine personification of Philosophy, it remained important for its place in Christian thinking for more than a thousand years, though it is not certain that Boethius was formally a Christian. Chaucer translated it, as King Alfred had done and Queen Elizabeth was to do (both royal scholars presumably enjoying professional help!), and in the great works of his middle period, such as *Troilus and Criseyde* and *The Knight's Tale*, included verse translations of parts of it. In both these major poems, the protagonists take up Boethian positions in face of their fortunes and fates.

Boethius faced his Job-like situation – that of the just man undergoing the injustice of suffering – with sophisticated discussion of notions relating to divine will, providence and vicissitude. In its Christian aspect, this discussion involved the nature and extent of free will, God's foreknowledge and control of destiny, and the urgent question for the individual soul of the award of God's grace. For the fourteenth-century Christian, two of the questions upon which Boethius focused were, 'If the good God is all-powerful, whence and why comes evil?' – the doubters' question; and 'How can there be good, unless God exists?' – the riposte of the faithful. On the burning questions of whether everything that happens has been sanctioned in the mind of God, and what effect the answer has on the notional free will of human beings which allows them choice of action, the broadly orthodox answer to the first has remained, almost until our own times, as Milton put it in the mouth of the God of *Paradise Lost*:

> ... because I am who fill
> Infinitude, nor vacuous the space,
> Though I uncircumscribed my self retire,
> And put not forth my goodness, which is free
> To act or not, Necessitie and Chance
> Approach not mee, and what I will is Fate.
>
> (VII, 168–73)

The term of special use there has to be understood: 'necessity', which often crops up in Chaucer's development of Boethius's ideas, is that force which makes ordained things happen.

The classical pre-Christian thinking upon which Boethius and other early Christian philosophers worked ran something like this: a group of divinities was imagined in a kind of triangular relationship; at the apex of this triangle was an all-powerful God, and at its lower points stood

Nature and Fortune, both of whom were usually represented as female. God created everything in Nature, inherent in whom was the good reality and potential of all creation, the harmony of which worked by divine reason. Opposite Nature stood Fortune, who represented, very broadly, the forces of chance and irrationality, and both were subject to Necessity. In literature from Virgil to Shakespeare, Fortune presides, with allies (who are often siblings, as when Chaucer, in *The House of Fame*, makes Fame her sister) who represent different facets of her operation: Destiny, Fame, Reputation, Rumour. Fortune's prevalent form in medieval literature is as the turner of a huge wheel, to which humans are attached. A person at the top is graced by luck and rejoices in plenitude and freedom (the king or queen enthroned in power, the warrior triumphing in victory, the merchant surrounded by piles of gold, the beautiful girl holding court among suitors); but as the wheel rotates under Fortune's hand, people formerly fortunate are crushed as the part of the rim to which they cling reaches the ground. As Boethius's Fortune explains, 'I am glad to chaungen the loweste to the heyeste, and the heyeste to the loweste' (III, Prose 2, 50). Fortune is characteristically shown as blind because she distributes her good and bad destinies arbitrarily, and not according to the deserving of recipients.

St Augustine was later to explain that 'misfortune' was the result of a bad use of free choice by people withdrawn from the grace of God; but of course God could restore grace. However, there is nothing religious about the knockabout way in which Fame, Fortune's sister, judges her suitors in Book III of *The House of Fame* (1360–867), which amusingly disposes of the idea that Fame comes to those who deserve it on account of their virtue. As for Chaucer's representation of Nature, he relies mainly on the *De Planctu Naturae* (*The Complaint of Nature*) of the twelfth-century writer Alanus de Insulis, reinforcing it or posing a counter-current of ideas about her, as his poetic invention determines. Alanus follows Boethius in representing her as a lofty creative power, promoting and affecting the government of things by her laws which, in accordance with Providence, determine the way the world works (III, metre 2). She is, in the main, just that lofty kind of power in *The Parliament of Fowls* but, since the poem is about mating, and hence to some extent moves according to the precepts of courtly love, Nature allows the mating debate to be conducted and structured on the assumed precedence of aristocratic birds. This is contrary to the teaching of Boethius that 'Alle the lynage of men that ben in erthe ben of semblable [equal] birthe ... Thanne comen alle mortel folk of noble seed' (III, metre 6).

So, from these two examples from among many which could be cited, it may be seen that Chaucer's use of Boethius was often dictated more by cultural and literary convenience than by specific commitment to his ideas. This might not be thought true of *Troilus and Criseyde* and *The Knight's Tale*, because in them Boethius's ideas are expressed by major characters in such a way as to affect the fundamental nature of the poems. They account for states of mind in the characters which in part determine the aesthetic upshot. For example, in Book I V of *Troilus and Criseyde*, when the blissful lovers learn that they are to be separated owing to the decree that Criseyde must leave Troy to be with her father in the Greek camp, Troilus prays in a temple to 'the pitouse goddes everichone', and to Jove in particular, to have pity on his sorrow, either by bringing him speedy death, or ridding Criseyde and himself of their distress. His long soliloquy is an agonized attempt to understand the ways of God which have unjustly brought him misery, and forced him to accept that

> '. . . al that comth, comth by necessitee:
> Thus to be lorn, it is my destinee.'
>
> (I V, 958–9)

Troilus argues throughout in terms of the apparent dichotomy between free will and predestination:

> 'But natheles, allas! whom shal I leeve?[1]
> For ther ben grete clerkes many oon,
> That destyne[2] thorugh argumentes preve;[3]
> And som men seyn that, nedely, ther is noon,
> But that fre chois is yeven us everychon.
> O, welaway! so sleighe[4] arn clerkes olde,
> That I not[5] whos opynyoun I may holde.
>
> 'For som men seyn,[6] if God seth al biforn,
> Ne God may nat deceyved ben, parde,
> Than moot it fallen,[7] theigh men hadde it sworn,
> That purveiance[8] hath seyn before to be.
> Wherfore I sey, that from eterne if he
> Hath wist byforn oure thought ek as oure dede,
> We han no fre chois, as thise clerkes rede.'[9]
>
> (967–80)

There, in what is presented as speech and thought issuing as Troilus's personal response to his wretchedness, Chaucer offers a verse rendering

1. believe   2. destiny   3. prove   4. subtle   5. know not   6. say   7. must it be   8. providence   9. counsel

of his own prose translation of part of Prose 3 of Book V of *De Consolatione Philosophiae*. It is a fatalistic proposition, to which Boethius
provides the reply of philosophy that human beings nevertheless have
freedom. But such a reply would not be germane to the mood of the
despairing Troilus, and Chaucer omits it. All the same Troilus, while
bitterly resisting his 'destinee', voices a constant concern of fourteenth-
century thought. Though he takes no consolation in his lifetime, in
death his immortal soul is consoled by the full felicity of heaven, from
which vantage point he laughs at the wretched world below him, where
people are grieving for him, and where blind desire such as his for
Criseyde continues to bring misery.

Boethius had tried to explain the problem of free will and predestination by defining different scales of knowing – the lower scale
being appropriate to human beings and the higher to God. Within the
lower scale of human comprehension, humans did have what was, for all
rational purposes of which they could conceive, 'free will'. But the ways
of God are unknowable, in this as in other matters, so that only he can
know what is 'predetermined', and how it can be defined when it is done.
Humans can strive to approach the 'intelligence' (a term often reserved
in medieval writing specifically to describe the working of God's mind)
of God through loving him in their worship.

The Boethian solution to the problem of free will and predestination
arose in part from Boethius's understanding of the Platonic doctrine of
Forms, and his desire to reconcile it with Christian belief. Behind every
particular thing – another person, an animal, an inanimate object – which
we can apprehend, though only as far as our nature and wits permit, lies
not only the particular thing's own nature as it is in essence, but also the
classifying 'comune spece' (general species) of which it is a type or form.
This, in its highest manifestation, resides perpetually in the mind of God,
where it is a part of the single principle which governs everything that
exists. Since, as both Platonists and Christians agreed, God (or the Prime
Mover, as he was often called) is good, humans must have faith in the
general beneficence of his creation, and if their particular lot is miserable,
bringing, say, oppression, poverty, torture, starvation, or disease, they
should face it with joyful acceptance, knowing that, as Voltaire's Dr
Pangloss in *Candide* professed with fatuous optimism, 'everything is for
the best in the best of all possible worlds'. This general cast of thinking
was in scholastic philosophy called Realism, because it attributed absolute existence, that is, total reality, to the universals which exist in God's
mind. Though its Boethian form is important in Chaucer, in theology it
is particularly associated with Thomas Aquinas (c. 1225–74).

Opposed to Realism was Nominalism, the extreme form of which was the belief that universals and comparable abstract conceptions were mere names, and had only a grammatical significance which did not explain reality. The medieval theologian who propounded a moderate nominalism was William Ockham (d. 1349), who thought that a thing which was real was always individual, and had greater reality than any classificatory generalization about the kind of form in which it existed. The universal to which Realism allotted a higher reality was in Ockham's view only a 'term' or 'sign'. This 'cutting out' of the special significance of universals gave rise to the phrase 'Ockham's razor'. Nevertheless Ockham believed that we must study the likenesses between individual things, and thus arrive at knowledge, with a degree of generalization, by experience of what we know.

This is quite different from the view of Aquinas, whose Realism enabled him to accept universals as coming from the mind of God, and so to achieve perfect harmony between faith and reason. Nominalists, denying a scheme of certainty within which they could accommodate the unknowableness of God, thus appeared to have a less spiritual view of the world, and Ockham was in fact imprisoned for heresy. But the kind of thinking represented by his ideas, which in relation to the possibility of humans approaching God were more pessimistic than the ideas associated with Realism, allowed freer play for science and philosophy in the quest for knowledge. Neither Ockham nor the earlier Nominalists of the eleventh and twelfth centuries questioned the Christian revelation, but by rejecting the wholeness of the theological Realist position, such thinkers opened the way for people to ask questions about the world and the cosmos which appeared to challenge Christian belief. In particular, Nominalism seemed to open the way to the idea that man could be, perhaps even was, to a larger extent than orthodoxy propounded, master of his own destiny. Probably the most important early questioner was Roger Bacon (?1214–94), the Franciscan scientist and philosopher, who was twice confined for heresy.

The great English opponent of Ockham was Bishop Bradwardine (1280–1349) who died of the plague in the same year as his rival. Bradwardine's work of refutation was *De Causa Dei contra Pelagium* (*Concerning the Reason of God against Pelagius*), Pelagius having been a fifth-century British monk whose heretical view was that man, through his will, was capable of good without the interaction of divine grace. Bradwardine re-asserted the absolute power of God, through whose knowledge and grace the entire divine plan was fulfilled. Within this scheme, Bradwardine paradoxically claimed, human will was free, although every event, from a single person's virtuous action to such a national triumph as the English victory over the French at Crécy in 1346, was God's achievement rather than man's. Bradwardine, in re-affirming the largely deterministic orthodoxy of St Augustine, was thus claiming back for the Church the rights of faith and grace from Ock-hamists and others who operated, without loss of faith as they saw it, more through a modern kind of philosophic reasoning. Chaucer acknow-ledges this whole debate in *The Nun's Priest's Tale* when, comically speculating about destiny just before the fateful fox appears to tempt the vain cockerel Chauntecleer from his perch, he names Augustine, Boethius and Bradwardine, and says that he cannot sift the (essential) flour from the (disposable) bran in their arguments.

From the debate between Realism and Nominalism, and especially from the manner of arguing of the latter, arose Dissent in something like its modern form. It led eventually to the Reformation, firstly in the contribution of John Wycliff (?1320–84), whom Chaucer almost certainly knew as a fellow-protégé of John of Gaunt, and the work of later Con-tinental reformers such as John Huss, John Calvin and Martin Luther.

Wycliff's theology was developed in part as a reaction against Nominalism, and especially against Ockham. Wycliff re-asserted the importance of divine foreknowledge, but distinguished it from fore-ordaining, thus leaving intact the certitude of free will. He thought that God's knowledge contained both certainty about the future and the idea of contingency – the conceiving of future events as possible – and this necessarily involved a variable approach to the problem of time, since all God's thought, whether it relates to the past, the present or the future, is eternally existent. But more important to us is Wycliff's insistence on individuals' own responsibility for their state of grace. His reformism in this respect led to his work being banned by Pope Gregory XI, because he attacked the abuses he saw in Church practice both from a moral point of view, and as matters of principle. Thus, he preached that evil governors, whether lay or clerical, forfeit their right to power. He advo-cated clerical poverty, in fulfilment of the teaching of Jesus, and attacked the whole hierarchical system of the Church. After the Great Schism of 1378, in which two Popes, one to rule from Rome and the other from Avignon, were elected by the same college of cardinals, he attacked the Papacy itself, denied the doctrine of transubstantiation (by which it was held that the communion bread and wine do change into the body and blood of Christ), and asserted the right of all people to read the Bible without the intercession of the Church – a right he reinforced by making his great English translation of the Bible in the 1380s. 'Let each man put his first trust in Christ's mercy and in his own good life and not in false pardons and vanities,' he wrote. It seems that 'vanities' associated with religion made less headway in England than their largely Continental inventors wished: a famous example, from a little before Chaucer's time, was the failure of the Flagellants (whose style of worship included whipping themselves into a state of grace) to establish their practices in England, although they tried. The devout English generally went no further than Thomas à Becket and Chaucer's Second Nun's heroine, Cecilia, both of whom wore hair garments next to their skin.

Wycliff's advice sounds a note constantly heard in fourteenth-century England, where literature of all kinds reflected a concern with personal conduct. The centre of this activity was the vernacular sermon, which played a powerful role in liberating scholarly expression from the confines of Latin. Though Latin remained the conventional medium for learned written communication, the practical expression of its wisdom had to be in the language of the land; direct translation from Latin into English, and vice versa, was common. As the level of literacy among lay people rose, the readership for religious works in English increased; Chaucer's poems of strictly religious meaning appear to have gone into more manuscript copies than those of mainly secular import.

Among writers whose works were widely known as part of the background shared by Chaucer and his readers, three may be mentioned. Robert Mannyng of Brunne (1288–1338) wrote *Handlyng Synne* (*Concerning Sin*) (1303), a poem in Midland English which was formally a translation of a French work, but in the execution was much extended into a satire on social vices, and therefore was highly topical. It was written, its author claimed, 'in simple speech for love of simple men'. Then there was Robert Holcot (who died of the plague in 1349), a Dominican who, besides being an expositor of the Bible, moralized on history. Lastly there was Bromyarde – not the Dominican abbot of the 1390s who opposed Wycliff from a Cambridge base, as used to be thought, but an earlier Dominican whose work is widely quoted from the middle of the fourteenth century onwards. His *Summa Predicantium* (*The Whole of Preaching*) is a voluminous compilation of alphabetically arranged moral and anecdotal sermon materials. G. R. Owst (*Literature and Pulpit in Medieval England*, 1961, p. 224) calls it 'the gathered fruits of Mendicant Preaching in England'. It is often quoted by Langland and Chaucer, and its language of complaint and satire is echoed by Chaucer almost every time he satirizes Church or lay people in *The Canterbury Tales*.

The Tale of Melibee and *The Parson's Tale* in particular show

Chaucer's involvement with conduct-based devotional writing, and in most of his works, while never advancing religious heterodoxy, he develops a prudential morality and holds doctrinal rigidity at a distance. Sometimes he examines the latter speculatively, through a dramatic character's mind, as in the Wife of Bath's thoughts about the respective merits of virginity and the married state.

Other religious writings in English were those of the mystics, prominent among whom were the Yorkshireman Richard Rolle of Hampole (c. 1300–1349), Dame Julian of Norwich (1343–1413) and the Augustinian Walter Hilton (d. 1395), who wrote both burningly and tranquilly of the love of God from the vantage point of a reclusive monastic spirituality. Rolle's lyrical poems and Hilton's prose work, *The Scale of Perfection*, otherwise known as *The Ladder of Perfection*, have deservedly survived. The number of manuscripts of mystical works which exist points to their popularity; their spirit shows occasionally in Chaucer's religious tales and their tellers in *The Canterbury Tales*.

Of interest to students of Chaucer, and especially to those who judge his attitude towards religion to have been to some extent independent, is his connection at court with supporters of the Lollards, the name (meaning 'mumblers') given to those who followed Wycliff. These were the seven so-called 'Lollard knights', four of whom are known to have had literary, or legal, or social relations with Chaucer. They were generally regarded as heretical, and whether or not they were formally Lollards, it is clear that, besides upholding the ideal of secular knighthood, they believed in a pure kind of Christianity, in which the dispensations and decrees of the Church were somewhat loosened in favour of direct illumination from the Bible. To Sir Philip la Vache, the son-in-law of one of them, Chaucer addressed his poem 'Truth', a 'Balade de Bon Conseyl' in which the 'conseyl' to the young man is to renounce the pursuits of this world in something like Boethian style and concentrate on the kind of truth which will bring him to God:

> That thee is sent, receyve in buxumnesse;[10]
> The wrestling for this world axeth a fal.
> Her is non hoom, her nis but wildernesse:
> Forth, pilgrim, forth! Forth, beste, out of thy stal!
> Know thy contree, look up, thank God of al:[11]
> Hold the heye[12] wey, and lat thy gost[13] thee lede;
> And trouthe thee shal delivere, it is no drede.[14]

(15–21)

---

10. submissive obedience   11. for everything   12. high   13. spirit   14. without doubt

'Truth' is a late poem – indeed, by one tradition, it is Chaucer's deathbed composition – but has the spareness and moral punchiness found in the best of English devotional versifying of the thirteenth and fourteenth centuries.

Perhaps it should be noted, with regard to Chaucer's religious poetry, that some of it is translated, and some may have been commissioned, which reduces the need to think of it as expressing Chaucer's beliefs. Considering his poetry as a whole, I think Chaucer uses religion as he uses classical ideas or themes, or history, or science, in the service of his own poetic essence, which is mostly conveyed through a many-faceted humour laced with humane pathos. Destructive and anarchic humour rarely offers a coherent corrective point of view, but Chaucer's humour seems to me firmly anchored in a pragmatic and even analytical mode of charitable morality that we often feel is in tune with that of our own times – a statement which it would take a whole book to justify.

Among the greatest of Chaucer's poems are those in which high seriousness and delicate feeling prevail, while such *Canterbury Tales* as those of the Clerk, the Man of Law, the Prioress and the Second Nun are essentially pious. Yet when the whole range of his poetry is considered, we must be ready for matters of faith and morals to be subject to the devices of a great writer whose special forte is humour: approval heartfelt or feigned, hostile scorn or sentimental indulgence, misrepresentation, tedious enlargement or exuberant summarizing, wit both verbal and metrical, shifting perspective, and the alternating foci which mark debate among fictitious characters – a list of techniques and attributes which could be much extended.

Chapter 15. Science and Pseudo-science

There would be no point in encouraging the reader of a general book on Chaucer to find out about the sciences mentioned and discussed in the poetry, if our author's general procedure were simply to show off his knowledge of various sciences and what we now classify as pseudo-sciences. We need to know a little about these teasing fields of medieval intellectual and practical endeavour in order to assess what essence of this or that story, or of event in a story, depends on a Chaucerian perception, or comic distortion, of an accepted belief of his time. That is to say, the full fun or deepest meaning of a poem or passage cannot be savoured without two ingredients being tasted: the state of knowledge of the day, and the Chaucerian version in its poetic context. It takes time to master the relevant branches of knowledge, but fortunately medieval sciences seem to be items in the same parcel of knowledge: religion governs and frames all, and astrology insinuates its lore into almost every other field. It is not too extravagant to suggest that it is when Chaucer is at the very top of his investment form that he is most likely to make secure literary capital out of his learning. This can be seen on a small scale in the Wife of Bath's *Prologue* and on a larger one in *The Knight's Tale* and *Troilus and Criseyde*.

Astronomy and Astrology

In considering the many and important ways in which what we now call 'astronomy' and 'astrology' figure in Chaucer's works, we must first of all understand that in the medieval scheme of knowledge, there was no distinction between the two; they became separate in meaning only in the seventeenth century. Yet Chaucer does use both words. 'Astronomye' was a combination of two things: 'observational astronomy', which was the study, scientific in method, of all the heavenly bodies, including earth though, before the advent of the telescope, it was limited by what could be seen by the naked eye; and 'judicial astronomy', a largely fanciful scheme of the consequences for human beings of astronomical data obtained by observation. To judge by the detail and clear explanation of these matters in Chaucer's *A Treatise on the Astrolabe* (a hand instrument for measuring altitudes and angles in observation of heavenly bodies), and the still more sophisticated exposition in *The*

Equatorie of the Planets, which may be his translation of the Latin version of a work of Arab origin, Chaucer spent much time on 'astronomye'. So it is not surprising that time and again he builds it into his poetry, often making it a motivational key to the action in a serious vein, and at other times, because he is a comic poet, making comic use of it and putting knowledge of quite complicated astronomical calculations into the heads of such unlikely characters as the Host, and the cock in *The Nun's Priest's Tale*. Though Thomas Aquinas (c. 1225–74) managed to build judicial astronomy into the Christian system, Chaucer evidently felt at liberty to write sceptically about it. But his main use of what we now call astrology, apart from locating the time of day or season, is to give significance or psychological explanation to the event or frame of mind it introduces. Its importance in Chaucer's poetic art is proved by his habit of adding astrological embroidery to stories in which his original authors, such as Boccaccio, had none.

The heavens were conceived according to the system of the Greek astronomer Ptolemy (*fl.* second century A.D.), in whose most influential work, *The Almagest*, the Earth was an unmoving body at the centre of the cosmos, round which all the other planets (the word means 'wanderers') revolved in different ways, while the great mass of other stars and constellations, the so-called 'fixed stars', all worked to one rule as they turned from east to west. The planets were Saturn, Jupiter, Mars, the Sun, Venus, Mercury and the Moon, the latter being nearest to Earth and Saturn being farthest from it. Each planet was thought to be placed on an invisible sphere at the centre of which was Earth. On the eighth sphere, beyond the sphere of Saturn, were all the fixed stars, and beyond that was the ninth sphere, the Primum Mobile (First Mover), which the love of God, who was outside even that, turned so as to give motion to all the spheres.

The fixed stars on that eighth sphere revolved from east to west in just under twenty-four hours, so that each new night they would be seen to have shifted a tiny bit to the west. They in fact moved thirty degrees per month, and since there are 360 degrees in the complete circle, they took a year to come back to their starting point. Against their united movement the planets, including the Sun, circled, slightly waveringly. In relation to the Sun's circling path, which was called the *eccentric*, the six others moved, each at its own speed, and never more than eight degrees away from this eccentric.

To go back to those 360 degrees of the circle: in relation to the band round the heavens in which the Sun circled the Earth, each sector of 30 degrees was named after a nearby fixed star or constellation, and was

209

thus given a zodiacal sign. When Chaucer in *The House of Fame* (932) writes of 'the eyryssh bestes', he presumably means the signs of the zodiac, since most of the signs have the names of animals (the Greek *zoon* means animal). In astrology, these signs have characteristics which, to some extent, determine their influence. The signs are: Aries (Ram); Taurus (Bull); Gemini (Twins); Cancer (Crab); Leo (Lion); Virgo (Virgin); Libra (Scales); Scorpio (Scorpion); Sagittarius (Archer); Capricornus (Goat); Aquarius (Water Carrier); and Pisces (Fishes).

At any time of the day or night, six of these would be above the horizon and six below, in one or other of the twelve 'houses'. Unlike the twelve zodiacal divisions, which rotated in the sky with, indeed as essential components of, the fixed stars, the houses, like the hour figures on a clock, remained stationary, the first being just below the eastern horizon. Since any sign or planet that happened to be in it would soon rise above the horizon, that first house was known as the ascendant. As soon as a sign or planet rose above the horizon, it would begin to exert more influence. To pursue the clock simile, the sign or planet in so doing would be like a clock hand leaving the last hour of the night and moving into the first hour of daylight.

Clearly, since day and night vary in length throughout the year, the size of the houses must vary too, as well as the two-hour time divisions notionally allotted to each of them for the placing of planets – or anything else for that matter. So we come to the 'hours inequal' which Chaucer often mentions. In midwinter, the hours inequal of daylight will be only about forty minutes long, and at midsummer they will be eighty minutes long. Ordinary clock time was rendered as 'hours equal', or 'hours of the clock'. The planets as they rotated presided over each of the 'hours inequal' in turn, and the planet which occupied the first hour after daybreak (note that, in contrast, the first *house* is the one just *before* daybreak) gives its name to the day. Since there are seven planets and twenty-four hours, and seven divides into twenty-four three times, leaving three over, for each succeeding day you must go three planets along the established order to find the name of the day. The order, which I now repeat, is Saturn, Jupiter, Mars, Sun, Venus, Mercury, Moon. So, starting at the beginning, Saturn rules Saturday, Sun Sunday, Moon Monday, Mars Tuesday (*mardi* in French), Mercury Wednesday (*mercredi* in French), Jupiter Thursday (*jeudi* in French), and Venus Friday (*vendredi* in French). The following table, slightly modified from that which appears in M. W. Grose, *Chaucer*, 1967, p. 51, shows the days of the week, the 'inequal hours' and the planets which dominate them throughout the week:

Inequal hours	Saturday	Sunday	Monday	Tuesday	Wednesday	Thursday	Friday
1	Saturn	Sun	Moon	Mars	Mercury	Jupiter	Venus
2	Jupiter	Venus	Saturn	Sun	Moon	Mars	Mercury
3	Mars	Mercury	Jupiter	Venus	Saturn	Sun	Moon
4	Sun	Moon	Mars	Mercury	Jupiter	Venus	Saturn
5	Venus	Saturn	Sun	Moon	Mars	Mercury	Jupiter
6	Mercury	Jupiter	Venus	Saturn	Sun	Moon	Mars
7	Moon	Mars	Mercury	Jupiter	Venus	Saturn	Sun
8	Saturn	Sun	Moon	Mars	Mercury	Jupiter	Venus
9	Jupiter	Venus	Saturn	Sun	Moon	Mars	Mercury
10	Mars	Mercury	Jupiter	Venus	Saturn	Sun	Moon
11	Sun	Moon	Mars	Mercury	Jupiter	Venus	Saturn
12	Venus	Saturn	Sun	Moon	Mars	Mercury	Jupiter
13	Mercury	Jupiter	Venus	Saturn	Sun	Moon	Mars
14	Moon	Mars	Mercury	Jupiter	Venus	Saturn	Sun
15	Saturn	Sun	Moon	Mars	Mercury	Jupiter	Venus
16	Jupiter	Venus	Saturn	Sun	Moon	Mars	Mercury
17	Mars	Mercury	Jupiter	Venus	Saturn	Sun	Moon
18	Sun	Moon	Mars	Mercury	Jupiter	Venus	Saturn
19	Venus	Saturn	Sun	Moon	Mars	Mercury	Jupiter
20	Mercury	Jupiter	Venus	Saturn	Sun	Moon	Mars
21	Moon	Mars	Mercury	Jupiter	Venus	Saturn	Sun
22	Saturn	Sun	Moon	Mars	Mercury	Jupiter	Venus
23	Jupiter	Venus	Saturn	Sun	Moon	Mars	Mercury
24	Mars	Mercury	Jupiter	Venus	Saturn	Sun	Moon

The next table gives a general idea of the kinds of influence the seven planets were supposed to exert. Special astral events, such as the unusual conjunction of the Moon, Saturn and Jupiter in the sign of Cancer, which caused a storm and forced Criseyde to stay in Pandarus's house and so enable Troilus to become her lover, cannot be dealt with here, and should be considered individually while reading the particular poems in which they occur:

Planet	Representative Metal	Attributes, effects or influence
Saturn	Lead	Ill-luck and malevolence; cold, dull and heavy; sickness; old age.
Jupiter	Tin	Good luck; prophecy.
Mars	Iron	Evil; bloodshed; boasting; anger.
Sun	Gold	Life; good luck; speed; wisdom; generosity.

Planet	Representative Metal	Attributes, effects or influence
Venus	Copper	Beauty; love of two kinds: tender, loving, motherly; passionate, lascivious, promiscuous.
Mercury	Quicksilver	Changeableness; science and commerce; theft.
Moon	Silver	Fickleness; madness; frustration.

In concluding these brevities on astronomy and astrology, I note the prominence of classical, pagan deities and their influence. As Derek Brewer puts it (*An Introduction to Chaucer*, 1984, p. 99):

The ancient gods and goddesses, Jupiter, Mars, Venus, Mercury, etc. were still strong enough to be violently attacked by St Augustine in his *The City of God* (413–27 A.D.). The attacks by him and others were successful, and by the sixth century they were finished as sacred powers. This released them for other valuable purposes in the Christian Middle Ages.

These purposes, as far as we readers of Chaucer are concerned, were literary, involving psychological, metaphorical, tragic and comic enrichment of the poetry. Chaucer is our first great exemplar of such uses, though not the only one in the fourteenth century.

Medicine

In the frequency with which Chaucer displays medical knowledge and gives details of medical processes he shows that, as with astrology, he is particularly fascinated by the subject. He parades his interest in it in much the same way as he parades anything else in his poetry: with knowledge and sly humour, often equivocally, and with his eye fixed serenely with benedictory or condemnatory glow on its practitioners, whether they be divine or human. So it is instructive for a reader of Chaucer to learn a little about medieval medicine as it is reflected in the poetry, and a start might be made by reading the description of the Doctor of Physic in the *Prologue* to *The Canterbury Tales* (411–44).

That Doctor, I am afraid, is one of his creator's many targets for satire, and not only because his job brought him such profits that he wore rich clothes and 'lovede gold in special'. To begin with, 'he was grounded in astronomye', and we know that 'judicial astronomy' (see p. 208) is meant because

> Wel koude he fortunen the ascendent
> Of his ymages for his pacient.

(I, 417–18)

In more than one place in his poetry, Chaucer expresses the same distrust of astrology that he makes plain to his son in his *Treatise on the Astrolabe*:

Natheles these ben observaunces of judicial matere and rytes of payens,[1] in whiche my spirit hath no feith, ne knowing of her *horoscopum*.

(II, 4, 57–60)

'The cause of everich maladye' was to be found in the disposition of matter in the patient. The fundamental properties of all matter were thought to lie in two pairs of contraries, Hot and Cold, and Dry and Moist; four properties which in paired combinations constituted the four elements, Fire, Air, Earth and Water. Hot and Dry produced Fire; Hot and Moist produced Air; Cold and Dry produced Earth; and Cold and Moist produced Water. The constitution of human beings, as of anything else below the Moon, was made up of varieties of these combinations, and the resulting dominant physical characteristics were called Humours.

To humours we must add the term Complexion, which meant not the colour and quality of the facial skin, as it does today, but temperament; and temperament was determined by the combination of elements which produced a person's humour. Accordingly, there were four main kinds of complexion:

Choleric   partaking of fire, which is hot and dry. Choleric people tend to be thin, bad-tempered and quarrelsome, like the Reeve. Its body liquid is yellow bile.

Sanguine   partaking of air, which is hot and moist. Sanguine people tend to be generous, happy and attracted to the opposite sex. Chaucer tells us that his Franklin was sanguine of complexion (I, 333). Its body liquid is blood.

Phlegmatic   partaking of water, which is cold and moist. Phlegmatic people tend to be fattish, lethargic, dull and slow-tempered. Its body liquid is phlegm.

Melancholy   partaking of earth, which is cold and dry. Melancholy people tend to be gloomy, sullen and covetous. The concept had not yet developed the richness of its sixteenth-century meaning, involving sensitive meditation and introspection. But Troilus is surely melancholy in this sense when languishing for his lost Criseyde amid the concern of his friends for the cause of his pallor:

1. pagans

> And al this nas but his malencolie,
> That he hadde of hymself swich fantasie.

(V, 622)

The body liquid of melancholy is black bile, an imaginary fluid.

People were thought to have something of every humour in their constitutions, and the balance they possessed came out not only in character, but also in their health; and this is where the Doctor of Physic comes in, with his knowledge of 'astronomye'. He knew that the four humours each dominated a different six-hour stretch of the twenty-four hours: blood from midnight till six in the morning, choler from six a.m. till noon, melancholy from noon till six in the evening, and phlegm from six p.m. till midnight. He also knew that each sign of the zodiac influenced both character and health, and that each sign governed a particular part of the body, thus: Aries governs the head and face; Taurus the neck and Adam's apple; Gemini the shoulders, arms and hands; Cancer the breasts, sides, spleen and lungs; Leo the stomach, heart and back; Virgo the belly and intestines; Libra the navel and groin; Scorpio the genitals, bladder and bowels; Sagittarius the thighs; Capricorn the knees; Aquarius the lower legs; and Pisces the feet.

The planets also ruled parts of the body and the humours. So, when a patient's humours were out of balance – a condition assumed in all ill-health – the physician had to make a number of astronomical calculations to find out what was wrong, and how and when to treat the condition. Blood-letting and purgation were common, and of course herbal and dietary remedies were used. Chaucer seems to have known about herbs, and besides often raiding the herbal pharmacopoeia to send characters to sleep, or to heal them, or give them sweet breath as in the case of Absalom, he felicitously credits the Garden of Love in *The Parliament of Fowls* with every natural quality, including herbs, which will preserve people's health and youth:

> Th'air of that place so attempre was
> That nevere was ther grevaunce of hot ne cold;
> There wex ek every holsom spice and gras;
> No man may there waxe sek ne old . . .

(204–7)

And in Chaucer's brilliant burlesque of so many genres and fields of knowledge, *The Nun's Priest's Tale*, the wife of that proud cockerel Chauntecleer, the 'faire damoysele Pertelote', believing that his ominous dream derives from the unsettled state of his body, advises him:

> A day or two ye shul have digestyves
> Of wormes, er ye take your laxatyves
> Of lawriol,[2] centaure,[3] and fumetere,[4]
> Or elles of ellebor,[5] that groweth there,
> Of katapuce,[6] or of gaitrys beryis,[7]
> Of herbe yve, growing in oure yeerd, ther mery is;
> Pekke hem up right as they growe and ete hem yn.
>
> (VI, 2961–7)

Alchemy

For us, this is a less important pseudo-science than astrology or physiognomy, both of which are often met in Chaucer's poetry; but brief mention of it must be made, not only for the sake of *The Canon's Yeoman's Tale*, which is a satire upon it, but because in medieval thinking, which was largely based on inherited authority, it had links with religion and magic and so was an element of which account must be taken. Alchemy was the predecessor of chemistry, to which genuine science – that is, inquiry based upon experimentally sound observation – it gave its physical bases of operation. The word 'alchemy' comes to us from Greek through Arabic, and means, 'transmuting'. Alchemy was concerned with the transmutation of base metals into gold or other precious metal, and with the search for the philosopher's stone, which was imagined as a solid substance that was supposed to work as a catalyst in the transmuting. An alchemist or any other magician was often called a philosopher, an appellation glanced at unfavourably by Chaucer in his idealized portrait of the Clerk in the *General Prologue*:

> But al be that he was a philosophre,
> Yet hadde he but litel gold in cofre . . .
>
> (I, 297–8)

Since transmutation figures in Christian belief, not only in the transubstantiation (of bread and wine during communion), but also in the process of regeneration which leads to redemption, the alchemists claimed that their work was in harmony with the divine purpose. Their statements describing their theory and practice were conducted in an arcane terminology which drew on existing disciplines such as astrology and religious philosophy, and thus constituted an occult mystery.

Several critics, in writing on Chaucer's references to alchemy, and on *The Canon's Yeoman's Tale* in particular, mention comparable

2. spurge-laurel 3. centaury 4. fumitory 5. hellebore 6. lesser spurge 7. dogwood

pseudo-sciences which have currency in our own age, their aim being to warn us against feeling superior to our medieval forbears. Chaucer's treatment of the subject of alchemy here is satirical. One interesting, and I believe tenable, theory is that the alchemical work described in *The Canon's Yeoman's Tale* is allegorical, a figurative black mass which parallels the Sacrament and in fact accomplishes – in a downward direction to hell – the transmutation of the souls of the practitioners. It is one measure of the difference between Chaucer and his friend and fellow-poet, Gower, that in Book I V of his *Confessio Amantis* the latter gives a straightforward account of the discipline of alchemy without suggesting that it is a bogus science. Chaucer, at the end of *The Canon's Yeoman's Tale*, neither comments on the validity or otherwise of alchemy nor allows his narrator to do so. The Yeoman, after quoting an imaginary Plato to the effect that Christ only allows discovery of the philosopher's stone to men especially preferred by him, includes in his last thoughts on the subject only a slightly equivocal condemnation of alchemists:

> Thanne conclude I thus, sith that God of hevene
> Ne wil nat that the philosophres nevene [8]
> How that a man shal come unto this stoon,
> I rede, as for the beste, lete it goon.
> For whoso maketh God his adversarie,
> As for to werken any thyng in contrarie
> Or his wil, certes, never shal he thryve,
> Thogh that he multiplie terme of his lyve.

> (VIII, 1472–9)

The connection between alchemy and astrology is made by the well-understood relation between particular planets and metals. The Yeoman speaks of the 'foure spirites and the bodies seven' which are essential to alchemical operations. The four spirits were quicksilver, trisulphide of arsenic ('orpyment'), sal ammoniac and brimstone, and the 'bodies sevene' were gold which comes from the Sun, silver from the Moon, iron from Mars, quicksilver from Mercury, lead from Saturn, tin from Jupiter and copper from Venus. These associations appear in many places in Chaucer's poetry. The process which eventually produced the philosopher's stone was also sevenfold, involving distillation, congelation, solution, descension, sublimation, calcination and fixation. The great literary monument to the bogus art is Ben Jonson's play *The Alchemist*, in which the terms and processes are absorbed in an uproarious satire directed at Avarice, the plot of which Coleridge considered the best in all

8. make known

English plays. As an afterthought, I might add that there is, and was in the Middle Ages, a scientific method of 'increasing' gold, though not exactly of 'transmuting' other metals into it.

Numerology and Number Symbolism

Numerology began as a branch of ancient mathematics with religious connotations, but is now scarcely a factor in either scientific knowledge or orthodox religious belief, though it has currency in such fields as astrology and necromancy. But in the Middle Ages it was an essential part of the body of theological knowledge and practice, expounded and blessed as it was by such chief fathers of the Church as St Augustine, who saw in it one way to the understanding of God and his visible creation. It was a branch of knowledge taken over from the Greeks and Hebrews during the establishment of Christianity and, as such, was as important for artists as for theologians. Most of the important poets of the Middle Ages, including Chaucer, used it both as a system which helped them to find significant poetic structure and point meaning, and as a reservoir for significant metaphor, especially whenever the subject of their poetry related to religion.

Along with other branches of pseudo-knowledge which until the Renaissance had been used in the interpretation of classical and Biblical literature, numerology became discredited in Bible studies when Erasmus (1466–1536) developed scholarly criticism of the Bible. But it survived as an aesthetic discipline, and has been shown to be of cardinal importance in the major works of Spenser and Milton, and to have exercised symbolic force in poems by Dryden and Shadwell which were composed in the last years of the seventeenth century. In the eighteenth century Fielding used symbolic numbers in the structure of *Joseph Andrews*, and in this century Alban Berg has used them as a factor in musical composition. Without the minor key of numerology, therefore, the music of much traditional English literature can be heard only imperfectly.

Numerology originated in the ideas of Pythagoras and Plato, both of whom thought that mathematics could help to explain the principles upon which creation and the cosmos worked. Mathematics, Plato considered, made it possible for the inquirer to see beyond the changeable phenomena of life, and to contemplate the pure Forms behind the particular and the temporal. Number gave structure to things both concrete and abstract, and so helped to explain order, one of the main principles of creation, permanence and morality. Early Christianity, guided by the Fathers whose culture depended not only on the Bible, but on the inherited wisdom of classical Greece and Rome, sought and found, in many areas of thought, unity with the past. As far as number was concerned, the Bible must be found to reflect the theological values and insights of Pythagoras and Plato. Solomon's words to God about Creation, in the Book of Wisdom, seemed to confirm the rightness of this approach: 'Thou hast ordered all things in number and measure and weight' (XI, 21).

There is, of course, a qualitative difference between Biblical number-lore, with its largely metaphorical and mystical bearings which were partly derived from Cabbalistic practice, and the sophisticated mathematical theories of Pythagoras which, as in the case of music, were often scientific as well as religious. Plato developed mystical approaches to number – 'mystical' indicating a spiritual level of meaning over and above the purely literal level – which Christians found congenial, and it was this amalgam upon which medieval poets drew. Some idea of the system familiar to Chaucer and his contemporaries must now be given.

Pythagoras's greatest discovery concerning the mathematical ratios involved in harmonic relationships in music produced the 'divine tetraktus', that is, the number 10 considered as the sum of 1,2,3,4. These first four numbers (though 1, being an indivisible unity, was 'no number') were thought of geometrically: thus 1 was a point, 2 a line, 3 a triangle or surface, and 4 a tetrahedron, which was solid. Next in importance to the tetraktus came Plato's perception of two series, which he evoked to explain creation and the 'world soul'. Both series started at unity, one moving thence through the first even number, and the other through the first odd number, thus: 1,2,4,8; 1,3,9,27.

The culmination of Platonic thought in this respect was that everything was essentially number, a concept to which the more pragmatic Aristotle – whose philosophy was also triumphantly accommodated to the medieval Christian system – was hostile. He observed that if everything was conditioned by number, many things would turn out to be the same as each other. But correspondences and symbols were the very stuff of medieval thinking.

In number symbolism, the divisors and multiples of all numbers, as well as their potentialities in addition and subtraction, could be important. Numbers such as 6 and 28, which are the sum of all their divisors, excluding themselves, were considered perfect; numbers whose divisors added up to more than themselves, such as 12, were thought superabundant, and were especially revered on that account. Some of the applications of the above appear in the following brief selection of medieval, largely Christian, number symbols. I give first the mathematical idea or ideas, and then examples of their significance which a sophisticated reader or listener would have been expected to know and to apply.

1 Unity; God.

2 Diversity; unlimit; evil, disorder, strife.

3 Perfect harmony (unity + diversity); limit, good; the Trinity.

4 Perfection (the first square, 2 × 2); gospels, apostles, cardinal graces, senses of allegory; the quadrivium; elements, humours; seasons, winds, points of the compass.

5 The union of the first even and odd numbers, and hence the prevailing number in nature and art; Christ's wounds.

6 The sum of the first three numbers; the Trinity; the days of Creation.

7 Prime number: the sum of 3 and 4, which are both good numbers; mystical in many contexts; the climacteric of all diseases; the sins; the virtues; the Joys of the Virgin; the Sorrows of the Virgin; innumerable biblical and other referents.

8 The first cube, 2 × 2 × 2; new beginning and stability; eternity; Christ; baptism; Resurrection; circumcision; Beatitudes; the number who survived the Flood.

10 The Tetraktus; the Commandments; the number of strings on David's harp.

12 'Superabundant'; the New Jerusalem (see Revelation); the Apostles; 144 Virgins, 144,000 population of the twelve tribes, etc.

Of Chaucer's works, the one most obviously numerological in structure is *The Book of the Duchess*. Its subject, the restoration of the soul to unity in spite of being disharmonized by grief, is the same as that of *Pearl* by the Gawain-poet. *Pearl* and *Sir Gawain and the Green Knight* both have 101 stanzas (101 being a prime number, in which unity figures twice) and those of *Pearl* are in twenty linked sets, all but one of which are fives. Consideration of number is often linked with astrological insights (the signs of the zodiac are twelve in number), as in the Parson's *Prologue*. The line total of *The Book of the Duchess* is 1333, the digits of which add up to the important 10, and the line total of *The Parliament of Fowls*, which is written almost entirely in seven-line stanzas, is 699, the digits of which add up to 24, and not 700. 24 is twice the superabundant dozen, and therefore particularly auspicious.

Other Science and Lore

It remains to consider briefly some other branches of knowledge given literary transcendence in Chaucer's poetry, and firstly, physiognomy, on which he drew increasingly in his later works. Physiognomy is the art of judging both character and disposition from the features of the face or the form of the body, and derives ultimately from Aristotle's observations of animals. The bulldog jaw and the high forehead, which presuppose determination and strong intellect respectively, are examples of a still common popular lore. Physiognomy remains a potential field for strictly scientific inquiry on the borders of physiology and psychology, and should not be thought of as quaint medieval superstition.

As early as *The Book of the Duchess*, in the idealized description by the 'man in blak' of his lady, we learn that nobody who had ever lived could have detected 'Yn al hir face a wikked sygne' (917), in which the word 'sign' takes us beyond the conventional Platonic association of virtue with physical beauty, into the mystery of physiognomy. Particular features (a word which reminds me that late nineteenth- and early twentieth-century slang vocabulary contained the word 'fizzogg' – physiognomy – for face) indicated particular qualities of character or disposition.

In *Troilus and Criseyde* there is a full physiognomical description of the ill-fated couple and Diomede (Book V, 799–840), and in the *General Prologue* to *The Canterbury Tales* many of the characters are described in such terms, their chief qualities being presented through analysis of the appearance of face and body, in which the eyes and complexion (in the modern sense) seem to be most important. The Monk, for example, after his preferred activities and his clothes have been described, is summed up with the confirmatory physiognomical evidence:

> His heed was balled, that shoon as any glas,
> And eek his face, as he hadde been enoynt.
> He was a lord ful fat and in good poynt;
> His eyen stepe, and rollynge[9] in his heed,
> That stemed as a forneys[10] of a leed[11] ...

> (I, 198–202)

A distinctly Sanguine type, no doubt. The Prioress, Miller, Pardoner and Summoner among other characters in the *Prologue*, are given the treatment, but the subtlest physiognomical description is probably that given to the Wife of Bath. It comes in odd lines interspersed with details of her clothing, life history and character:

9. big 10. furnace 11. cauldron

> Boold was hir face, and fair, and reed of hewe ...
> Gat-toothed was she ...
> A foot-mantel aboute her hipes large.

> (I, 458, 468, 472)

People with teeth set wide apart were considered by physiognomists to be tricksters, gluttons and lechers, and women with wide hips were thought to be lascivious. But the Wife herself, in the wonderful self-revelations in the *Prologue* to her tale, elevates the explanation of her spaced teeth to a goddess-like level of lovingness:

> Gat-tothed I was, and that bicam me wel;
> I had the prente of seinte Venus seel.[12]

> (III, 603–4)

Her ensuing self-analysis confirms the importance of astrological lore in all such matters.

Many characters in *The Tales*, both subtle ones and grotesques, are considered physiognomically, and of the latter the miller's daughter in *The Reeve's Tale* is the most vivid, in that her listed characteristics at the beginning prepare us for her immediate accord with the strange student, Aleyn, when she finds him in her bed:

> This wenche thikke and wel ygrowen was,
> With kamus[13] nose, and eyen greye as glas,
> With buttokes brode, and brestes rounde and hye;
> But right fair was hire heer, I wol nat lye.

> (I, 3973–6)

Branches of knowledge or lore which are of minor importance in the way they figure in Chaucer's poetry are optics and lapidary lore. Optics is romanced about when mirrors come into the story in *The Squire's Tale*, and fantastically resorted to by the adulterous May in *The Merchant's Tale* when the old man January recovers his sight and sees her coupling with young Damian in the pear tree. Lapidary lore, which gives precise significance to precious stones, figures occasionally: the little choirboy in *The Prioress's Tale* is referred to as

> This gemme of chastite, this emeraude,
> And eek of martirdom the ruby bright ...

> (VII, 1799–1800)

Emerald indicates success in life as well as chastity, and ruby has many

12. the print of holy Venus's seal   13. snub

virtuous powers: banishing grief, diverting the mind from evil thought, and counteracting poison, all of which fit the context.

Dream-lore, like physiognomy, is related to psychology. I shall discuss it separately from the medieval literary convention of dream poetry (see Chapter 9), in which the matter of a poem is set in motion and largely contained within the frame of a dream or vision. Yet it is in the *Proem* to Book I of just such a poem, *The House of Fame*, that Chaucer, at a comparatively early stage of his writing life, speculates on the nature of dreams and their interpretation. In all three of his Love Visions, Chaucer mentions the commentary by Macrobius (*fl.* 400 A.D.) on Cicero's *Somnium Scipionis* (*The Dream of Scipio*), in which the classification of dreams is attempted, and he often draws upon comparable material from *The Romance of the Rose*, which is itself a dream poem in which discussion of dream-lore is as indebted to Macrobius as Chaucer was.

Chaucer's speculation on the classification and interpretation of dreams in *The House of Fame* proceeds with a hesitancy and absence of clear definition quite different from the certitude of Macrobius, who lists five types of dream, the first of which, *somnium*, exists in five varieties. The five types are: *somnium*, *visio* and *oraculum*; *insomnium* and *phantasma*. Of the first three, all of which are prophetic, the *somnium* is the commonest form, and it requires a skilled interpreter; in the *visio* a vision of a future event appears; in the *oraculum* a person, spirit or divinity appears and, as an oracle, says what is going to happen. The *insomnium* and *phantasma* are not prophetic, but indicate the physical or mental state of the dreamer; an *insomnium* is dreamt as a result of stress of some kind, and a *phantasma* is what it sounds like, a delusion. Chaucer simply poses the possibilities – slightly inaccurately – and remains doubtfully questioning. The literary sense of such a stance emerges with humour in the almost surrealistic confusion of the poem's main narrative material, which of course is dreamt. But in Book V of *Troilus and Criseyde*, as the hero moves towards his tragic disillusion, his dreams figure with as much atmospheric power as the dreams of, say, Shakespeare's Clarence in *Richard III*, Antigonus in *The Winter's Tale*, or Katharine of Aragon in *Henry VIII*.

Not surprisingly in view of his scepticism about dreams, which parallels his impatience with judicial astronomy, Chaucer's most memorable treatment of dream-lore is the wonderful burlesque debate about it in *The Nun's Priest's Tale*. When Chanticleer relates to Pertelote his dream of the predatory fox, which in the terms of Macrobius would be a *visio*, she, with wifely concern, chides him and treats it as an *insomnium*, the remedy for which is dietary and herbal. Chanticleer's extremely long and earnest riposte – it goes on for 190 lines – is full of historical examples of dreamers, comically treated; and of course, in the upshot of the *Tale*, Chanticleer is right and Pertelote wrong.

To conclude this selective tour round Chaucer's scientific sites, I refer briefly to the subject lectured on by that early, satirical example of a pedantic schoolmaster, the eagle in *The House of Fame*. His lecture which occupies most of the last 400 lines of Book II, turns to comic use two seriously held medieval propositions. The first is that everything in nature has a habitat, to which it strives to go by instinct:

> ... every kyndely thyng that is
> Hath a kyndely stede ther he
> May best in hyt conserved by;
> Unto which place every thyng,
> Thorgh his kyndely enclynyng,
> Moveth for to come to,
> Whan that hyt is away therfro ...

$$(730-36)$$

This idea preceded the theory of gravitation. The second proposition concerns the way in which sound is defined and its working explained, beginning with the bald statement: 'Soun ys noght but eyr ybroken' (765). But the eagle rapidly turns this into a new and ludicrous assertion that all sounds fly upward to the House of Fame, that being their natural habitat; and the House of Fame, when we come to it, is an extraordinary building which behaves like a Palace of Rumour. Most ludicrous of all, the eagle describes the transformation of speech, when it reaches the House of Fame, into the physical form of the person who spoke it. The transition from accepted medieval scientific belief, as stated by Boethius and Vincent of Beauvais, which is where the eagle's lecture began, to the fantastic and absurd application at the end, is a nice example of Chaucer's literary method.

Select Bibliography

Listed in order of recommendation within each section:

Text

F. N. ROBINSON, (ed.), *The Works of Geoffrey Chaucer*, second edition (Oxford, 1957). Source of all quotations and many annotations and comments in this book. The standard work.

Language

NORMAN DAVIS, Douglas Gray, Patricia Ingham, Anne Wallace-Hadrill, *A Chaucer Glossary* (Oxford, 1979). Essential as a check, especially when working with varied editions of the poems.

DAVID BURNLEY, *A Guide to Chaucer's Language* (Macmillan, 1983). Exhaustive and especially good on register, but fails to include guidance on pronunciation.

Criticism

DEREK PEARSALL, *The Canterbury Tales* (Allen and Unwin, 1985). Invaluable for study of *The Canterbury Tales*. Sane and thorough, and takes account of a wide range of criticism. Good reading.

J. A. BURROW (ed.), *Geoffrey Chaucer* (Penguin, 1969). Fine selection of short critical extracts from all periods, including the medieval, with informative connecting editorial matter.

EDWARD WAGENKNECHT (ed.), *Chaucer: Modern Essays in Criticism* (Oxford, 1959). The standard selection of mid-century criticism.

P. M. KEAN, *Chaucer and the Making of English Poetry* (Routledge and Kegan Paul, 1972). Volume I: Love Vision and Debate; Volume II: The Art of Narrative. Deals with almost all the major poetry, and emphasizes themes.

PIERO BOITANI (ed.), *Chaucer and the Italian Trecento* (Cambridge, 1983). Authoritative contributions by various hands on the Italian influence in Chaucer, centring on what he drew on from Dante, Petrarch and Boccaccio.

CHARLES MUSCATINE, *Chaucer and the French Tradition* (University of California, 1957). Still the best book on this essential matter.

JOHN M. FYLER, *Chaucer and Ovid* (Yale, 1979). Possibly a bit specialized, but makes clear an aspect of Chaucer's work which is often taken for granted.

J. MANN, *Chaucer and Medieval Estates Satire* (Cambridge, 1973). Places a main aspect of Chaucer's work securely within its period.

D. W. ROBERTSON JR, *A Preface to Chaucer: Studies in Medieval Perspectives* (Princeton, 1962). An immensely scholarly reading of Chaucer, which has been challenged owing to its insistence on a religious dimension to virtually everything Chaucer wrote.

Background and Sources

DEREK BREWER (ed.), *Geoffrey Chaucer, Writers and their Background Series* (Bell, 1974). An authoritative detailed anthology which I find indispensable.

ROBERT P. MILLER (ed.), *Chaucer: Sources and Backgrounds* (Oxford, 1977). Useful extracts, with summary accounts and judgements, from many of Chaucer's source authors and writers who influenced him.

N. R. HAVELY (ed. and trans.), *Chaucer's Boccaccio* (Brewer, Rowman and Littlefield, 1980). Illuminates *Troilus and Criseyde*, *The Knight's Tale* and *The Franklin's Tale* by presenting and introducing relevant extracts from Boccaccio and his sources.

MURIEL BOWDEN, *A Commentary on the General Prologue to the Canterbury Tales* (Condor, 1967). Voluminous information about the characters and their places within fourteenth-century society.

Index

227

FOR THE BEST IN PAPERBACKS, LOOK FOR THE 🐧

In every corner of the world, on every subject under the sun, Penguin represents quality and variety – the very best in publishing today.

For complete information about books available from Penguin – including Puffins, Penguin Classics and Arkana – and how to order them, write to us at the appropriate address below. Please note that for copyright reasons the selection of books varies from country to country.

In the United Kingdom: Please write to *Dept E.P., Penguin Books Ltd, Harmondsworth, Middlesex, UB7 0DA.*

If you have any difficulty in obtaining a title, please send your order with the correct money, plus ten per cent for postage and packaging, to *PO Box No 11, West Drayton, Middlesex*

In the United States: Please write to *Dept BA, Penguin, 299 Murray Hill Parkway, East Rutherford, New Jersey 07073*

In Canada: Please write to *Penguin Books Canada Ltd, 2801 John Street, Markham, Ontario L3R 1B4*

In Australia: Please write to the *Marketing Department, Penguin Books Australia Ltd, P.O. Box 257, Ringwood, Victoria 3134*

In New Zealand: Please write to the *Marketing Department, Penguin Books (NZ) Ltd, Private Bag, Takapuna, Auckland 9*

In India: Please write to *Penguin Overseas Ltd, 706 Eros Apartments, 56 Nehru Place, New Delhi, 110019*

In the Netherlands: Please write to *Penguin Books Netherlands B.V., Postbus 195, NL–1380AD Weesp*

In West Germany: Please write to *Penguin Books Ltd, Friedrichstrasse 10–12, D–6000 Frankfurt/Main 1*

In Spain: Please write to *Longman Penguin España, Calle San Nicolas 15, E–28013 Madrid*

In Italy: Please write to *Penguin Italia s.r.l., Via Como 4, I-20096 Pioltello (Milano)*

In France: Please write to *Penguin Books Ltd, 39 Rue de Montmorency, F-75003 Paris*

In Japan: Please write to *Longman Penguin Japan Co Ltd, Yamaguchi Building, 2–12–9 Kanda Jimbocho, Chiyoda-Ku, Tokyo 101*

FOR THE BEST IN PAPERBACKS, LOOK FOR THE

PENGUIN CLASSICS

Saint Anselm	**The Prayers and Meditations**
Saint Augustine	**The Confessions**
Bede	**A History of the English Church and People**
Chaucer	**The Canterbury Tales**
	Love Visions
	Troilus and Criseyde
Froissart	**The Chronicles**
Geoffrey of Monmouth	**The History of the Kings of Britain**
Gerald of Wales	**History and Topography of Ireland**
	The Journey through Wales and **The Description of Wales**
Gregory of Tours	**The History of the Franks**
Henryson	**The Testament of Cresseid and Other Poems**
Walter Hilton	**The Ladder of Perfection**
Julian of Norwich	**Revelations of Divine Love**
Thomas à Kempis	**The Imitation of Christ**
William Langland	**Piers the Ploughman**
Sir John Mandeville	**The Travels of Sir John Mandeville**
Marguerite de Navarre	**The Heptameron**
Christine de Pisan	**The Treasure of the City of Ladies**
Marco Polo	**The Travels**
Richard Rolle	**The Fire of Love**
François Villon	**Selected Poems**

FOR THE BEST IN PAPERBACKS, LOOK FOR THE

PENGUIN CLASSICS

ANTHOLOGIES AND ANONYMOUS WORKS

The Age of Bede
Alfred the Great
Beowulf
A Celtic Miscellany
The Cloud of Unknowing and Other Works
The Death of King Arthur
The Earliest English Poems
Early Christian Writings
Early Irish Myths and Sagas
Egil's Saga
King Arthur's Death
The Letters of Abelard and Heloise
Medieval English Verse
Njal's Saga
Seven Viking Romances
Sir Gawain and the Green Knight
The Song of Roland

FOR THE BEST IN PAPERBACKS, LOOK FOR THE 🐧

PENGUIN CLASSICS

FOR THE BEST IN PAPERBACKS, LOOK FOR THE 🐧

PENGUIN CLASSICS

William Hazlitt	**Selected Writings**
Thomas Hobbes	**Leviathan**
Samuel Johnson/ James Boswell	**A Journey to the Western Islands of Scotland and The Journal of a Tour to the Hebrides**
Charles Lamb	**Selected Prose**
Samuel Richardson	**Clarissa**
	Pamela
Richard Brinsley Sheridan	**The School for Scandal and Other Plays**
Adam Smith	**The Wealth of Nations**
Tobias Smollett	**The Expedition of Humphry Clinker**
	The Life and Adventures of Sir Launcelot Greaves
Richard Steele and Joseph Addison	Selections from the **Tatler** and the **Spectator**
Laurence Sterne	**The Life and Opinions of Tristram Shandy, Gentleman**
	A Sentimental Journey Through France and Italy
Jonathan Swift	**Gulliver's Travels**
Sir John Vanbrugh	**Four Comedies**

FOR THE BEST IN PAPERBACKS, LOOK FOR THE 🐧

PENGUIN LITERARY CRITICISM

The English Novel   Walter Allen

In this 'refreshingly alert' (*The Times Literary Supplement*) landmark panorama of English fiction, the development of the novel is traced from *Pilgrim's Progress* to Joyce and Lawrence.

Film as Film   V. F. Perkins

Acknowledging the unique qualities of cinema as essentially a bastard medium – neither purely a visual nor a dramatic art – this pioneering text remains 'one of the most sophisticated and commendable works of film criticism' – *Tribune*

A Short History of English Literature   Ifor Evans

'He relates the arts to society instead of penning them in his study ... He is fair to all and gushes over none ... a mastery of phrase which makes the writing lively without being exhaustingly exhibitionistic' – Ivor Brown in the *Observer*

The Modern World   Ten Great Writers   Malcolm Bradbury

From Conrad to Kafka, from Proust to Pirandello, Professor Bradbury provides a fresh introduction to ten influential writers of the modern age and the Modernist movement. Each, in their individual way, followed Ezra Pound's famous dictum – 'Make it new'.

Art and Literature   Sigmund Freud

Volume 14 of the *Penguin Freud Library* contains Freud's major essays on Leonardo, Dostoyevsky and Michelangelo, plus shorter pieces on Shakespeare, the nature of creativity and much more.

The Literature of the United States   Marcus Cunliffe

'Still the best short history [of American literature] ... written with notable critical tact' – Warner Berthoff. 'Cunliffe retains the happy faculty (which he shares with Edmund Wilson) of reading familiar books with fresh eyes and of writing in an engaging style' – Howard Mumford Jones

PENGUIN LITERARY CRITICISM

Modernism Malcolm Bradbury and James McFarlane (eds.)

A brilliant collection of essays dealing with every aspect of literature and culture during the period 1890–1930 – from Apollinaire and Brecht to Yeats and Zola.

The New Pelican Guide to English Literature Boris Ford (ed.)

The indispensable critical guide to English literature in eight volumes, erudite yet accessible. From the ages of Chaucer and Shakespeare, via Georgian satirists and Victorian social critics, to the leading writers of the 1980s, all literary life is here.

The Theatre of the Absurd Martin Esslin

This classic study of the dramatists of the Absurd examines the origins, nature and future of a movement whose significance has transcended the bounds of the stage and influenced the whole intellectual climate of our time.

The Theory of the Modern Stage Eric Bentley (ed.)

In this anthology Artaud, Brecht, Stanislavski and other great theatrical theorists reveal the ideas underlying their productions and point to the possibilities of the modern theatre.

Introducing Shakespeare G. B. Harrison

An excellent popular introduction to Shakespeare – the legend, the (tantalizingly ill-recorded) life and the work – in the context of his times: theatrical rivalry, literary piracy, the famous performance of *Richard II* in support of Essex, and the fire which finally destroyed the Globe.

Aspects of the Novel E. M. Forster

'I say that I have never met this kind of perspicacity in literary criticism before. I could quote scores of examples of startling excellence' – Arnold Bennett. Originating in a course of lectures given at Cambridge, *Aspects of the Novel* is full of E. M. Forster's habitual wit, wisdom and freshness of approach.

FOR THE BEST IN PAPERBACKS, LOOK FOR THE

PENGUIN CRITICAL STUDIES

Described by *The Times Educational Supplement* as 'admirable' and 'superb', Penguin Critical Studies is a specially developed series of critical essays on the major works of literature for use by students in universities, colleges and schools.

titles published or in preparation include:

Absalom and Achitophel
The Alchemist
William Blake
The Changeling
Doctor Faustus
Dombey and Son
Don Juan and Other Poems
Emma *and* Persuasion
Great Expectations
The Great Gatsby
Gulliver's Travels
Heart of Darkness
The Poetry of Gerard
   Manley Hopkins
Jane Eyre
Joseph Andrews
Mansfield Park
Middlemarch
The Mill on the Floss
Milton's Shorter Poems
Nostromo

Paradise Lost
A Passage to India
The Poetry of Alexander Pope
Portrait of a Lady
A Portrait of the Artist as a
   Young Man
Return of the Native
Rosenkrantz and Guildenstern
   are Dead
Sons and Lovers
Tennyson
The Waste Land
Tess of the D'Urbervilles
The White Devil/
   The Duchess of Malfi
Wordsworth
Wuthering Heights
Yeats

FOR THE BEST IN PAPERBACKS, LOOK FOR THE 🐧

PENGUIN CRITICAL STUDIES

Described by *The Times Educational Supplement* as 'admirable' and 'superb', Penguin Critical Studies is a specially developed series of critical essays on the major works of literature for use by students in universities, colleges and schools.

titles published or in preparation include:

SHAKESPEARE
Antony and Cleopatra
As You Like It
Henry IV Part 2
Henry V
Julius Caesar
King Lear
Macbeth
Measure for Measure
Much Ado About Nothing
Richard II
Richard III
Romeo and Juliet
A Shakespeare Handbook
Shakespeare's History Plays
Shakespeare – Text into Performance
The Tempest
Troilus and Cressida
Twelfth Night
A Winter's Tale

CHAUCER
A Chaucer Handbook
The Miller's Tale
The Nun's Priest's Tale
The Pardoner's Tale
The Prologue to the Canterbury
   Tales